Big Book of Skill Builders

Parts of Speech
Nouns and Pronouns 7
Nouns and Pronouns 9
Common and Proper Nouns 11
Plural Nouns 13
Pronouns 15
Nouns and Adjectives 17
Adjectives 19
Action Verbs 21
Action Verbs 23
Adverbs 25
Adjectives and Adverbs 27

Sentence Skills
Subjects and Predicates 29
Subject-Verb Agreement 31
Rambling Sentences 33
Subjects and Predicates 35
Fragments and Run-Ons 37
Adding Detail 39
Combining Sentences 41
Subject-Verb Agreement 43

Punctuation
Commas 45
Quotation Marks 47
Apostrophes 49
Using the Correct Mark 51

Writing
Paragraphs 53
Paragraphs 55
Narrative Paragraphs 57
Expository Paragraphs 59
Descriptive Paragraphs 61
Persuasive Paragraphs 63
Similes and Metaphors 65
Onomatopoeia, Alliteration, and
    Personification 67
Figurative Language 69

Literacy Continued

Word Analysis

Homophones 71
Prefixes and Suffixes 73
Prefixes and Suffixes 75
Base Words 77
Prefixes 79
Suffixes 81
Word Roots 83
Multiple-Meaning Words 85
Analogies 87

Using Reference Books

Using the Dictionary 89
Using an Encyclopedia 91
Using an Almanac 93
Using an Atlas 95
Choosing the Best Reference 97

Reading Comprehension

Reading for Details 99
Predicting Outcomes 101
Sequencing 103
Drawing Conclusions 105
Main Idea 107
Main Idea 109
Series of Events 111
Drawing Conclusions 113
Drawing Conclusions 115
Jean C. George: Reading
    comprehension 117
Jean C. George: Reading
    comprehension 119
Tiger Woods: Reading comprehension 121
Tiger Woods: Reading comprehension 123
Jane Goodall: Reading comprehension 125
Jane Goodall: Reading comprehension 127
Colin Powell: Reading comprehension 129
Colin Powell: Reading comprehension 131

Literary Response and Analysis

The Lion, the Witch and the Wardrobe:
    Root words 133

Literacy Continued

The Lion, the Witch and the Wardrobe:
    Character traits 135
The Lion, the Witch and the Wardrobe:
    Story elements.......................................137
Maniac Magee: Character traits..............139
Maniac Magee: Problem resolution 141
Shiloh: Vocabulary 143
Shiloh: Characterization 145
Shiloh: Summarizing.................................147
The BFG: Vocabulary 149
The BFG: Reading for details 151
The BFG: Creative writing 153

Math

Numbers and Operations

Number Forms..155
Comparing Whole Numbers 157
Place Value to 100 Millions......................159
Comparing Numbers Game 161
Place Value to 100 Millions......................163
Estimation and Addition Game 165
Subtraction Game......................................167
Multiplication-Facts Game 169
Division Game 171
Multiplying by a One-Digit Number 173
Estimation Game 175
Multiplication of Larger Numbers.............177
Division 179
Unit Pricing 181
Decimals to Thousandths 183
Standard Form and Word Names of
    Decimals 185
Comparing and Ordering Decimals 187
Rounding Decimals 189
Fractions 191
Equivalent Fractions 193
Simplifying Fractions.................................195
Comparing Fractions 197
Improper Fractions and Mixed Numbers ...199
Addition and Subtraction of Fractions......201
Changing Fractions to Percents 203

Math Continued

Measurement
- Metric Units of Length Game 205
- Customary Units of Length 207
- Customary Units of Length 209
- Metric Units of Length 211
- Metric Units of Weight and Capacity 213
- Customary Units of Weight 215
- Customary Units of Length, Weight, and Capacity 217
- Customary Units of Weight and Capacity 219
- Area 221
- Area and Perimeter 223

Geometry
- Slides, Turns, and Flips 225
- Space Figures 227
- Types of Angles 229

Data Analysis and Graphing
- Bar Graph 231
- Double Bar Graph 233
- Pictograph 235
- Line Graph 237
- Circle Graph 239

Patterns
- Completing a Pattern 241
- Identifying a Pattern 243
- Completing a Pattern, Attributes 245

Science

Earth
- Layers of the Earth 247
- Volcanoes 249
- Earthquakes 251
- Plate Tectonics 253
- Outer Space 255
- Outer Space 257
- Outer Space 259
- Storms and Weather 261

Science Continued

Physical
Electricity 263
Simple Circuits 265
The Lightbulb 267

Life
Animal Movement 269
Animal Movement 271
Animal Adaptations 273
Animal Defenses 275
Skeletal System 277
Respiratory System 279
Muscular System 281
Digestive System 283
Circulatory System 285

Social Studies

Map Skills
Cardinal and Intermediate Directions 287
Map Scale 289
Latitude and Longitude 291
Cardinal and Intermediate Directions 293
Map Symbols 295

U.S. Geography
State-Study Game 297
State-Study Game 299
Natural Resources 301
Natural Resources 303
States and Capitals Game 305

U.S. Government
Amendments 307
Amendments 309
Checks and Balances 311
The Preamble 313

Economics
Economics Vocabulary 315
Supply and Demand 317
Wants and Needs 319

Big Book of Skill Builders

About This Book
Engage your students and build a solid foundation in basic skills with *Big Book of Skill Builders*! The editors of *The Mailbox®* have compiled the best teacher-tested ideas from the grades 4–5 edition of *Teacher's Helper®* magazine to bring you this valuable, timesaving resource. Inside you'll find a wealth of activity pages that build skills in all of the major curriculum areas at your grade level. Eye-catching and educationally sound activities are delivered in formats that engage students and make learning fun! Units are organized by curriculum area and include the skills you use throughout the year. Each page is clearly labeled with skills and a subject area icon so you can see at a glance how an activity fits with your curriculum. In addition, a detailed table of contents makes it easy for you to quickly locate the specific pages you want to use in your lessons. Organized for the way you teach and ready for you to use, *Big Book of Skill Builders* is a tremendous resource that you can use to build skills all year long!

Managing Editor: Debra Liverman
Editor at Large: Diane Badden
Copy Editors: Tazmen Carlisle, Amy Kirtley-Hill, Karen L. Mayworth, Kristy Parton, Debbie Shoffner, Cathy Edwards Simrell
Cover Artist: Clevell Harris
Artists: Pam Crane, Theresa Lewis Goode, Clevell Harris, Ivy L. Koonce, Sheila Krill, Clint Moore, Greg D. Rieves, Rebecca Saunders, Barry Slate, Donna K. Teal
The Mailbox® Books.com: Jennifer Tipton Bennett (DESIGNER/ARTIST); Stuart Smith (PRODUCTION ARTIST); Karen White (INTERNET COORDINATOR); Paul Fleetwood, Xiaoyun Wu (SYSTEMS)

President, The Mailbox Book Company™: Joseph C. Bucci
Director of Book Planning and Development: Chris Poindexter
Curriculum Director: Karen P. Shelton
Book Development Managers: Cayce Guiliano, Elizabeth H. Lindsay, Thad McLaurin
Editorial Planning: Kimberley Bruck (MANAGER); Debra Liverman, Sharon Murphy, Susan Walker (TEAM LEADERS)
Editorial and Freelance Management: Karen A. Brudnak; Sarah Hamblet, Hope Rodgers (EDITORIAL ASSISTANTS)
Editorial Production: Lisa K. Pitts (TRAFFIC MANAGER); Lynette Dickerson (TYPE SYSTEMS); Mark Rainey (TYPESETTER)
Librarian: Dorothy C. McKinney

©2003 by THE EDUCATION CENTER, INC.
All rights reserved.
ISBN# 1-56234-559-1

Except as provided for herein, no part of this publication may be reproduced or transmitted in any form or by any means, electronic or mechanical, including photocopying, recording, or storing in any information storage and retrieval system or electronic online bulletin board, without prior written permission from The Education Center, Inc. Permission is given to the original purchaser to reproduce patterns and reproducibles for individual classroom use only and not for resale or distribution. Reproduction for an entire school or school system is prohibited. Please direct written inquiries to The Education Center, Inc., P.O. Box 9753, Greensboro, NC 27429-0753. The Education Center®, *The Mailbox®*, *Teacher's Helper®*, the mailbox/post/grass logo, and The Mailbox Book Company™ are trademarks of The Education Center, Inc., and may be the subject of one or more federal trademark registrations. All other brand or product names are trademarks or registered trademarks of their respective companies.

Manufactured in the United States
10 9 8 7 6 5 4 3 2 1

Name _____ Nouns and Pronouns

GREEDY KING MIDAS

Directions: Read the sentences below. Underline each noun and circle each personal pronoun.

1. There once lived a very greedy king.
2. He was asked to judge a music contest between two gods.
3. One of the gods in the contest was a friend of the king.
4. Instead of judging the contest fairly, the king selected his friend as the winner.
5. The other god became very upset and gave the king donkey ears.
6. One day the king helped a satyr—half man, half goat—who was lost.
7. The satyr granted the king one wish.
8. Instead of wishing for his donkey ears to be removed, he wished that everything he touched would turn to gold.
9. The king soon realized that his greed was a mistake.
10. Everything the king touched—his food, his pillow, his daughter—was turned to gold.
11. The king begged the gods to take away the dreadful wish.
12. They told the king to wash in the river, and the wish and the donkey ears would be removed.
13. The king listened to them and washed himself—and all that he had touched—with the river water.
14. He soon had his daughter back, as well as all the people and items he had touched.
15. The king was never greedy again.

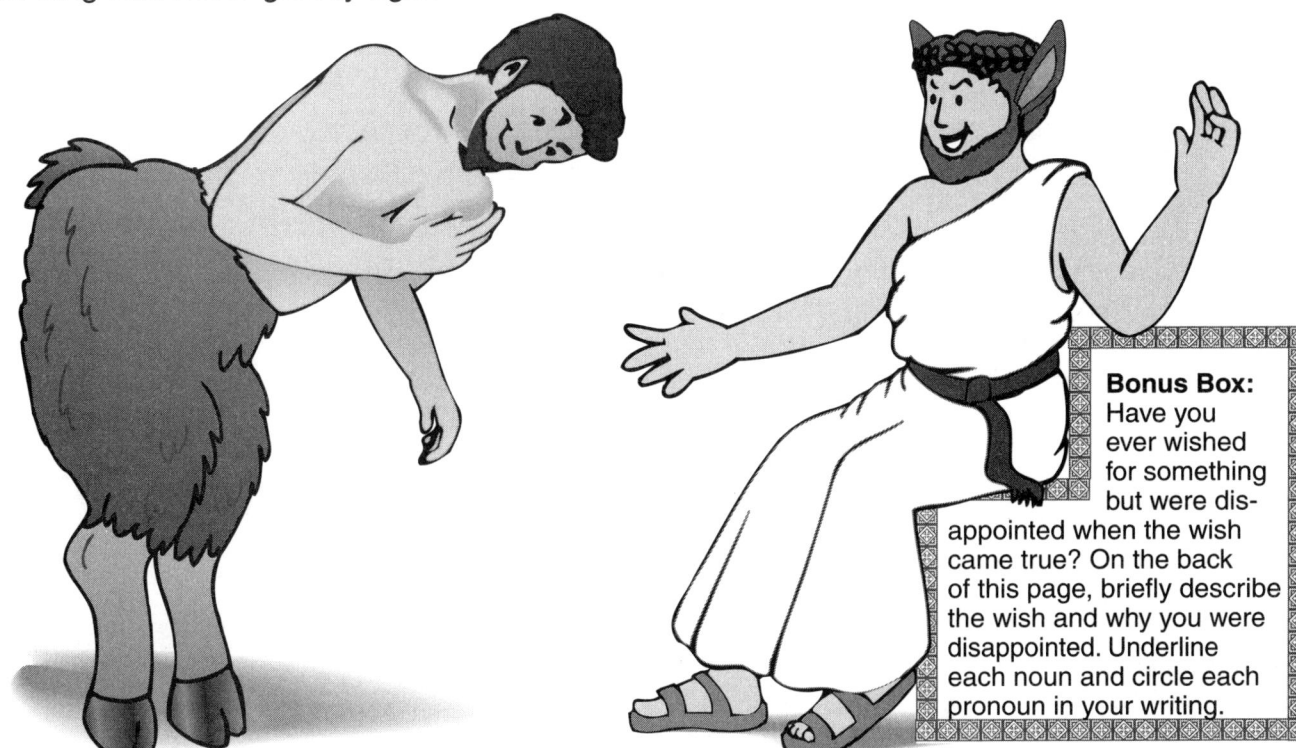

Bonus Box: Have you ever wished for something but were disappointed when the wish came true? On the back of this page, briefly describe the wish and why you were disappointed. Underline each noun and circle each pronoun in your writing.

©The Education Center, Inc. • *Big Book of Skill Builders* • TEC60797

 **Answer Key**

1. There once lived a very greedy <u>king</u>.
2. (He) was asked to judge a music <u>contest</u> between two <u>gods</u>.
3. One of the <u>gods</u> in the <u>contest</u> was a <u>friend</u> of the <u>king</u>.
4. Instead of judging the <u>contest</u> fairly, the <u>king</u> selected (his) <u>friend</u> as the <u>winner</u>.
5. The other <u>god</u> became very upset and gave the <u>king</u> donkey <u>ears</u>.
6. One <u>day</u> the <u>king</u> helped a <u>satyr</u>—half <u>man</u>, half <u>goat</u>—who was lost.
7. The <u>satyr</u> granted the <u>king</u> one <u>wish</u>.
8. Instead of wishing for (his) donkey <u>ears</u> to be removed, (he) wished that everything (he) touched would turn to <u>gold</u>.
9. The <u>king</u> soon realized that (his) <u>greed</u> was a <u>mistake</u>.
10. Everything the <u>king</u> touched—(his) <u>food</u>, (his) <u>pillow</u>, (his) <u>daughter</u>—was turned to <u>gold</u>.
11. The <u>king</u> begged the <u>gods</u> to take away the dreadful <u>wish</u>.
12. (They) told the <u>king</u> to wash in the <u>river</u>, and the <u>wish</u> and the donkey <u>ears</u> would be removed.
13. The <u>king</u> listened to (them) and washed himself—and all that (he) had touched—with the river <u>water</u>.
14. (He) soon had (his) <u>daughter</u> back, as well as all the <u>people</u> and <u>items</u> (he) had touched.
15. The <u>king</u> was never greedy again.

Name_____   Nouns and Pronouns

THE WOODEN HORSE

Directions: Read the myth below. Then fill in each blank with one noun or pronoun from the word box. Each word is used only once.

Word Box
- battles
- them
- king
- army
- he
- years
- it
- wife
- heroes
- her
- woman
- horse
- she
- they

   There once was a beautiful _____ named Helen. _____ was married to old King Menelaus of Greece. Paris, the prince of Troy, fell in love with Helen and took her to Troy. The _____ was very sad. His sadness grew into anger, and ____ formed an _____ of 50,000 soldiers. _____ sailed to Troy to retrieve their king's _____. Menelaus also took three great _____ with him—Achilles, Odysseus, and Ajax. Menelaus and his men fought the Trojans for ten _____. Many men died in the _____.

   Odysseus came up with a plan to get inside the city gates of Troy. Odysseus told Menelaus to build a huge wooden horse and leave it standing outside the city walls. When the Trojans opened the city gates, the Greeks were gone. Only the huge wooden horse stood before _____. The curious Trojans dragged the wooden horse inside the city.

   All was not what it seemed, however. Hidden inside the _____ were several of Menelaus's men. During the night the men opened a secret door in the horse, climbed out, and opened the gates to the city. Menelaus's army entered the city and destroyed _____. At last Helen was returned to _____ home in Greece.

Bonus Box: Have you ever thought you knew what was inside a gift, but when you opened it you were totally surprised? On the back of this sheet, write about a time when you were surprised by a gift. Underline each noun and pronoun in your writing.

Answer Key

There once was a beautiful __woman__ named Helen. __She__ was married to old King Menelaus of Greece. Paris, the prince of Troy, fell in love with Helen and took her to Troy. The __king__ was very sad. His sadness grew into anger, and __he__ formed an __army__ of 50,000 soldiers. __They__ sailed to Troy to retrieve their king's __wife__. Menelaus also took three great __heroes__ with him—Achilles, Odysseus, and Ajax. Menelaus and his men fought the Trojans for ten __years__. Many men died in the __battles__.

Odysseus came up with a plan to get inside the city gates of Troy. Odysseus told Menelaus to build a huge wooden horse and leave it standing outside the city walls. When the Trojans opened the city gates, the Greeks were gone. Only the huge wooden horse stood before __them__. The curious Trojans dragged the wooden horse inside the city.

All was not what it seemed, however. Hidden inside the __horse__ were several of Menelaus's men. During the night the men opened a secret door in the horse, climbed out, and opened the gates to the city. Menelaus's army entered the city and destroyed __it__. At last Helen was returned to __her__ home in Greece.

Name_____ Common and Proper Nouns

THESEUS AND THE MINOTAUR

Directions: Help Theseus get through the labyrinth and find the Minotaur. Then look back at each noun lurking in the maze. Decide if the noun is *common* or *proper* and write it in the appropriate box below. **Note:** Capitalize each proper noun.

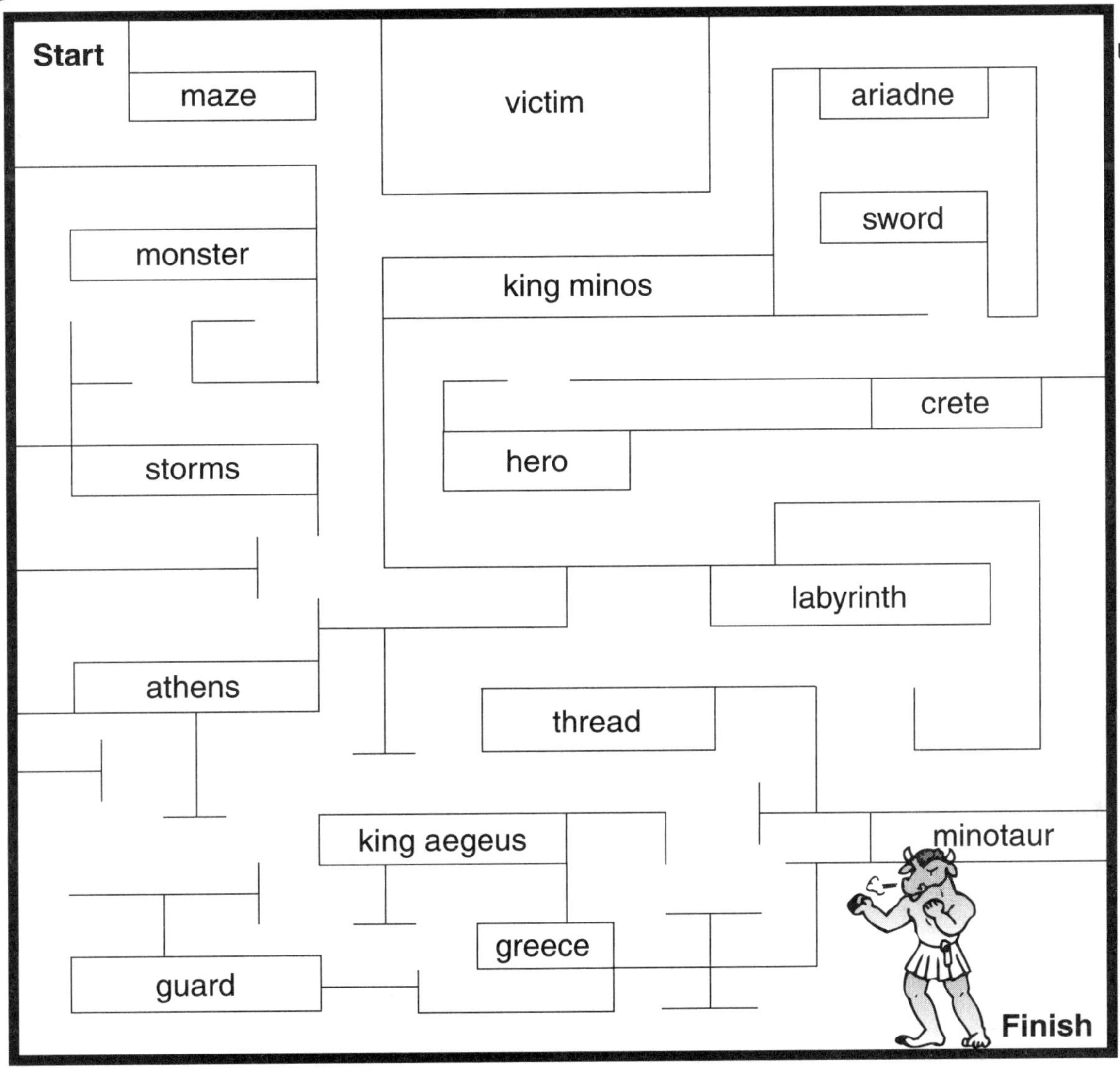

Nouns in the maze:
- maze
- victim
- ariadne
- monster
- sword
- king minos
- crete
- storms
- hero
- labyrinth
- athens
- thread
- king aegeus
- minotaur
- greece
- guard

Common Nouns	Proper Nouns

Bonus Box: Create your own maze for Theseus and the Minotaur on the back of this page.

©The Education Center, Inc. • *Big Book of Skill Builders* • TEC60797

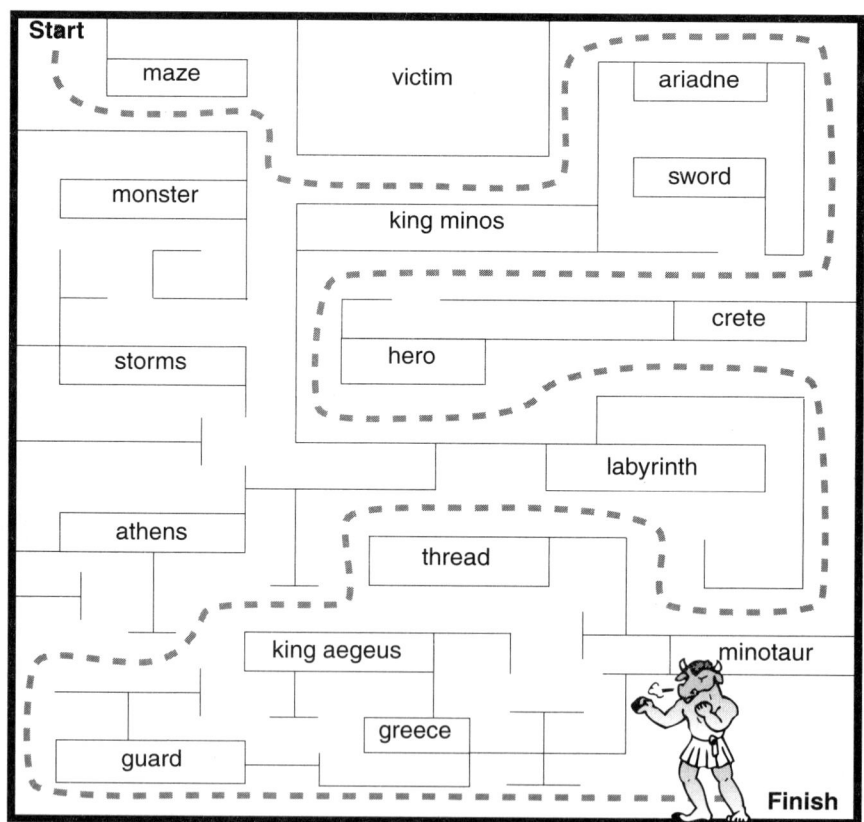

Common Nouns: maze, monster, storms, hero, victim, sword, labyrinth, thread, guard

Proper Nouns: King Minos, Ariadne, Crete, Athens, King Aegeus, Minotaur, Greece

Name _____ Plural Nouns

UP, UP, AND AWAY!

Directions: Write the plural form of each noun in the appropriate blank.

1. bird
2. valley
3. maze
4. window
5. buddy
6. ray
7. wing
8. enemy
9. body
10. island
11. journey
12. shoulder
13. feather
14. wind

Bonus Box: On another sheet of paper, write a short story about the tale of Daedalus and Icarus. Include each noun above in your story. You may use the singular form, the plural form, or both forms of each noun in your writing.

Answer Key

1. birds
2. valleys
3. mazes
4. windows
5. buddies
6. rays
7. wings
8. enemies
9. bodies
10. islands
11. journeys
12. shoulders
13. feathers
14. winds

Name _____ Pronouns

Survival at Valley Forge

Read the following true story about George Washington at Valley Forge; then use the pronouns in the ink bottle to fill in the blanks. Some of the pronouns will be used more than once. Two will not be used at all.

    As Americans, many of _____ have heard the story of Valley Forge. _____ is a story about George Washington, his men, and _____ courage. It is a legend that _____ should never forget.

    The War of Independence began in 1775. _____ was fought between Britain and 13 of its colonies in North America. Washington was the commander in chief of the Continental Army. _____ led his troops in many battles.

    The winter of 1777 was especially bad. Bitter cold temperatures and snow made fighting almost impossible. When _____ was time to make camp, the British had no problems because _____ troops could rest comfortably in Philadelphia. That's because British Redcoats had captured the city earlier. But American soldiers weren't so lucky. Washington led _____ ragged army to an area northwest of Philadelphia. _____ chose a hilly site in Valley Forge.

    Nearly 10,000 soldiers made camp. _____ suffered horrible conditions. Food and clothing were scarce. Washington's men were so hungry that _____ even tried to make soup from leaves picked from trees and bushes. About half of the soldiers were barefooted and without even a blanket. Those who were barefooted wrapped _____ feet with rags and tree bark. Washington realized that _____ men would freeze unless _____ built huts. Soldiers who were strong enough to work in the cold chopped down trees to construct log huts. To encourage _____, Washington offered a $12 prize to the soldiers who finished _____ hut first. However, many men did not have warm clothing and were already too weak to help. _____ just huddled together on hillsides, sleeping under frost or snow.

    By spring, over one-quarter of Washington's soldiers had died from disease, cold, and exposure to the weather. These men gave up _____ lives to fight for America. Like Washington, _____ believed in a new nation with freedom and justice for all. Surely the American cause was right. Surely _____ was a cause worth fighting for!

them	us
we	our
it	his
their	my
he	they

Bonus Box: Pretend that you are a soldier at Valley Forge. Write a letter to a friend or family member telling about the winter of 1777.

 **Answer Key**

As Americans, many of __us__ have heard the story of Valley Forge. __It__ is a story about George Washington, his men, and __their__ courage. It is a legend that __we__ should never forget.

The War of Independence began in 1775. __It__ was fought between Britain and 13 of its colonies in North America. Washington was the commander in chief of the Continental Army. __He__ led his troops in many battles.

The winter of 1777 was especially bad. Bitter cold temperatures and snow made fighting almost impossible. When __it__ was time to make camp, the British had no problems because __their__ troops could rest comfortably in Philadelphia. That's because British Redcoats had captured the city earlier. But American soldiers weren't so lucky. Washington led __his__ ragged army to an area northwest of Philadelphia. __He or They__ chose a hilly site in Valley Forge.

Nearly 10,000 soldiers made camp. __They__ suffered horrible conditions. Food and clothing were scarce. Washington's men were so hungry that __they__ even tried to make soup from leaves picked from trees and bushes. About half of the soldiers were barefooted and without even a blanket. Those who were barefooted wrapped __their__ feet with rags and tree bark. Washington realized that __his__ men would freeze unless __they__ built huts. Soldiers who were strong enough to work in the cold chopped down trees to construct log huts. To encourage __them__, Washington offered a $12 prize to the soldiers who finished __their__ hut first. However, many men did not have warm clothing and were already too weak to help. __They__ just huddled together on hillsides, sleeping under frost or snow.

By spring, over one-quarter of Washington's soldiers had died from disease, cold, and exposure to the weather. These men gave up __their__ lives to fight for America. Like Washington, __they__ believed in a new nation with freedom and justice for all. Surely the American cause was right. Surely __it__ was a cause worth fighting for!

Name _____

Nouns and Adjectives

Food Fit for a King!

King Ferdinand is quite fond of food. Each day throughout the week, he writes his court cook a note. Find the nouns and adjectives in each note below (do not include articles). Then write them in the correct serving dishes below. Use a dictionary for help, if needed.

1 Monday
The pheasant was perfectly cooked! The queen was fond of the tender turnips and warm, white bread.

2 Tuesday
Meat pie would provide an appetizing dinner. But I am so hungry now! Send me a platter of sugary quinces and cooked apples.

3 Wednesday
The tarts were the tastiest! Were they made with nuts and dates? I would like mincemeat pie for lunch tomorrow.

4 Thursday
Prepare the Great Hall for a royal feast! Be certain to serve the freshest fish, the most savory sausage, and the finest fowl.

5 Friday
The cider you served was as refreshing as the trickling brook beside the manor. I toast the apple orchard!

6 Saturday
Lady Margaret of Devonshire will visit on Sunday. Treat her to a table with the most sumptuous delights.

7 Sunday
Please bring the custards to the fireside. Young Edward has engaged me in a grueling game of chess.

Kiss the Cook!

Nouns

Adjectives

Bonus Box: Draw another serving platter on the back of this sheet. Write the proper nouns from the notes above in it.

©The Education Center, Inc. • *Big Book of Skill Builders* • TEC60797

17

Answer Key

Nouns
1. pheasant, queen, turnips, bread
2. pie, dinner, platter, quinces, apples
3. tarts, nuts, dates, pie, lunch
4. Great Hall, feast, fish, sausage, fowl
5. cider, brook, manor, orchard
6. Lady Margaret, Devonshire, Sunday, table, delights
7. custards, fireside, Edward, game, chess

Adjectives
1. fond, tender, warm, white
2. Meat, appetizing, hungry, sugary, cooked
3. tastiest, mincemeat
4. royal, certain, freshest, savory, finest
5. refreshing, trickling, apple
6. sumptuous
7. Young, grueling

Bonus Box: Great Hall, Lady Margaret, Devonshire, Sunday, Edward

Name _____   Adjectives

Feast on These Descriptions!

Cotton candy, ice cream, and hot dogs—how would you describe foods like these to a king of long ago?

Directions: Think about each food shown below. On each numbered picture, write an adjective describing how each food (1) looks, (2) tastes, (3) smells, (4) feels, and (5) sounds as it is eaten.

Example: An ice-cream cone is (1) creamy and crunchy, (2) sweet, (3) flavorful, (4) cold, and (5) quiet.

Bonus Box: On the back of this sheet, draw a shopping cart. Label the cart with adjectives that describe a favorite food. Exchange papers with a classmate to see if he or she can guess the food item.

©The Education Center, Inc. • *Big Book of Skill Builders* • TEC60797

How to Use Page 19

Whet your students' appetites for the activity on page 19 with the following game.

1. Place three mystery foods in separate paper lunch bags.
2. Choose a student volunteer for each bag.
3. Quietly direct each student to use her senses—sight, taste, smell, touch, and hearing—to describe the food in her bag. Explain to each volunteer that she must only use a one-word adjective for each sense, such as *yellow, sweet, fruity, soft,* and *squishy.*
4. After each volunteer shares her clues, direct remaining students to guess what the food item is in each bag. Then have students identify the part of speech the volunteers used to describe each food *(adjective).*
5. Distribute a copy of page 19 to each student. Discuss the example on the page; then have each student complete the page as directed on the sheet. Afterward share students' responses.

Answer Key

Students' answers will vary; however, each descriptive word should be an adjective.

Name _____

Action Verbs

Recipes for Action

Directions: Choose two of your favorite activities. Write a recipe for participating in each activity. Include at least five action verbs that show actions used in each one. Underline each action verb you use.

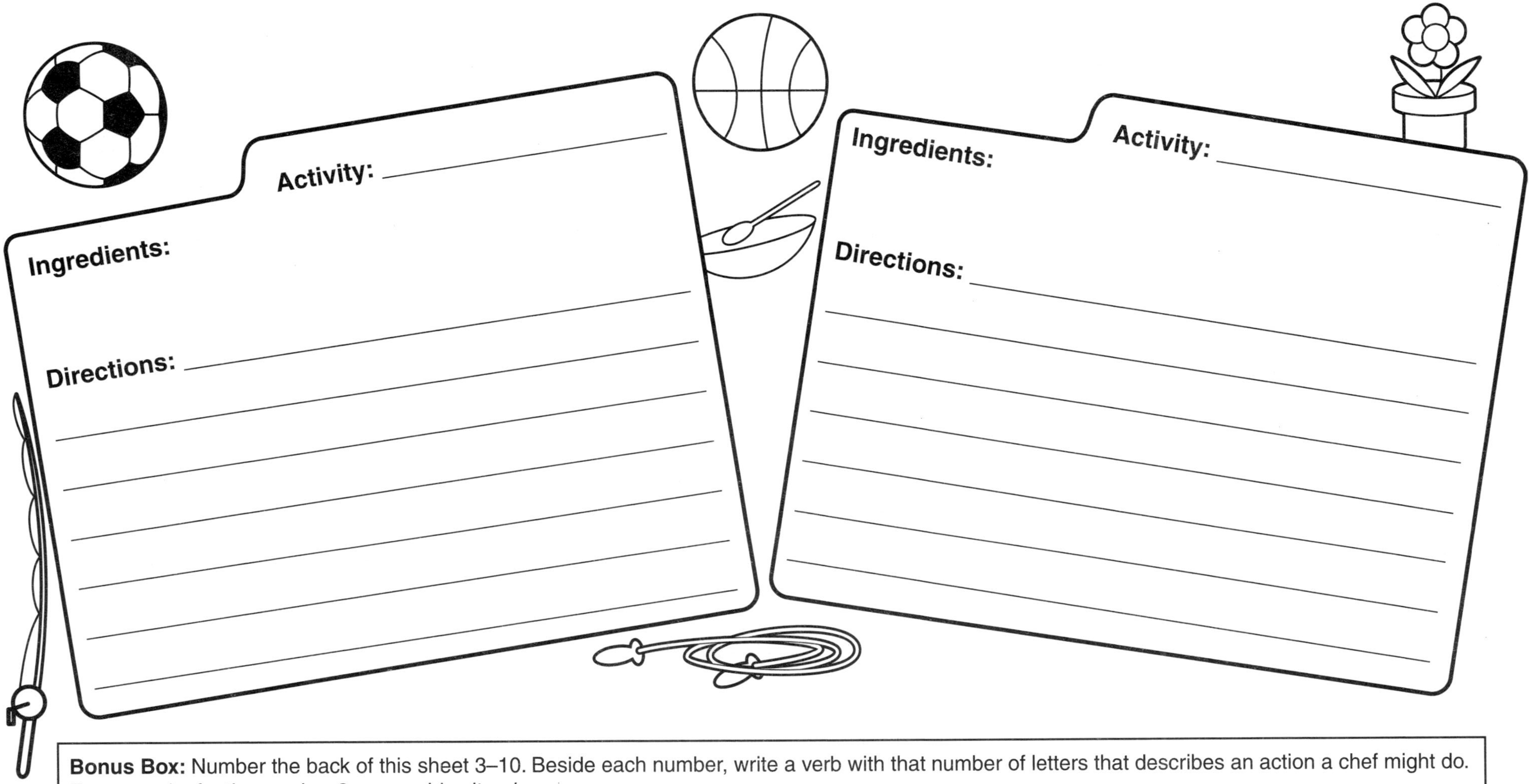

Activity: _____

Ingredients:

Directions:

Activity: _____

Ingredients:

Directions:

Bonus Box: Number the back of this sheet 3–10. Beside each number, write a verb with that number of letters that describes an action a chef might do. For example, for the number 3 you could write *sip*.

©The Education Center, Inc. • *Big Book of Skill Builders* • TEC60797

How to Use Page 21

1. Before introducing the activity, remind students that an *action verb* shows action.
2. Brainstorm with students a list of favorite activities, such as playing basketball, gardening, fishing, and baking. Record their responses on the chalkboard.
3. Have students explain some of the actions or particular movements associated with each activity. For example, dribbling, shooting, running, and jumping are involved in playing basketball.
4. Give a copy of page 21 to each student. Discuss the directions; then share the sample recipe shown below. Point out the parts of a recipe, including the list of ingredients and the directions.
5. Have students complete the page as directed and then share their fun-filled recipes.

Sample Recipe

Activity: biking

Ingredients:

bike   protective elbow and knee pads
helmet   neighborhood or park

Directions:

1. <u>Put</u> on your helmet and protective pads.
2. <u>Choose</u> a place to ride, such as the sidewalks in your neighborhood or a bike path in the park.
3. <u>Get</u> on your bike and <u>pedal</u>.
4. Always <u>watch</u> where you <u>are going</u>.
5. <u>Follow</u> the rules of the road. <u>Obey</u> traffic signs.
6. <u>Enjoy</u> your ride!

Students' recipes will vary, but each should include at least five action verbs.

Bonus Box: Accept reasonable responses. Possible answers include the following: *sip, stir, knead, freeze, combine, sprinkle, apportion, substitute.*

Name _____ Action Verbs

Action-Packed Vacations

A variety of action verbs can be found around the world—and around the alphabet too! For each state or country listed below, write a phrase that includes an action verb and describes something you might do while vacationing there. The verb must begin with the letter of the state or country named. Use a dictionary or thesaurus for help.

Example: *Attend* a concert in Australia

A _____ in **A**ustralia
B _____ in the **B**ahamas
C _____ in **C**anada
D _____ in **D**enmark
E _____ in **E**ngland
F _____ in **F**lorida
G _____ in **G**reece
H _____ in **H**awaii
I _____ in **I**taly
J _____ in **J**apan
K _____ in **K**ansas
L _____ in **L**uxembourg
M _____ in **M**exico
N _____ in **N**orway
O _____ in **O**regon
P _____ in **P**oland
Q _____ in **Q**atar
R _____ in **R**ussia
S _____ in **S**witzerland
T _____ in **T**aiwan
U _____ in **U**zbekistan
V _____ in **V**enezuela
W _____ in **W**est Virginia
X You're e**X**cused from this one!
Y _____ in **Y**emen
Z _____ in **Z**imbabwe

Bonus Box: Choose four of the countries or states and their matching verbs. For each pair, write a silly sentence using words that repeat the same beginning letter. For example, you may write "Ned and Nancy nibble noodles in Norway." Write your sentences on the back of this sheet.

©The Education Center, Inc. • Big Book of Skill Builders • TEC60797

Answer Key

Accept reasonable answers. Possible action verbs include the following:

- **A:** amble, antique
- **B:** boogie, bicycle
- **C:** camp, communicate
- **D:** dine, drive
- **E:** eat, eavesdrop
- **F:** fly, frolic
- **G:** gab, guzzle
- **H:** hitchhike, hula
- **I:** imitate, investigate
- **J:** jaywalk, jump
- **K:** kick, kiss
- **L:** laugh, lunge
- **M:** motorbike, meditate
- **N:** navigate, nuzzle
- **O:** oar, overeat
- **P:** parachute, party
- **Q:** quarrel, quest
- **R:** refresh, reserve
- **S:** ski, scour
- **T:** tip, troupe
- **U:** unpack, unwind
- **V:** view, videotape
- **W:** waddle, waltz
- **Y:** yacht, yawn
- **Z:** zigzag, zone

Name _____   Adverbs

Pleasing Pancakes

Chef Geoff knows the king absolutely flips over pancakes! So just how does Geoff make these king-pleasing pancakes? Complete the activity below to find out.

Directions: Circle the adverb in each sentence below. Draw an arrow to the word that the adverb is describing. Then color the pancake to show if the adverb is telling *where, how,* or *when.* The first one is done for you.

	Where	How	When
1. The stove temperature should be (fairly) hot.	A	F	L
2. This first pancake is completely burned!	B	C	M
3. Oh, no! The batter has spilled everywhere.	A	W	Q
4. The king is terribly fond of fresh berries on his pancakes.	P	R	V
5. Pancakes must be flipped properly.	X	Y	I
6. This pancake is almost done.	E	L	H
7. The king often eats three or more stacks of pancakes.	S	K	E
8. Chocolate chip pancakes are quite tasty.	J	U	G
9. The king is positively picky about his pancakes!	A	V	Z
10. I always cook my pancakes to perfection!	T	O	Y
11. Here is a new stack.	E	C	A
12. A batch of fresh pancakes will be made tomorrow.	M	K	R

Write the letter that you colored for each number shown below.

___ ___ ___ ___   ___ ___ ___ ___ ___ ___ ___ ___ ___ !
 9 11 4   5   2   3 12 7 1   8   6   6 10

Bonus Box: Write the word *cook* on the back of this sheet. Write an *-ly* adverb beginning with each letter of the alphabet (except *X*) that tells how the cooking is done. For example, *artfully, bravely, continuously,* and so on.

Answer Key

1. **fairly,** hot, how
2. **completely,** is burned, how
3. **everywhere,** has spilled, where
4. **terribly,** fond, how
5. **properly,** must be flipped, how
6. **almost,** done, how
7. **often,** eats, when
8. **quite,** tasty, how
9. **positively,** picky, how
10. **always,** cook, when
11. **here,** is, where
12. **tomorrow,** will be made, when

Riddle:

<u>V</u> <u>E</u> <u>R</u> <u>Y</u>   <u>C</u> <u>A</u> <u>R</u> <u>E</u> <u>F</u> <u>U</u> <u>L</u> <u>L</u> <u>Y</u>!
9 11 4 5   2 3 12 7 1 8 6 6 10

Bonus Box: Students' answers will vary. Accept reasonable responses. Possible answers include the following: *artfully, bravely, continuously, devoutly, earnestly, flawlessly, grandly, hurriedly, inattentively, joyously, kindly, loudly, messily, nobly, orderly, placidly, quietly, rapidly, sheepishly, tenderly, unhappily, vocally, wastefully, yearningly, zealously.*

Name _____   Adjectives and Adverbs

Exploring the Great Outdoors

Sign up today to take part in a host of activities sponsored by the Great Outdoor Sports Association. Membership is easy! Choose two items from each category below. On the line beside each item you choose, write an adjective that describes the piece of equipment, plus an adverb that describes how it is used. On the back of this sheet, write a sentence about each item you chose. Include both the adjective and adverb that you listed beside that item.

Example
hiking boots: leather (adj.) comfortably (adv.)
sample sentence: These **leather** hiking boots will help me walk **comfortably** over mountain trails.

Hikers of America
1. compass _____
2. backpack _____
3. map _____
4. canteen _____
5. emergency kit _____

Happy Campers Club
1. poncho _____
2. tent _____
3. sleeping bag _____
4. pocketknife _____
5. knapsack _____

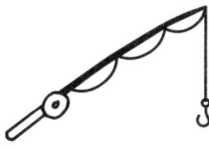

Association of Avid Fishers
1. tacklebox _____
2. lure _____
3. bait _____
4. waders _____
5. rod _____

Explorers of the Sea
1. wet suit _____
2. flippers _____
3. regulator _____
4. oxygen tanks _____
5. snorkel _____

Bird-Watchers Society
1. binoculars _____
2. camera _____
3. notebook _____
4. field guide _____
5. film _____

Rock Climbers Club
1. piton _____
2. helmet _____
3. rope _____
4. rock-climbing shoes _____
_____
5. harness _____

Bonus Box: Pretend you're a spokesperson for one of the above groups. You must persuade others to participate in this activity. Write a 30-second radio spot that includes the following descriptive words: *spectacular, essential, enjoyable, adventurous, awesome.*

Name _____   Subjects and Predicates

The Subject Is Columbus!

Poor Mr. San-Diego! His class is having trouble identifying complete subjects and predicates. He meets the challenge by using the one and only Christopher Columbus as the topic of his lesson!

Mr. San-Diego wants his class to understand that

> The complete subject tells what the sentence is about and usually comes before the verb.
> Example: The earth
> The complete predicate tells something about the subject and begins with the verb.
> Example: is not flat

Directions: In each sentence below, draw a / line between the complete subject and complete predicate.

1. The salty smell of the sea filled the air of Genoa, Italy.
2. This city was my birthplace.
3. The people of Europe wanted spices, silks, and jewels from the Far East.
4. These treasures were carried overland from the Orient by caravan.
5. A shorter route by sea may be possible.
6. I know that the earth is round!
7. The Orient can be reached by sailing west.
8. Men and ships were requested from the king of Portugal.
9. The king said no to my request.
10. The king and queen of Spain were then asked.
11. They also said no.
12. The rulers changed their minds though.
13. My three tiny ships soon headed west into unknown waters.
14. My crew and I sailed westward.
15. My men began to talk of mutiny.
16. One of my men spotted land on October 12, 1492!
17. We went ashore early the next morning.

Exploring the Skill

Pretend that you are one of the sailors on Columbus's ship. On the back of this page, write your journal entry for October 13, 1492. In each sentence that you write, underline the complete subject once and the complete predicate twice.

Answer Key

1. The salty smell of the sea / filled the air of Genoa, Italy.
2. This city / was my birthplace.
3. The people of Europe / wanted spices, silks, and jewels from the Far East.
4. These treasures / were carried overland from the Orient by caravan.
5. A shorter route by sea / may be possible.
6. I / know that the earth is round!
7. The Orient / can be reached by sailing west.
8. Men and ships / were requested from the king of Portugal.
9. The king / said no to my request.
10. The king and queen of Spain / were then asked.
11. They / also said no.
12. The rulers / changed their minds though.
13. My three tiny ships / soon headed west into unknown waters.
14. My crew and I / sailed westward.
15. My men / began to talk of mutiny.
16. One of my men / spotted land on October 12, 1492!
17. We / went ashore early the next morning.

Name _____ Subject-Verb Agreement

Why Don't We Agree?

Where in the world is Harmon San-Diego taking his class in this lesson? He's using information about Marco Polo while teaching the students that

> The subject and verb of a sentence must agree in number:
>   When a subject is singular, the verb must also be singular.
>   When a subject is plural, the verb must be plural.
>
> Examples: The **explorer wants** to discover new lands. (singular)
>   The **explorers want** their ships to be seaworthy. (plural)

Marco Polo

Directions: Circle the correct form of the verb for each sentence. Then write *singular* or *plural* after the sentence.

1. Hundreds of years ago, Venice (was, were) a great center of trade. 1. _____
2. I (was, were) born there around 1254. 2. _____
3. Seventeen years later, my father, my uncle, and I (go, goes) on a trip to China. 3. _____
4. We (are, am) going to meet the great Kublai Khan. 4. _____
5. We (cross, crosses) deserts and mountains that were almost impassable. 5. _____
6. The trip (last, lasts) about three years. 6. _____
7. In China, I (learn, learns) many new things. 7. _____
8. The Chinese (use, uses) paper money. 8. _____
9. As the years (goes, go) by, I travel to many lands. 9. _____
10. In 1292, we (asks, ask) the Great Khan whether we may return to Venice. 10. _____
11. Our journey home (take, takes) over a year. 11. _____
12. We (is, are) gone for a total of 24 years! 12. _____
13. Upon our return, we find that Venice (is, are) at war with Genoa, Italy. 13. _____
14. Unfortunately, I (am, are) captured and put into prison. 14. _____
15. Here, I (write, writes) a book about my adventures. 15. _____
16. Those who read my book (learn, learns) a lot about the world. 16. _____

Exploring the Skill

On the back of this page, write eight sentences about a place that you have "explored." In each sentence, underline the subject and circle the verb. Exchange papers with a partner. Proofread your partner's sentences to see whether the subjects and verbs agree.

 **Answer Key**

1. Hundreds of years ago, Venice **was** a great center of trade.
2. I **was** born there around 1254.
3. Seventeen years later, my father, my uncle, and I **go** on a trip to China.
4. We **are** going to meet the great Kublai Khan.
5. We **cross** deserts and mountains that were almost impassable.
6. The trip **lasts** about three years.
7. In China, I **learn** many new things.
8. The Chinese **use** paper money.
9. As the years **go** by, I travel to many lands.
10. In 1292, we **ask** the Great Khan whether we may return to Venice.
11. Our journey home **takes** over a year.
12. We **are** gone for a total of 24 years!
13. Upon our return, we find that Venice **is** at war with Genoa, Italy.
14. Unfortunately, I **am** captured and put into prison.
15. Here, I **write** a book about my adventures.
16. Those who read my book **learn** a lot about the world.

1. singular
2. singular
3. plural
4. plural
5. plural
6. singular
7. singular
8. plural
9. plural
10. plural
11. singular
12. plural
13. singular
14. singular
15. singular
16. plural

Name _____   Rambling Sentences

Too Many *Ands*!

Mr. San-Diego has discovered that his students use too many *and*s in the stories that they write. Too many *and*s join good sentences into long, rambling sentences.

Directions: Read the story below about Roald Amundsen. Cross out the unneeded *and*s. Cross out each word that needs to be capitalized and write it correctly in the space above the word. Add ending punctuation where needed.

Roald Amundsen was born near Oslo, Norway, in 1872 and he always dreamed of being the first person to reach the North Pole and he was disappointed when he learned that Robert E. Peary had reached it first and Amundsen then changed his plans to find the South Pole instead and he would have to sail from Norway across the equator to Antarctica and in June 1910, he began his journey with a crew of 19 men and about 100 Eskimo dogs and by the middle of January 1911, Amundsen had made his way to the eastern edge of Antarctica and there was not time to reach the pole before the hard winter began and so the party set up a base camp and when spring arrived the following October, Amundsen and four companions set off for the South Pole and the dogs pulled sledges while the men traveled on skis and along the way they built depots where supplies could be stored for their return trip and at 3:00 P.M. on December 14, 1911, Amundsen and his men reached the South Pole.

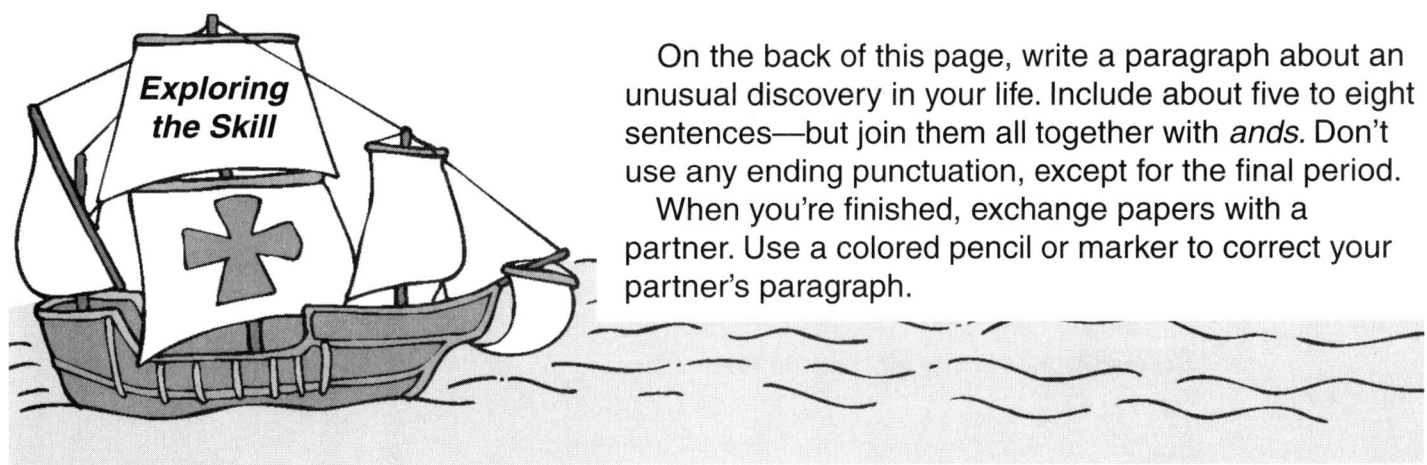

Exploring the Skill

On the back of this page, write a paragraph about an unusual discovery in your life. Include about five to eight sentences—but join them all together with *and*s. Don't use any ending punctuation, except for the final period.

When you're finished, exchange papers with a partner. Use a colored pencil or marker to correct your partner's paragraph.

Roald Amundsen was born near Oslo, Norway, in 1872. ~~and~~ He always dreamed of being the first person to reach the North Pole. ~~and~~ He was disappointed when he learned that Robert E. Peary had reached it first. ~~and~~ Amundsen then changed his plans to find the South Pole instead. ~~and~~ He would have to sail from Norway across the equator to Antarctica. ~~and~~ In June 1910, he began his journey with a crew of 19 men and about 100 Eskimo dogs. ~~and~~ By the middle of January 1911, Amundsen had made his way to the eastern edge of Antarctica. ~~and~~ There was not time to reach the pole before the hard winter began. ~~and~~ So the party set up a base camp. ~~and~~ When spring arrived the following October, Amundsen and four companions set off for the South Pole. ~~and~~ The dogs pulled sledges while the men traveled on skis. ~~and~~ Along the way they built depots where supplies could be stored for their return trip. ~~and~~ At 3:00 P.M. on December 14, 1911, Amundsen and his men reached the South Pole.

Name_____ Subjects and Predicates

Winter Warm-Ups

After a long day of skiing, nothing beats warming up at the lodge! Warm up your sentence skills by following the directions below.

Directions: Read the complete subjects and complete predicates on the skis below. Make a complete sentence by matching a subject to a predicate. Write the matching numbers in each snowflake; then write the sentences on the back of this sheet. The first one is done for you.

(The brown beagle in the lobby wore a bright red sweater.)

1. the brown beagle in the lobby
2. Beethoven and his buddies
3. Boxer
4. bought delicious funnel cakes covered with powdered sugar
5. a group of youngsters
6. the family of six
7. played cards in the loft
8. soaked their sore muscles in the spa
9. Betty's brother
10. wore a bright red sweater

1, 10

11. ate a bowl of chicken noodle soup
12. covered up with a warm flannel blanket
13. the ski instructors
14. watched videos
15. the bulldog with the broken leg
16. relaxed by the glowing fire
17. watched skiers speeding down the mountain's slopes
18. weary skiers
19. a lodge employee
20. ordered a cup of steaming hot chocolate

Bonus Box: Write a paragraph about an imaginary ski trip. Be sure to include a subject and predicate in each sentence.

©The Education Center, Inc. • *Big Book of Skill Builders* • TEC60797

Answer Key

Students' sentences and the order of answers may vary.

1, 10 — The brown beagle in the lobby wore a bright red sweater.

2, 4 — Beethoven and his buddies bought delicious funnel cakes covered with powdered sugar.

3, 20 — Boxer ordered a cup of steaming hot chocolate.

5, 14 — A group of youngsters watched videos.

6, 7 — The family of six played cards in the loft.

18, 8 — Weary skiers soaked their sore muscles in the spa.

15, 11 — The bulldog with the broken leg ate a bowl of chicken noodle soup.

9, 12 — Betty's brother covered up with a warm flannel blanket.

13, 17 — The ski instructors watched skiers speeding down the mountain's slopes.

19, 16 — A lodge employee relaxed by the glowing fire.

Fragments and Run-Ons

Stormy Sentences

Being caught in a blizzard isn't exactly what Beethoven had in mind when he and his family went on a ski trip! Read Beethoven's journal entry below. Then follow the directions for each numbered group of words. The remaining answer will tell you where Beethoven was skiing when the blizzard occurred.

1 What a day I had! 2 After we arrived at the ski resort. 3 I quickly gathered my poles, skis, and bindings and headed for the slopes. 4 The lift took me to the top of the mountain I noticed that the powdery snow was perfect! 5 I enjoyed schussing down the smooth, wide slopes for most of the afternoon. 6 Then, all of a sudden. 7 Huge snowflakes began to fall, and the wind picked up speed. 8 I decided that I needed to pick up some speed myself I raced downhill. 9 Frost on my goggles made seeing difficult I barely missed a tree! 10 I got to the bottom of the mountain and raced toward our cabin. 11 Opened the door. 12 I heard the radio blasting a warning to skiers about the blizzard. 13 Boy, was I glad I made it home just in time!

1. If this is a complete sentence, cross out Sun Valley, Idaho.
2. If this is a sentence fragment, cross out Aspen, Colorado.
3. If this is a run-on sentence, cross out Stowe, Vermont.
4. If this is a run-on sentence, cross out Killington, Vermont.
5. If this is a complete sentence, cross out Jackson Hole, Wyoming.
6. If this is a sentence fragment, cross out Wintergreen, Virginia.
7. If this is a run-on sentence, cross out Hidden Valley, Pennsylvania.
8. If this is a run-on sentence, cross out Stowe, Vermont.
9. If this is a sentence fragment, cross out Big Sky, Montana.
10. If this is a complete sentence, cross out Bear Valley, California.
11. If this is a sentence fragment, cross out Snowbird, Utah.
12. If this is a complete sentence, cross out Hidden Valley, Pennsylvania.
13. If this is a complete sentence, cross out Steamboat Springs, Colorado.

Jackson Hole, Wyoming
Wintergreen, Virginia
Aspen, Colorado
Snowbird, Utah

Sun Valley, Idaho
Killington, Vermont
Steamboat Springs, Colorado
Hidden Valley, Pennsylvania

Bear Valley, California
Big Sky, Montana
Stowe, Vermont

Answer Key

1. complete sentence; ~~Sun Valley, Idaho~~
2. sentence fragment; ~~Aspen, Colorado~~
3. complete sentence; Stowe, Vermont
4. run-on sentence; ~~Killington, Vermont~~
5. complete sentence; ~~Jackson Hole, Wyoming~~
6. sentence fragment; ~~Wintergreen, Virginia~~
7. complete sentence; Hidden Valley, Pennsylvania
8. run-on sentence; ~~Stowe, Vermont~~
9. run-on sentence; Big Sky, Montana
10. complete sentence; ~~Bear Valley, California~~
11. sentence fragment; ~~Snowbird, Utah~~
12. complete sentence; ~~Hidden Valley, Pennsylvania~~
13. complete sentence; ~~Steamboat Springs, Colorado~~

Students should identify Big Sky, Montana, as the area Beethoven was visiting when the blizzard occurred.

Name_____ Adding Detail

Freestyle Sentences

Add some style to simple sentences by using words with pizzazz! Choose words from the Snowbank to replace dull words or add detail to each sentence below. Rewrite each sentence on the blank. Then count the number of new words you used to determine your freestyle score!

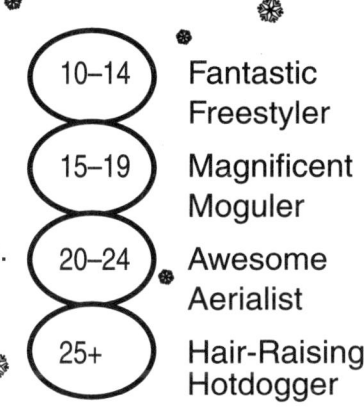

10–14 Fantastic Freestyler
15–19 Magnificent Moguler
20–24 Awesome Aerialist
25+   Hair-Raising Hotdogger

1. Beethoven dressed in ski clothes.
   _____

2. Boxer skied down the slope.
   _____

3. The lines were very long.
   _____

4. The slopes were full of people.
   _____

5. The friends skied down a trail.
   _____

6. The group went down the mountain.
   _____

7. Beauregard did a stunt.
   _____

8. The snow was cold.
   _____

9. The mountain was beautiful.
   _____

10. Betty fell into the snow when she hit a bump.
    _____

Snowbank

clad	lengthy	powdery	apparel	icy	competitors
tourists	incredibly	gear	experienced	schussed	screamed
smashed	thrilling	powder	donned	lift	soared
blasted	mogul	slippery	plunged	challenging	huge
executed	maneuver	frigid	expert	packed	magnificent

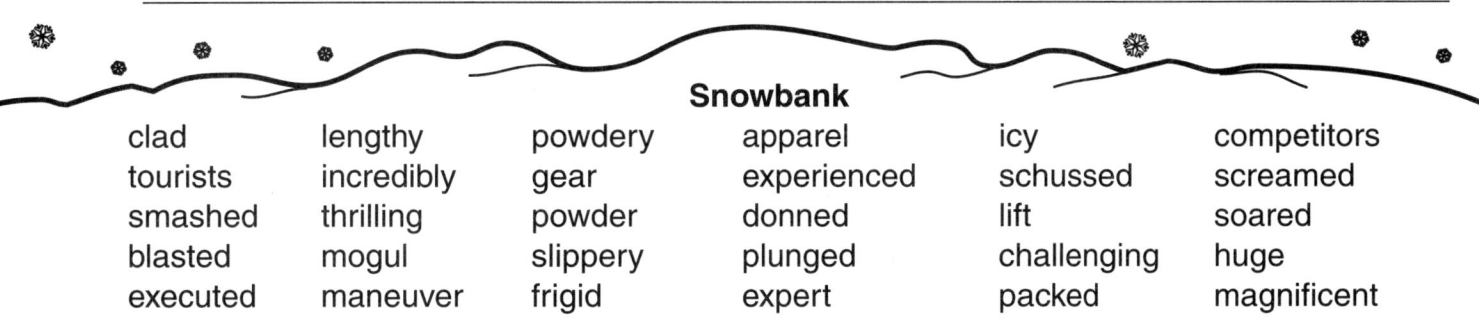

Name _____

Sentence Slalom

Slalom skiing isn't the only activity that requires skill. Combining short, choppy sentences into longer, stronger ones does too!

Directions for Two Players:
1. Cut out the cards along the bold lines.
2. Place the cards facedown on a playing surface.
3. Player 1 draws two cards. If the numbers on the cards match, Player 1 combines the sentences and states which rule he or she used. If the cards do not match, they are returned to the playing surface and play resumes with Player 2.
4. Player 2 takes a turn in the same manner.
5. Continue play until all matches have been made. The player with the most cards at the end of the game wins.

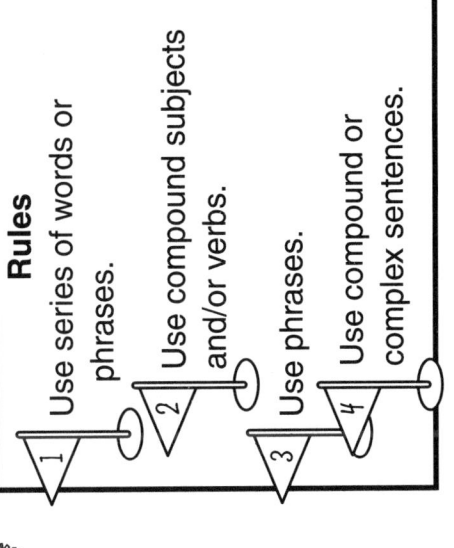

Rules
1. Use series of words or phrases.
2. Use compound subjects and/or verbs.
3. Use phrases.
4. Use compound or complex sentences.

1. Alpine skiing is a popular form of skiing.	9. Slalom is a downhill skiing technique.	2. Skis are narrow runners.	5. Schussing is a technique used to ski downhill.
10. Beginning skiers like to ski downhill and cross-country.	4. Moguls are bumps on a ski slope.	6. In ski jumping, skiers perform leaps from slopes.	1. Cross-country skiing is a popular form of skiing.
8. Skiing is an exhilarating sport.	7. Turning is a difficult part of skiing.	2. Skis curve at the tips.	4. Moguls are used in freestyle competitions.
3. Downhill equipment includes boots and poles.	6. Slopes can be as high as 90 meters.	7. Turning enables skiers to change direction and control speed.	8. Skiing is a challenging and sometimes dangerous sport.
3. Downhill equipment includes skis and bindings.	9. Slalom refers to high-speed turning on slopes.	10. Advanced skiers like to ski downhill and cross-country.	5. Traversing is a technique used to ski downhill.

How to Use Page 41

1. Pair students. Give a copy of page 41 and scissors to each pair.
2. Copy the background information on this page onto a sheet of chart paper, make a transparency, or duplicate it and give a copy to each student.
3. Discuss the information and game directions with students, instructing them to use the information to help them form their sentences. If desired, provide each pair with an answer key for self-checking.
4. Have each pair play the game as directed.

Background for the Teacher

Combining Sentences

- **Use series of words or phrases.**
  Example: The snow is new. The snow is cold. The snow is deep.
  The snow is new, cold, and deep.

- **Use compound subjects and/or verbs.** (A sentence with a compound subject includes two or more subjects. A sentence with a compound predicate includes two or more verbs.)
  Example: Boomer likes to compete in freestyle events. Betty likes to compete in freestyle events.
  Boomer and Betty like to compete in freestyle events.
  Example: Boomer tripped over his skis. He fell headfirst into a snow bank.
  Boomer tripped over his skis and fell headfirst into a snowbank.

- **Use phrases.**
  Example: Beethoven enjoys downhill skiing. Beethoven is a dog.
  Beethoven, a dog, enjoys downhill skiing.

- **Use compound or complex sentences.** (A compound sentence is made up of two simple sentences joined by conjunctions, such as and, but, or, for, and yet.)
  Example: Ballet skiing looks very simple. It requires a lot of skill.
  Ballet skiing looks very simple, but it requires a lot of skill.

  (A complex sentence is made up of two simple sentences combined using words such as while, which, and that.)
  Example: Ski clothing is made to be warm and waterproof. It should fit snugly.
  Ski clothing, which is made to be warm and waterproof, should fit snugly.

 Answer Key

Students' sentences and sentence-combining techniques may vary. Accept reasonable responses.

1. Alpine and cross-country skiing are popular forms of skiing. **2**
2. Skis are narrow runners that curve at the tips. **4**
3. Downhill equipment includes skis, bindings, boots, and poles. **1**
4. Moguls, bumps on a ski slope, are used in freestyle competitions. **3**
5. Schussing and traversing are techniques used to ski downhill. **2**
6. In ski jumping, skiers perform leaps from slopes that can be as high as 90 meters. **4**
7. Turning is a difficult part of skiing, but it enables skiers to change direction and control speed. **4**
8. Skiing is an exhilarating, challenging, and sometimes dangerous sport. **1**
9. Slalom, a downhill skiing technique, refers to high-speed turning on slopes. **3**
10. Beginning and advanced skiers like to ski downhill and cross-country. **2**

Name_____   Subject-Verb Agreement

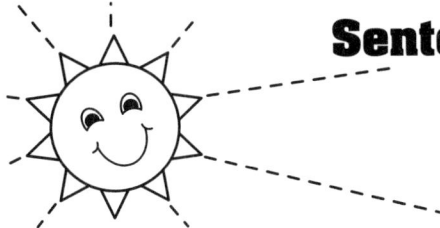

Sentences Seasoned With Summertime!

You have to agree—summertime is a season filled with fun! Each sentence below is not only seasoned with a summertime activity but with a subject and verb too.

Directions: Read each sentence below. Circle the subject in each one. Next, decide whether you *agree* or *disagree* with the verb used in each sentence. Color the sun that shows your decision. The first one is done for you.

Agree   Disagree

#	Sentence	Agree	Disagree
1.	(Sally and Sam) surf from sunrise to sunset.	B	Q
2.	Hamburgers tastes terrific when served hot off a grill.	C	E
3.	We roller-skate regularly near Rolling Rock River.	P	F
4.	Wanda water-skis wonderfully.	R	L
5.	The Higgins family hikes high in the mountains each summer.	K	S
6.	Gertrude grow flowers in her garden.	D	N
7.	I rides horses at The Triple R Ranch.	Y	A
8.	Bailey watches birds in his backyard.	Z	G
9.	Carmen camps at her cousin's country cabin.	M	H
10.	Terrel travel on a tour bus throughout Texas.	V	J
11.	Sabrina says sunbathing is simply sensational.	U	X
12.	Five friends fish at Fairview Farm.	I	B
13.	They pack a picnic of pasta and pickles.	O	W

Write the letter that you colored for each number shown below.

___ ___ ___ ___ ___ ___   ___ ___   ___   ___ ___ ___ ___ ___   ___ ___ ___ ___ ___ ___ !
 5   11   9   9   2   4   12   5   7   5   11   3   2   4   5   2   7   5   13   6

Bonus Box: On the back of this sheet, draw a picture of one of your favorite summertime activities. Write two sentences about it. Be sure that your subjects and verbs agree.

©The Education Center, Inc. • *Big Book of Skill Builders* • TEC60797   43

Answer Key

1. Sally and Sam; **Agree**
2. Hamburgers; **Disagree**
3. We; **Agree**
4. Wanda; **Agree**
5. The Higgins family; **Disagree**
6. Gertrude; **Disagree**
7. I; **Disagree**
8. Bailey; **Agree**
9. Carmen; **Agree**
10. Terrel; **Disagree**
11. Sabrina; **Agree**
12. Five friends; **Agree**
13. They; **Agree**

S U M M E R   I S   A   S U P E R   S E A S O N!
5 11 9 9 2 4   12 5   7   5 11 3 2 4   5 2 7 5 13 6

Name _____ Commas

A "Beary" Special Season!

Bernard Bear has just waked from his long winter's nap. He's writing a letter to his friend Brenda. He's still a little sleepy, so he needs help completing it.

Directions: Read the letter below and the comma rules your teacher shares with you. Using a colored pencil, complete the letter by placing commas where needed. In each paw print at the end of a group of words, write the number of the rule you used to decide where to place the comma(s).

Hint: There are 18 missing commas.

March 21 2003 🐾

Dearest friend 🐾

My what a good rest I had! 🐾 I could no longer bear my dreary stuffy den. 🐾 So I ventured outside. There I found some roots fruit and mice on which to nibble. 🐾 Brenda I was quite taken by the sights and sounds of the glorious spring morning! 🐾 The air was filled with the fragrant smell of blossoming flowers the voices of birds singing melodious tunes and the soft cry of hungry baby animals. 🐾

I remained outside most of the morning and by late afternoon I was as hungry as a bear! 🐾 My cousin Beatrice a most capable cook lives but a short distance from my home. 🐾 As I set out for my visit I found myself wandering toward the meadow. 🐾 There is a grassy slope that is just perfect for performing a good somersault or two. As I approached the meadow you'll never guess whom I saw. 🐾 Beatrice! We had a marvelous time rolling down the hill. Afterward we shared a picnic lunch she had packed.

I must close for now. There is a bothersome bug a bee hovering around my honey jar! 🐾 (Beatrice always says "Bears and bees just do not mix!") 🐾 I wish you a most pleasant spring!

Yours truly 🐾
Bernard B. Bear

Bonus Box: Imagine that you are an animal. Then, on the back of this sheet, write a letter to a friend describing your favorite things about spring. Be sure to correctly use at least five commas in your letter.

©The Education Center, Inc. • *Big Book of Skill Builders* • TEC60797

How to Use Page 45

1. Copy the rules from the background information onto a transparency or a sheet of chart paper.
2. Remind students that commas tell the reader where to pause in a sentence; then discuss each rule and its example.
3. Give a copy of page 45 to each student. Have the student complete the page as directed.

Background for the Teacher

Commas Rules
Use a comma...

1. to separate words, phrases, or clauses in a series
   Example: Birds use materials like bits of yarn, cotton, and hair for building their nests.

2. to separate items in addresses and dates
   Example: We're having a picnic on March 28, 2003, in Asheville, North Carolina.

3. to set off long phrases and clauses
   Example: Four times a year, we experience a change of seasons.

4. after a greeting or a closing in a letter
   Example: Dear Edward,
   Sincerely,
   Eleanor

5. after introductory words at the beginning of a sentence or after an interjection
   Example: Hey, why don't we meet at the zoo?

6. to separate the name of the person being spoken to from the rest of the sentence
   Example: Mary Ann, look at those beautiful flowers!

7. to set off the exact words of a speaker
   Example: "It's time for our annual spring cleaning," explained Margaret.

8. between independent clauses joined by or, and, or but
   Example: I would love to go biking, but I believe it's going to rain.

9. to set off an appositive
   Example: Shadow, our dog, had a litter of six puppies.

10. to separate adjectives that modify the same noun
    Example: Birds are lovely, colorful creatures.

March 21, 2003 (2)

Dearest friend, (4)

My, what a good rest I had! (5) I could no longer bear my dreary, stuffy den. (10) So I ventured outside. There I found some roots, fruit, and mice on which to nibble. (1) Brenda, I was quite taken by the sights and sounds of the glorious spring morning! (6) The air was filled with the fragrant smell of blossoming flowers, the voices of birds singing melodious tunes, and the soft cry of hungry baby animals. (1)

I remained outside most of the morning, and by late afternoon I was as hungry as a bear! (8) My cousin Beatrice, a most capable cook, lives but a short distance from my home. (9) As I set out for my visit, I found myself wandering toward the meadow. (3) There is a grassy slope that is just perfect for performing a good somersault or two. As I approached the meadow, you'll never guess whom I saw. (3) Beatrice! We had a marvelous time rolling down the hill. Afterward we shared a picnic lunch she had packed.

I must close for now. There is a bothersome bug, a bee, hovering around my honey jar! (9) (Beatrice always says, "Bears and bees just do not mix!") (7) I wish you a most pleasant spring!

Yours truly, (4)
Bernard B. Bear

Name _____

Quotation Marks

Animal Talk

Dana Dolots is assistant to the famous Dr. Dolittle. While Dana was caring for the doctor's pets during his spring vacation, she left a note for the doctor stating what each animal said. But Dana got so busy that she forgot to put quotation marks around the animals' exact words!

Directions: Read each statement below. Use a colored pencil to put quotation marks around the exact words of the speaker. Add other punctuation marks if needed. Use the rules below to help you. The first one is done for you.

Punctuating Direct Quotations

🐾 Place quotation marks before and after the speaker's exact words. (Do not put marks around words that tell who is speaking.)

🐾 Begin a speaker's exact words with a capital letter.

🐾 Use a comma to separate the quotation from the words that tell who is speaking.

🐾 Place a comma or a period inside quotation marks.

🐾 Place a question mark or an exclamation point inside the quotation marks if it belongs to the quotation.

1. "The silk in my web is so strong that even the heavy dew of a spring morning cannot damage it," said the spider.
2. I said the puma can jump 12 to 15 feet straight up into a tree!
3. The polar bear bellowed My thick coat keeps me warm while I enjoy a good springtime sparring.
4. I use my stomach as a table remarked the sea otter. I place a rock on it so I can break open clam shells to get to the meat inside.
5. During the spring and summer I have about 300 spots that cover my coat so wolves, bears, and other prey can't see me as easily replied the fawn.
6. Don't you know that I faithfully follow my mother wherever she goes questioned the duckling.
7. I eventually leave the pond and turn into a frog cried the tadpole.
8. Cooling off on a warm spring or summer day is easy commented the bird. I dip my feet and legs into cool water.
9. The bee answered I help pollinate many beautiful flowers.
10. I've been called the world's finest engineer barked the beaver I build dams more than 8 feet high and 40 feet wide.

Bonus Box: What would your pet or favorite animal say if it could talk? On the back of this sheet, write a sentence showing the animal's exact words. Be sure to punctuate it correctly.

Answer Key

1. "The silk in my web is so strong that even the heavy dew of a spring morning cannot damage it," said the spider.
2. "I," said the puma, "can jump 12 to 15 feet straight up into a tree!"
3. The polar bear bellowed, "My thick coat keeps me warm while I enjoy a good springtime sparring!"
4. "I use my stomach as a table," remarked the sea otter. "I place a rock on it so I can break open clam shells to get to the meat inside."
5. "During the spring and summer I have about 300 spots that cover my coat so wolves, bears, and other prey can't see me as easily," replied the fawn.
6. "Don't you know that I faithfully follow my mother wherever she goes?" questioned the duckling.
7. "I eventually leave the pond and turn into a frog!" cried the tadpole.
8. "Cooling off on a warm spring or summer day is easy," commented the bird. "I dip my feet and legs into cool water."
9. The bee answered, "I help pollinate many beautiful flowers."
10. "I've been called the world's finest engineer," barked the beaver. "I build dams more than 8 feet high and 40 feet wide."

Name _____   Apostrophes

Antsy Apostrophes

It's springtime, and Alvin Ant is getting *antsy!* He needs help finding a path to the picnic basket filled with food. Read the sentences below. Then, beginning at **START**, color a path showing the correct use of the word *ant*. Use the Color Code below to show the words that are singular possessive and plural possessive. Use a different color to show the ones that are not. The first one is done for you. What color should it be shaded?

1. _____ homes are often underground.
2. Worker _____ are all female.
3. An _____ doesn't need to work out; it can lift things 50 times heavier than its body!
4. An _____ body has three main parts.
5. _____ nests can be made from tree leaves.
6. _____ deserve straight As for their work effort!
7. Some _____ jobs include building nests, searching for food, and caring for the young.
8. The size of an _____ colony varies from a dozen to a million members.
9. _____ outer skeletons are hard, shell-like coverings.
10. A baby _____ room is called a nursery.
11. In some species, a soldier _____ chief job is to defend the colony from enemies.
12. _____ aren't all the same size.

Color Code
🐜 singular possessive = pink
🐜 plural possessive = purple

START: Ants'

Path stones: Ant's, Ants, ant's, ants, ants', ant, ants', ant, ants, Ant's, ants', ant, ants, ant's, ant, ant's, Ants, ant's, Ants', ant, ant's, Ants', Ants, ants, Ants', ants, ants', ant's, ant

"Boy, there are ants everywhere!"

©The Education Center, Inc. • *Big Book of Skill Builders* • TEC60797   49

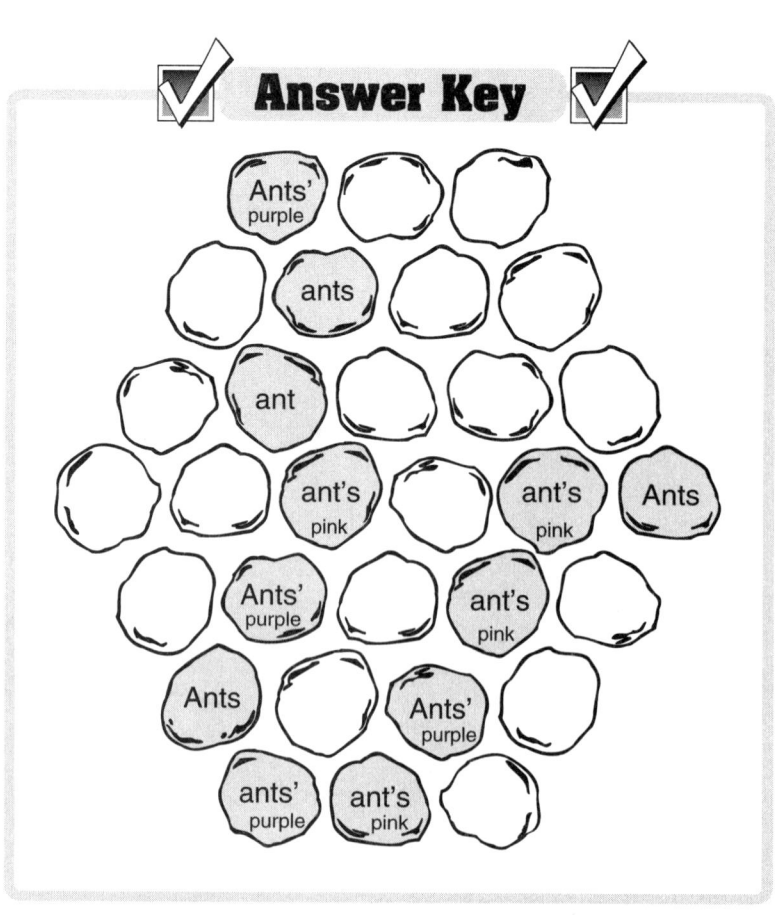

Name _____ Using the Correct Mark

Punctuation Picnic

Survey your class to complete the information below. Have a different classmate answer each item. Write each answer in a complete sentence in the space provided. Be sure to punctuate each sentence correctly.

Example: Jenny's favorite hobby is in-line skating.

Name three things that remind you of spring.	Tell your birthday, including the year.	What is your favorite hobby?	Name a contraction that you most often use.
Estimate how much money is in your wallet.	Estimate the number of miles from Earth to its nearest neighbor.	What does your parent say when you get an A on a test?	What time do you usually go to bed on Saturday night?
Name the title of your favorite song.	Name your least favorite TV program.	Share a quote from a favorite song, movie, or book.	What is your family's favorite springtime outing?
Share a sibling's name, including the middle initial.	What do you like to do after you finish your homework?	Make a statement that begins with the word *wow*.	Name four places you've visited during the year.

©The Education Center, Inc. • Big Book of Skill Builders • TEC60797

How to Use Page 51

1. Give a copy of page 51 to each student.
2. Share the background information at the right; then have students complete the activity as directed on the page. If desired, copy the rules onto a transparency sheet or sheet of chart paper. Have lower-level students use the rules to complete the activity, writing the answer and the number of the rule used in each square.
3. Discuss the students' answers, having students identify each punctuation mark and rule used.

Background for the Teacher

Punctuation Rules

1. Use a comma to separate words, phrases, or clauses in a series.
2. Use a comma between the day and year in a date.
3. Use an apostrophe to show possession.
4. Use an apostrophe in a contraction.
5. Use a period as a decimal point and to separate dollars and cents.
6. Use a comma between groups of three digits, counting from the right.
7. Use quotation marks to set off the exact words of a speaker.
8. Use a colon between the hour and minutes of the time of day.
9. Use quotation marks to show the title of a song.
10. Use italics (or underlining) to show the title of a play, book, magazine, television program, movie, or CD.
11. Use a period after an initial.
12. Use a comma after a dependent clause at the beginning of a sentence.
13. Use an exclamation point to show strong feeling after a word, a phrase, or an exclamatory sentence.

Answer Key

Students' sentences will vary.

Name three things that remind you of spring.	Tell your birthday, including the year.	What is your favorite hobby?	Name a contraction that you most often use.
1	2	3	4
Estimate how much money is in your wallet.	Estimate the number of miles from Earth to its nearest neighbor.	What does your parent say when you get an A on a test?	What time do you usually go to bed on Saturday night?
5	6	7	8
Name the title of your favorite song.	Name your least favorite TV program.	Share a quote from a favorite song, movie, or book.	What is your family's favorite springtime outing?
9	10	7	3
Share a sibling's name, including the middle initial.	What do you like to do after you finish your homework?	Make a statement that begins with the word *wow*.	Name four places you've visited during the year.
11	12	13	1

Name _____ Paragraphs

Paint a Paragraph With Details

A well-written paragraph paints a complete and interesting picture for a reader. The first sentence of a paragraph is called the *topic sentence.* The topic sentence tells what the paragraph is about. The last sentence is called the *conclusion.* It restates the topic sentence.

In between the topic sentence and the conclusion are the *details.* Detail sentences prove, explain, or support the topic sentence. Just as you can't paint a beautiful picture without colors, you can't "paint" a good paragraph without interesting details.

Directions: Fill in the blanks with details that support each topic sentence below. Use the back of this sheet if you need more space.

There are many interesting places to visit in my town.

a. _____
b. _____
c. _____
d. _____
e. _____

My town is an interesting place to visit.

Smoking is bad for your health.

a. _____
b. _____
c. _____
d. _____
e. _____

There are many reasons not to smoke.

Kittens make great pets.

a. _____
b. _____
c. _____
d. _____
e. _____

A cat is a wonderful addition to any family.

There are several ways to annoy a little brother or sister.

a. _____
b. _____
c. _____
d. _____
e. _____

It is not hard to drive a little brother or sister crazy.

Bonus Box: Choose one of the four topics listed above. On another sheet of paper, write your own paragraph using the topic sentence, details, and conclusion.

Name _____

Paragraphs

Art Museum Adventure

The sentences in the body of a paragraph should be organized in a logical order. One way to do this is by using *transition* words, such as *first, second, next,* and *finally.*

Read the sentences below about one student's trip to an art museum. Think about the order in which the sentences would occur in a paragraph. Write a number from 1 to 11 in the blank next to each sentence. Then rewrite the sentences in paragraph form. The first one has been done for you.

I had a super time when my class visited the art museum.

___ The painting was so realistic that it seemed the dancers would twirl right off the canvas!
___ In the last gallery, we saw art from ancient Egypt.
___ Finally, it was time for us to return to school.
_1_ I had a super time when my class visited the art museum.
___ The tour books described the exhibits displayed throughout the museum.
___ I will never forget my awesome adventure at the art museum.
___ As we entered the first gallery, we saw a beautiful painting of ballerinas.
___ In the next gallery was a painting of a knight on a horse.
___ As soon as we arrived, we bought our tickets and tour books.
___ My favorite in this gallery was the Egyptian mummy case.
___ In the background of the painting, I could see the knight's castle.

Bonus Box: On the back of this sheet, write a paragraph about an interesting place you have visited. Be sure to include transition words to help the sentences flow in a logical order.

55

Answer Key

5	The painting was so realistic that it seemed the dancers would twirl right off the canvas!
8	In the last gallery, we saw art from ancient Egypt.
10	Finally, it was time for us to return to school.
1	I had a super time when my class visited the art museum.
3	The tour books described the exhibits displayed throughout the museum.
11	I will never forget my awesome adventure at the art museum.
4	As we entered the first gallery, we saw a beautiful painting of ballerinas.
6	In the next gallery was a painting of a knight on a horse.
2	As soon as we arrived, we bought our tickets and tour books.
9	My favorite in this gallery was the Egyptian mummy case.
7	In the background of the painting, I could see the knight's castle.

Name_____   Narrative Paragraphs

Use Your Imagination!

A *narrative* paragraph tells a story by sharing details of an experience. It should include colorful details to make the experience come to life.

- Imagine that you woke up one morning and your favorite cartoon character was sitting on your bed. Write a paragraph telling how you spent the morning.

- Imagine that you have created a magic potion. Write a paragraph telling what you would do with it.

- Imagine that you could trade places with any person for one day. Write a paragraph telling about your day.

- Imagine that you went to school only until you were 12 years old. Write a paragraph telling about your last day of school.

- Imagine that you could become invisible by snapping your fingers. Write a paragraph telling what happened one time when you were invisible.

_____
name

©The Education Center, Inc.

©The Education Center, Inc. • *Big Book of Skill Builders* • TEC60797

How to Use Page 57

1. Make one copy of page 57 and one copy of the graphic organizer below for each student.
2. Have each student read and then select one of the five writing prompts on page 57.
3. Have the student use the graphic organizer to plan a narrative paragraph.
4. Instruct the student to refer to the organizer to write his paragraph on a sheet of loose-leaf paper.
5. Allow students to peer-edit each other's paragraphs.
6. Have each student write the final draft of his paragraph on the pattern at the bottom of page 57 and then color and cut out the pattern. Post the completed paragraphs on a bulletin board titled "Use Your Imagination!"

Graphic Organizer

Topic Sentence: _____

Supporting Detail #1: _____

Supporting Detail #2: _____

Supporting Detail #3: _____

Concluding Sentence: _____

©The Education Center, Inc. • Big Book of Skill Builders • TEC60797

Name _____ Expository Paragraphs

Expository Express

An *expository* paragraph gives information about a topic. It may tell how to do something, explain ideas, or give directions.

Write a paragraph explaining…
- how to make your bed.
- how to make a paper airplane.
- how to buy lunch in your school's cafeteria.
- how to make your favorite snack.

_____
name

©The Education Center, Inc.

How to Use Page 59

1. Make a class supply of page 59 on light-colored construction paper and give one copy to each student.
2. Have the student read and then select one of the four writing prompts at the top of the page.
3. On a sheet of loose-leaf paper, have the student write a topic sentence for an expository paragraph related to that prompt and then list the steps that he will include.
4. Instruct the student to number his steps in the best possible order for his paragraph.
5. Have the student write a rough draft of his paragraph. Point out that *transition words* help guide the reader through the paragraph. (See the list in the box.)
6. Allow students to peer-edit each other's completed paragraphs.
7. Have each student write his final draft on the train-car pattern at the bottom of page 59 and then cut out the pattern. For a great classroom display, copy the engine pattern below and post it on a wall. Then use yarn to link your students' patterns one behind the other along the wall.

Transition Words
about
after
at
before
during
first
second
third
until
meanwhile
next
soon
later
finally
then
as soon as
when

Pattern

Name _____ Descriptive Paragraphs

Picture-Perfect Descriptions

A *descriptive* paragraph describes a person, a place, a thing, or an idea. It should include words that help the reader see, hear, smell, taste, and feel what you are describing.

- Describe your dream bedroom.
- Describe a pet you own or one you would like to own.
- Describe the car you would like to own one day.
- Describe the shoes that you are wearing.
- Describe the imaginary monster that lives in your bedroom closet.

_____
name

©The Education Center, Inc.

How to Use Page 61

1. Make copies of page 61 and give one to each student.
2. Have the student read and then select one of the five writing prompts at the top of the page.
3. Model how to use a web like the one shown below for prewriting; then have each student create one for his topic.
4. Instruct each student to write a draft of his descriptive paragraph on another sheet of paper. (Remind students to use adverbs, adjectives, similes, and metaphors in their writing.)
5. Allow students to peer-edit each other's completed paragraphs.
6. Direct each student to write his final draft on the frame pattern at the bottom of page 61.
7. Have students use crayons or colored pencils to decorate their frames as desired and then cut them out.
8. Have students glue the paragraphs on 9" x 6" sheets of black construction paper. Punch holes along the left side of each sheet of black paper and bind the pages between two construction paper covers. Store the booklet in your reading corner or in your writing center for free-time viewing.

Web

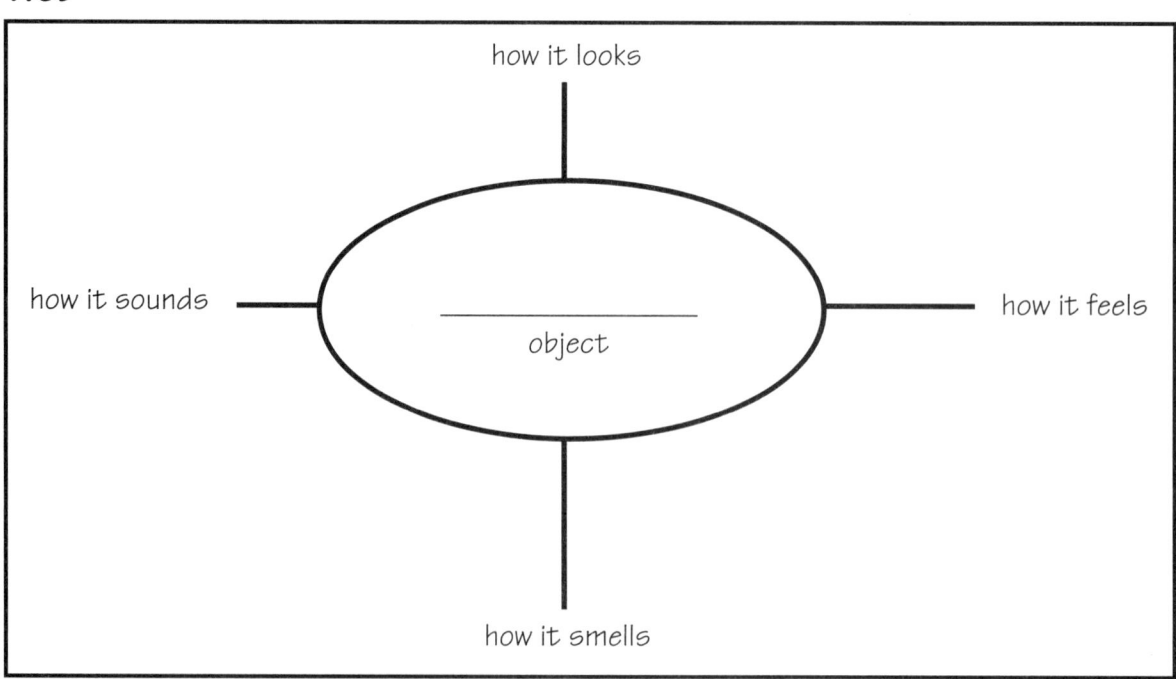

Name _____   Persuasive Paragraphs

The Power of Persuasion

A *persuasive* paragraph gives the writer's opinion on a topic. It includes strong facts and examples to convince the reader to agree with that opinion.

- Your school was given a gift of $20,000. Write a paragraph to convince your school's principal to spend the money a certain way.

- Your school does not allow students to wear hats. Write a paragraph to convince your school's principal to change this rule.

- Choose an animal. Write a paragraph to convince others that it would make a great pet.

- Choose a television show that you would either cancel or renew. Write a paragraph convincing the show's producer to either cancel or renew this show next season.

©The Education Center, Inc.

How to Use Page 63

1. Make copies of page 63 on light-colored construction paper and give one to each student.
2. Have the student read and then select one of the four writing prompts listed at the top of the page.
3. On a sheet of loose-leaf paper, have the student write a topic sentence for a persuasive paragraph and list three reasons to back up his statement.
4. Instruct the student to number his reasons in order of strength—starting with the weakest and ending with the strongest.
5. Have the student use his outline to write a rough draft of his paragraph. (Point out that transition words help guide the reader through a persuasive paragraph. See the list in the box.)
6. Allow students to peer-edit each other's completed paragraphs.
7. Have the student write his final draft on the weight pattern at the bottom of page 63 and then cut out the pattern. Enlarge a copy of the mouse with weights on page 63 and post it on a bulletin board titled "The Power of Persuasion." Staple the completed paragraphs around the board as shown.

Transition Words

in the same way	for this reason
similarly	in fact
likewise	another
like	besides
as	for example
also	for instance
but	next
yet	finally
otherwise	as well
however	along with
on the other hand	as a result of
still	therefore
although	in conclusion
even though	in summary
again	

Name _____   Similes and Metaphors

Striking It Rich!

Strike gold when you learn how to write a simile. A *simile* is a comparison of two things. The comparison is linked by the word *as* or the word *like*. For example:

His socks were as bright as a neon sign at midnight.

Complete the following sentences with similes.

1. The actor was as nervous as a _____

2. The waiter is as busy as a _____

3. Her blue eyes are like _____

4. Grandpa's laughter sounds like _____

5. The cool ocean breeze is as refreshing as _____

6. The baby's smile is as sweet as _____

7. Our class is as great as _____

A *metaphor* is a comparison linked by one of the following words: *is, are, was,* or *were*. For example: The desert was an endless sandbox under the noonday sun.

Complete the following sentences with metaphors.

8. A raindrop is _____

9. Fresh-baked cookies are _____

10. The line of cars was _____

11. The cat's purring is _____

12. Twinkling stars are _____

13. Wrapped packages are _____

14. Mom's hug was _____

©The Education Center, Inc. • *Big Book of Skill Builders* • TEC60797

Name_____   Onomatopoeia, Alliteration, and Personification

What a Gem!

Load up on these language gems! Read the definitions of *onomatopoeia, personification,* and *alliteration* below. Color code each sentence to match the technique used.

1. The ocean tickled my toes.
2. Lisa licks lime lollipops.
3. The hush of the crowd was eerie.
4. Sunshine kissed her cheek.
5. Tasty tomatoes tingle the tongue.
6. The bacon sizzled in the pan.
7. The slopes greeted the skiers.
8. Trucks whiz and zoom by.
9. Fred fries frankfurters on Friday.
10. The sunset paints the sky pink.
11. The bee buzzed by my ear.
12. The flashing light winked at the car.

Onomatopoeia is a word that sounds like the sound it names. Example: *The house creaks in the wind.* **Color these gems red.**

Personification is writing about a thing as if it were a person. Example: *Flowers danced in the yard.* **Color these gems green.**

Alliteration is repeating the beginning sounds of words in a sentence. Example: *Avoid angry alligators in the airport.* **Color these gems blue.**

Bonus Box: Create another example of each technique learned on this page. Write the sentences on the blank gems. Color code each sentence.

Answer Key

1. green (personification)
2. blue (alliteration)
3. red (onomatopoeia)
4. green (personification)
5. blue (alliteration)
6. red (onomatopoeia)
7. green (personification)
8. red (onomatopoeia)
9. blue (alliteration)
10. green (personification)
11. red (onomatopoeia) or blue (alliteration)
12. green (personification)

Name _____ Figurative Language

Diamonds in the Rough

Refine and polish each of the sentences below. Use the writing technique in parentheses as a tool to help you. The first one is done for you.

1. Dinner was delicious. (alliteration) _Dad's dinner was deliciously different._

2. The squirrels ran in the forest. (personification) _____

3. Sunrise was breathtaking. (metaphor) _____

4. Tonight there will be a full moon. (simile) _____

5. A little baby played in the crib. (onomatopoeia) _____

6. Each morning I rush to get ready for school. (simile) _____

7. The musician played a solo. (alliteration) _____

8. Peanut butter is my favorite snack. (metaphor) _____

9. The breeze stirred the trees. (personification) _____

10. Jets flew overhead. (simile) _____

11. The hens gather their chicks. (onomatopoeia) _____

Bonus Box: *Exaggeration* is a technique in which the writer goes beyond the truth. For example: *I am so thirsty I could drink an ocean!* Select two of the sentences from above. Change the meanings of the sentences by using exaggeration. Write the sentences on the back of this page.

Name _____   Homophones

Football Foul-Up

Fast Freddy, a freelance football reporter, is famous for fumbling his words. Read his notes below. In each sentence, there is a pair of *homophones* (words that have the same pronunciation, but different spellings or meanings) that may or may not be used correctly. Circle each homophone pair. Then, if the homophones are used correctly, color the football.

1. Before the game began, one of the players eight ate hot dogs.

2. Sum people paid a great some of money for their tickets.

3. Hear in the stadium, you could here the fans roar loudly.

4. After the first quarter, I went to buy a snack by the ticket booth.

5. A lineman ran for only four yards before being tackled.

6. At halftime, neither team had any points. I can't bare the sight of a bear scoreboard!

7. I just knew that the new quarterback would get sacked!

8. The official blue his whistle when a fan with his face painted blew came out onto the field.

9. Two of the players accidentally tackled the coach. I've never scene such a seen!

10. A player past the ball just passed the 50-yard line.

11. The defense was too weak to prevent the winning touchdown.

12. When his favorite team won, one fan did somersaults along the sidelines!

Bonus Box: Think of as many other homophone pairs as you can. Write the pairs on the back of this sheet.

©The Education Center, Inc. • *Big Book of Skill Builders* • TEC60797

Answer Key

1. Before the game began, one of the players (eight) (ate) hot dogs.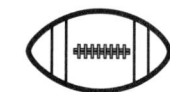

2. (Sum) people paid a great (some) of money for their tickets.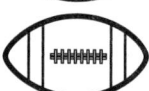

3. (Hear) in the stadium, you could (here) the fans roar loudly.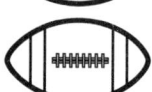

4. After the first quarter, I went to (buy) a snack (by) the ticket booth.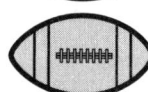

5. A lineman ran (for) only (four) yards before being tackled.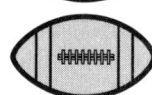

6. At halftime, neither team had any points. I can't (bare) the sight of a (bear) scoreboard!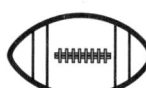

7. I just (knew) that the (new) quarterback would get sacked!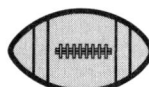

8. The official (blue) his whistle when a fan with his face painted (blew) came out onto the field.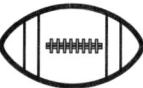

9. Two of the players accidentally tackled the coach. I've never (scene) such a (seen)!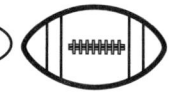

10. A player (past) the ball just (passed) the 50-yard line.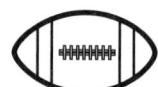

11. The defense was (too) weak (to) prevent the winning touchdown.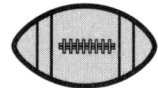

12. When his favorite team (won), (one) fan did somersaults along the sidelines!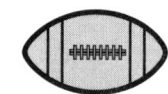

Bonus Box: Answers will vary. Possible answers include the following: *allowed/aloud, ant/aunt, board/bored, brake/break, cent/scent/sent, close/clothes, dear/deer, die/dye, eye/I, hare/hair, hi/high, knight/night, knows/nose, made/maid, meat/meet, pain/pane, peace/piece, rain/rein/reign, read/red, right/write, son/sun, tail/tale, wait/weight.*

Name _____ Prefixes and Suffixes

Operation Ex-Files

As a special agent for this project, you will use words that are unique to your job. Read each definition below. Then use the word parts on the file folders to make a new word that matches each definition. To do this, match a prefix or suffix on the left with a word or base word on the right. Be sure to spell each word correctly. Use the reference list your teacher gives you and a dictionary for help.

Example: *inter* (among, between) + *planetary* (of the planets) = *interplanetary* (something that is among or between the planets)

Prefix/Suffix
- -er
- bi-
- co-
- inter-
- extra-
- penta-
- pseudo-
- -ology
- micro-
- un-
- trans-

Word/Base Word
- *believable* .... capable of being believed
- *nym* .... from *onyma* meaning "name"
- *astronomy* ... the study of the stars, planets, and space
- *scope* .... an instrument for viewing
- *terrestrial* ..... of the earth
- *planetary* ..... of the planets
- *gon* .... figure having many angles
- *ped* .... of or relating to the foot
- *pilot* .... a person who steers a ship
- *UFO* .... an unidentified flying object
- *form* .... the shape of something

1. a five-sided building in Arlington, Virginia, that is the headquarters of the U.S. Department of Defense _____

2. a false name _____

3. someone who flies with and assists the main pilot _____

4. the study of unidentified flying objects _____

5. something so strange, amazing, or surprising that you find it difficult to accept as true _____

6. a person who studies the stars, planets, and space _____

7. a tool used to magnify small things so they may be observed and studied _____

8. something from outer space _____

9. a two-footed creature _____

10. to change the outward form or appearance _____

Bonus Box: Choose two prefixes and two suffixes from the list. Use a dictionary to find a word that includes each one. Write each word and its meaning on the back of this sheet.

How to Use Page 73

1. Remind students that a word's spelling may change when a prefix or suffix is added to it.
2. Review the prefix and suffix reference list below with students. Have them give examples of words that include these affixes. If desired, make a copy of the list for each student.
3. Give a copy of page 73 to each student. Instruct the student to follow the directions on the sheet to complete the activity.

 Answer Key

1. penta + gon = Pentagon
2. pseudo + nym = pseudonym
3. co + pilot = copilot
4. UFO + ology = ufology or UFOlogy
5. un + believable = unbelievable
6. astronomy + er = astronomer
7. micro + scope = microscope
8. extra + terrestrial = extraterrestrial
9. bi + ped = biped
10. trans + form = transform

Reference List

Use with "Operation Ex-Files" on page 73 and "Alien Transformations" on page 75.

Prefix and Suffix List

Prefix	Meaning	Prefix	Meaning	Suffix	Meaning
anti-	against	*multi-*	many, much	*-able, -ible*	able to
astro-	star	*oct-*	eight	*-al*	relating to, of the
auto-	self	*penta-*	five	*-er*	one who does
bi-	two	*poly-*	many	*-ful*	full of
circum-	around	*post-*	after	*-ic*	like
co-	with, together	*pre-*	before	*-ile*	capable of
deca-, deka-	ten	*pro-*	for, in favor of	*-ily*	in some manner
dis-	apart from, not	*pseudo-*	false	*-ion, -sion, -tion*	state of
ex-	out	*quad-*	four		
extra-	outside, beyond	*re-*	again	*-ist*	one who
fore-	before, earlier, in front	*sub-*	under	*-less*	without
hexa-	six	*super-*	above	*-ment*	act or result
il-, im-, in-, ir-	not	*trans-*	across, change	*-ness*	state of
in-	into	*tri-*	three	*-ology*	study or science of
inter-	among, between	*un-*	not	*-ous*	full of
micro-	small	*uni-*	one	*-y*	inclined to

©The Education Center, Inc. • Big Book of Skill Builders • TEC60797

Name _____ Prefixes and Suffixes

Alien Transformations

When you add a prefix or a suffix to a word, it can go through an unusual change! Read the directions below to complete each section. Be sure to spell your answers correctly. Use the reference list your teacher gives you and a dictionary for help.

Adding a prefix or a suffix to a word may change it to an *antonym*—a word that has an opposite meaning. Change the prefix or suffix in each word below, or add one to it, to make an antonym. Write your answer in the blank beside each word.

1. powerless _____
2. posttest _____
3. subhuman _____
4. careful _____
5. believable _____

6. pronuclear _____
7. fiction _____
8. export _____
9. known _____
10. regular _____

Adding a suffix to a word can change its part of speech. For example, when you add *-ment* to the verb *manage*, it becomes the noun *management*. Read each word below. Add a suffix to the word that changes it to the part of speech named (n = noun, v = verb, adj = adjective, and adv = adverb). Write your answers in the blanks beside each word.

1. itch (n)   + _____ = _____ (adj: likely to itch)
2. eerie (adj) + _____ = _____ (adv: in an eerie way)
3. infect (v) + _____ = _____ (n: state of being infected)
4. metal (n)   + _____ = _____ (adj: like metal)
5. dark (adj) + _____ = _____ (n: state of being dark)
6. awe (n)   + _____ = _____ (adj: full of awe)
7. like (v)   + _____ = _____ (adj: able to be liked)
8. poet (n)   + _____ = _____ (adj: like a poet)

Bonus Box: Imagine that you can change into an alien. Use four words from the above activities to describe how you change and what you look like. Write your description on the back of this sheet.

Answer Key

1. powerful
2. pretest
3. superhuman
4. careless
5. unbelievable
6. antinuclear
7. nonfiction
8. import
9. unknown
10. irregular

1. itch + y = itchy
2. eerie + ly = eerily
3. infect + tion = infection
4. metal + ic = metallic
5. dark + ness = darkness
6. awe + ful = awful
7. like + able = likable
8. poet + ic = poetic

Name _____ Base Words

Discovering Base Bones

Dinah is a *paleontologist*—a person who studies fossils. Help Dinah find the base word in each group of fossil bones below. Remember that a base word is the simplest form of a word before prefixes and suffixes are added to it.

Write the base word for each group of words in the blank fossil bone.

1. beheaded, headless, heady
2. appearance, disappear, appearing
3. disbelieve, believer, believable
4. historian, historical, prehistoric
5. loveless, lovable, unloved
6. deboned, boneless, bony
7. unarmed, armed, rearm
8. small-brained, brainless, brainy

Bonus Box: On the back of this sheet, write a sentence with one word from each group above. Choose a word other than the base word in each group.

Answer Key

1. head
2. appear
3. believe
4. history
5. love
6. bone
7. arm
8. brain

Name _____ Prefixes

Dinosaur Discoveries

Dinah is trying to discover the name of one of the largest and heaviest known dinosaurs ever to live. This giant, plant-eating creature was also very gentle. Do you know what it is called?

Help Dinah find the answer by solving the puzzle below. Use the number prefixes to make words that fit in the boxes. Write one letter per box. When you're finished, the answer will appear in the bold boxes.

Prefix	Meaning
semi-	half
uni-	one
bi-	two
tri-	three
quad-, quart-, quatr-	four
deca-	ten

Clues

1. a vehicle with two wheels, handlebars, and a seat
2. a coin equal to one-fourth of a dollar
3. a geometric shape with three sides and three angles
4. a mythical animal with one horn
5. a ten-event athletic contest
6. a set of three children born at the same time
7. identical clothing worn by everyone in the same group
8. half of a circle
9. a plane with two wings
10. a group of four singers or musicians
11. a flag made up of three colors
12. happening every half year
13. a punctuation mark that is half colon and half comma

Bonus Box: Use an encyclopedia or other resource to find out more about Dinah's dinosaur. On the back of this page, write a brief paragraph. What were some of the advantages of being such a big animal?

©The Education Center, Inc. • Big Book of Skill Builders • TEC60797

Answer Key

1. bicycle
2. quarter
3. triangle
4. unicorn
5. decathlon
6. triplets
7. uniform
8. semicircle
9. biplane
10. quartet
11. tricolor
12. semiannual
13. semicolon

Dinah's dinosaur is a **brachiosaurus.**

Bonus Box: The brachiosaurus is one of the most massive land creatures known to science. It lived about 140 million years ago. With its long neck, a brachiosaurus could reach food high up in trees. Predators would think twice before they would attack such a huge creature!

Name _____ Suffixes

All's Well That Ends Well

Dinah is preparing a report to present at the National Convention on Dinosaurs. She wants to use some words that contain suffixes in her report. Suffixes are word parts added to the ends of words.

Study the list of suffixes and their meanings below. Help Dinah make new words by adding suffixes to the base words in the word bank. Use the new words to complete the activities below. You may use a word more than one time.

Suffix	Meaning
-less	without
-ful	full of
-able	can be done
-ish	like, pertaining to
-er	compared to something
-ly	characteristic of
-ist	person who
-like	like
-ous	having the qualities of
-ness	state of, condition of

1. List three words that might appear in a paragraph about people who work with dinosaur fossils.

   _____ _____ _____

2. List three words that might appear in a paragraph about plant-eating dinosaurs.

   _____ _____ _____

3. List three words that might appear in a paragraph about meat-eating dinosaurs.

   _____ _____ _____

4. List three words that might appear in a paragraph about a human being going back in time to the age of dinosaurs.

   _____ _____ _____

5. List four words that might appear in a paragraph describing the earth during the dinosaur age.

   _____ _____ _____ _____

6. List three words that might appear in a paragraph about you and dinosaurs.

   _____ _____ _____

Word Bank					
agree	archaeology	art	biology	bright	care
cartoon	comfort	fear	friend	geology	gray
green	hope	large	love	sharp	small
soft	weak	wonder	work		

Bonus Box: Choose one of the six lists. Write a paragraph using all of the words in the list. Circle all words in your paragraph that have suffixes.

Answer Key

Answers will vary. Possible answers include the following:
1. cartoonist, archaeologist, artist, wonderful, biologist, workable, worker, geologist, careful
2. greenish, softness, fearful, largeness, grayish
3. brighter, careful, careless, fearless, greenish, grayish, smaller
4. agreeable, brighter, fearful, comfortable, comfortless, hopeful, friendly, friendless, smaller, careful
5. brighter, greenish, grayish, comfortable, lovely, hopeful, hopeless, sharper, wonderful, friendless, fearful
6. agreeable, careful, comfortable, fearful, fearless, friendly, hopeful, lovable, smaller, softer, weaker, wonderful

Name_____   Word Roots

Getting to the Root of the Problem

Dinah is interested in *archaeology*—the scientific study of the remains of past human life and activities. She's having trouble understanding some new words in her reading.

Use the word roots and their meanings below to help you decode the meanings of the words Dinah doesn't understand. The list of *affixes* (prefixes and suffixes) will also be helpful. Write your answers in the blanks provided.

Dinah's Problem Words   **Meanings**

1. revolve _____
   _____

2. geology _____
   _____

3. hemisphere _____
   _____

4. bisect _____
   _____

5. microscope _____
   _____

6. biped _____
   _____

7. visible _____
   _____

8. manuscript _____
   _____

9. biology _____
   _____

10. transform _____
    _____

Root	Meaning	Example	Affix	Meaning
vol, volv	roll, turn	revolt	re-	again
geo	earth	geography	hemi-	half
spher	ball	atmosphere	bi-	two
sec, sect	cut	insect	micro-	small
scope	watch	telescope	trans-	over, across
ped	foot	pedal	-logy	science of
vis	see	vision	-ible	can be done
scrib, script	write	describe		
bio	life	biography		
form	shape	uniform		
man	hand	manual		

Bonus Box: Would you like to be an archaeologist? Write a brief paragraph on the back of this sheet explaining your answer.

©The Education Center, Inc. • *Big Book of Skill Builders* • TEC60797   83

 **Answer Key**

Answers will vary. Suggested literal and specific answers:
1. revolve: to turn around again and again (to recur in cycles)
2. geology: the study of the earth (the scientific study of the origin, history, and structure of the earth)
3. hemisphere: half of a ball (half of a sphere)
4. bisect: to cut into two parts (to cut or divide into two equal parts)
5. microscope: an instrument to watch small things (an optical instrument that magnifies images of small objects)
6. biped: something with two feet (an animal with two feet)
7. visible: able to be seen (capable of being seen)
8. manuscript: something written by hand (a book or document written by hand)
9. biology: the science of life (the science of living organisms and life processes)
10. transform: to change over the shape (to change markedly the form or appearance of)

Name_____   Multiple-Meaning Words

Tracking Down Word Meanings

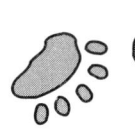        

Were these tracks made by a sleuth of bears or a gaggle of geese? Such words as *sleuth* and *gaggle* describe groups of things, particularly animals.

Below are other words used to name animal groups. Some of the words are not used much anymore, but they do make our language more colorful and vivid.

Write a sentence using each bold word as a group of animals. Then write a second sentence using a different meaning for the bold word.

Example: a **bale** of turtles   Joey found a *bale* of turtles near the lake.
Marti fed the cows a *bale* of hay.

1. a **band** of gorillas _____

2. a **brace** of ducks _____

3. a **cast** of hawks _____

4. a **charm** of goldfinches _____

5. a **watch** of nightingales _____

6. a **gang** of elks _____

7. a **knot** of toads _____

8. a **pride** of lions _____

9. a **clutter** of cats _____

10. a **leash** of foxes _____

11. a **mob** of kangaroos _____

12. a **pack** of wolves _____

13. a **pod** of whales _____

14. a **school** of fish _____

15. a **leap** of leopards _____

Bonus Box: Make a word game with ten small index cards. On one side of a card, draw a picture of an animal group. On the opposite side of the card, illustrate a different meaning of the word. Exchange cards with a friend and try to identify the words represented by the picture clues.

Name_____ Analogies

Investigating Analogies

An *analogy* compares a likeness between two objects that are otherwise unlike. Read the analogies below. Act like a detective and try to find the missing word for each one. The clue is to discover how the words in the first pair go together.

> **Example:** *Goose* is to *gosling* as *cow* is to _____.
>
> A gosling is a baby goose, so what is a baby cow? If you guessed *calf* you are absolutely correct!

Now use your detective brainpower to determine the clues that will help you solve each analogy below!

1. *Duck* is to *waddle* as *frog* is to _____.
2. *Hot dog* is to *eat* as *milk* is to _____.
3. *Water* is to *wet* as *desert* is to _____.
4. *Pickle* is to *sour* as *candy* is to _____.
5. *Boat* is to *water* as *airplane* is to _____.
6. *Skin* is to *humans* as *scales* are to _____.
7. *Flour* is to *wheat* as *sawdust* is to _____.
8. *Dog* is to *bark* as *cat* is to _____.
9. *Perfume* is to *nose* as *music* is to _____.
10. *Potato* is to *vegetable* as *apple* is to _____.
11. *Grass* is to *green* as *sky* is to _____.
12. *Spaghetti* is to *Italian* as *taco* is to _____.
13. *Baseball* is to *throw* as *soccer ball* is to _____.
14. *Curtains* are to *windows* as *sunglasses* are to _____.
15. *Apple* is to *skin* as *nut* is to _____.
16. *Foot* is to *big toe* as *hand* is to _____.
17. *Shower* is to *bathroom* as *refrigerator* is to _____.
18. *Lawyer* is to *courtroom* as *teacher* is to _____.
19. *Noise* is to *loud* as *whisper* is to _____.
20. *Smell* is to *nose* as *touch* is to _____.

Bonus Box: Think of some more analogies. Write each one on the back of this page, leaving out the last word. Exchange papers with a classmate and complete each other's analogies.

©The Education Center, Inc. • *Big Book of Skill Builders* • TEC60797

Answer Key

Suggested answers:
1. hop
2. drink
3. dry
4. sweet
5. air
6. fish
7. wood
8. meow
9. ears
10. fruit
11. blue
12. Mexican
13. kick
14. eyes
15. shell
16. thumb
17. kitchen
18. classroom
19. quiet
20. skin

Name _____ Using a Dictionary

Dictionary Dig

Professor I. Diggit, an anthropologist, found a mysterious box in the basement of the museum. The box was stamped with the word *frangible*, and inside it was a vase. Professor Diggit pulled out her handy reference book, the dictionary, to see what the strange word meant. Follow the directions to help her answer the questions below.

Directions: Study the dictionary entry for the word *frangible*. Read each of Professor Diggit's questions. In the vase beside each question, write the letter that matches the part of the entry where the answer can be found. Then answer each question in the space provided.

A. Word Entry **B. Pronunciation** **C. Definition** **D. Examples**

fran•gi•ble   ('fran-jə-bəl)   *adj.*   Easily broken: *Handle the frangible bowl with care.*

[Latin *frangere*, to break]   fran•gi•bil•i•ty   *n.*   **Syn:** *fragile*

E. Etymology (language the word comes from and its meaning)   **F. Other Forms**   **G. Synonym**

H. Parts of Speech Labels

---

1. How would you say the word *frangible?* Write its pronunciation. _____

2. What does *frangible* mean? _____

3. What part of speech is *frangible?* _____

4. What are the other forms of *frangible?* _____

5. What word means the same as *frangible?* _____

6. How could *frangible* be used in a sentence? _____
_____

7. From what language does *frangible* originally come? _____

8. What does its word of origin mean? _____

Bonus Box: Professor Diggit found several other items with strange words written on them. Use a dictionary to help her find the entry part in parentheses for each of the following words: *fresco* (part of speech), *archaic* (definition), *excavate* (pronunciation), *primitive* (example), *peculiar* (other forms).

Answer Key

1. B, 'fran-jə-bəl
2. C, easily broken
3. H, adjective
4. F, frangibility
5. G, fragile
6. D, Handle the frangible bowl with care.
7. E, Latin
8. E, to break

Bonus Box:

fresco—noun or verb
archaic—very old-fashioned, not used anymore
excavate—'ek-skə-ˌvāt
primitive—Cave dwellers hunted with primitive weapons.
peculiar—peculiarity, peculiarly

Name _____   Using an Encyclopedia

Encyclopedia Search

Professor I. Diggit has a big problem! She's leaving on a trip to Egypt tomorrow and she hasn't completed her research. Help Professor Diggit out by following the directions below.

Directions: Read each research note and the question that follows. Then choose the encyclopedia volume in which Professor Diggit can find the answer. Write the item number on the correct volume. Some volumes may not be used. Some may be used more than once.

1. I will travel to Egypt, a country in the Middle East. What other countries make up the Middle East?
2. I will fly into several airports before I reach Egypt. What are the world's busiest airports?
3. I will work in Egypt. What is the government like there?
4. I've heard that Egypt's court system has no juries. Is that true?
5. I will travel by boat down the Nile River. Into what body of water does the river flow?
6. I will travel by camel across the desert. What is the purpose of a camel's hump?
7. My plans include seeing great pyramids. Which pyramids are located in Egypt?
8. While in Egypt, I will study hieroglyphics. What are the meanings of some hieroglyphics?
9. I also plan to visit the Dead Sea. Is it true that this sea is actually a saltwater lake?
10. Anwar Sadat was a famous world leader. During which years was he president of Egypt?
11. Islam is the official religion in Egypt. What do you call a person who practices this religion?
12. After completing my work in Egypt, I will visit my sister in Madrid, Spain. What is the economy like there?

Volumes: A, B, C–Ch, Ci–Cz, D, E, F, G, H, I, J•K, L, M, N•O, P, Q•R, S–Sn, So–Sz, T, U•V, W•X•Y•Z

Bonus Box: Choose two questions from Professor Diggit's research. Use encyclopedias to help you answer the questions correctly.

Answer Key

1. M
2. A
3. E
4. E
5. N•O
6. C–Ch
7. P, E
8. H
9. D
10. S–Sn
11. I
12. M, So–Sz

Awesome "Al-moo-nacs"

Using an Almanac

Professor I. Diggit dug up an ancient vase in the shape of a cow. Around the cow's neck was a shiny gold bell. Why did the cow have a gold bell around her neck? Complete the activity below to find out.

Directions: Read each question below. Decide which almanac shown below would most likely contain the answer. Then lightly color the bell with the matching letter.

Almanac of Movies	The World Almanac of Transportation	Almanac of World Leaders	Almanac of Art Treasures	The Almanac of Inventions	The Almanac of Fashion	Famous People Almanac	The Sailor's Almanac	Farming Almanac	The Almanac of Rock Groups	The World Almanac of Careers
T	N	D	S	H	E	R	I	O	W	K

1. What was the most popular car of 1955? N T R
2. When did pleated skirts first come on the market? I E R
3. When was the Egyptian system of writing invented? H I O
4. When is the best time to plant corn? H N O
5. Who was the president of France in 1964? D W O
6. What year were the contents of King Tutankhamen's tomb discovered? T K S
7. Who were the 1988 Third World leaders? D E K
8. Who are the most well-known train robbers? W R D
9. What is a tide chart? N T I
10. When did the first hot-air balloon flight take place? S N I
11. What is the most money-making movie of all time? T H R
12. Who is the most popular lead singer? H W D
13. What is the highest paying occupation? E T K
14. How big was the largest tomato ever grown? K O H
15. Who was Mother Teresa? K S R
16. Where was Michael Jordan born? R H O
17. Who designed the first traffic light? I H K

Write the letter that you colored for each number shown below.

___ ___ ___ ___ ___ ___ ___ ___ ___ , ___ ___ ___ ___ ___ ___ ___ ___ !
 3   2   8   17 14 15   1   6   7   9   5 10 11 12   4 16 13

Answer Key

1.	N	10.	N
2.	E	11.	T
3.	H	12.	W
4.	O	13.	K
5.	D	14.	O
6.	S	15.	R
7.	D	16.	R
8.	R	17.	H
9.	I		

H E R H O R N S D I D N'T W O R K !

Name _____

Using an Atlas

Mapping Out the Atlas

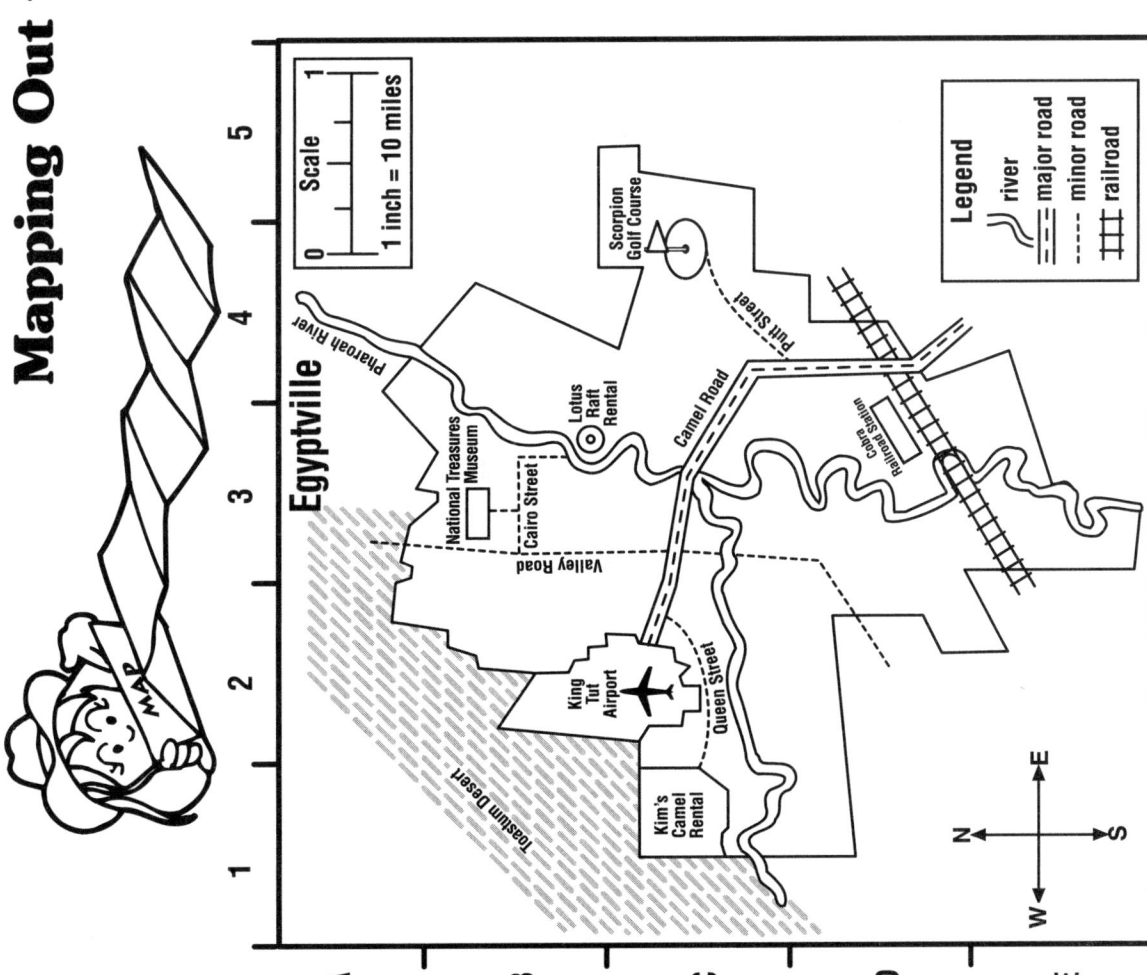

Directions: Read each statement below. To determine if the statement is true or false, study the map from Professor I. Diggit's atlas. If the statement is true, circle the T and write your proof on the line. If the statement is false, circle the F and rewrite the statement, making it true.

1. T F This is a map of Egypt. _____

2. T F This map gives information about roads, places, and the climate of Egyptville. _____

3. T F The index and grid provide the location of specific places on the map. _____

4. T F The distance from one place in Egyptville to another can be measured in miles. _____

5. T F There are several major roads in Egyptville. _____

6. T F There are at least two recreational areas in Egyptville. _____

7. T F A traveler can arrive in Egyptville by plane or train. _____

8. T F The only way to cross Toastum Desert is by automobile. _____

©The Education Center, Inc. • *Big Book of Skill Builders* • TEC60797

Answers may vary. Accept reasonable responses.

1. False; This is a map of Egyptville.
2. False; This map only gives information about the roads and the places in Egyptville.
3. True; Cobra Railroad Station is located at D3.
4. True; The distance from King Tut Airport to Scorpion Golf Course is about 25 miles.
5. False; Camel Road is the only major road in Egyptville.
6. True; Lotus Raft Rental and Scorpion Golf Course are two recreational areas in Egyptville.
7. True; King Tut Airport and Cobra Railroad Station are in Egyptville.
8. False; A person can rent a camel to cross Toastum Desert.

Name _____ Choosing the Best Reference

Reference Refresher

Professor I. Diggit is very confused! She has so many topics to research and she can't decide which reference book is best. Help the professor refresh her memory by following the directions below.

Directions: Think about how each reference book shown below is different. Decide which reference or references would be the best for each research topic. Write the number of the topic in the matching book. The first one is done for you.

1. the economy of China
2. synonyms of the word *good*
3. the pronunciation of the word *sponging*
4. a map of Florida towns, including an index
5. a map of Europe
6. how to use the word *range* in a sentence
7. synonyms and antonyms of the word *malevolent*
8. information on England

9. the highest-paying job in the year 2002
10. information about the Seven Cities of Cíbola
11. the time the next lunar eclipse will occur
12. inventions
13. the different parts of a saddle
14. the meaning of the word *slothful*
15. the different parts of speech of the word *object*
16. antonyms of the word *ashamed*

Bonus Box: If you could have only one reference book for the school year, which one would it be? On the back of this paper, write your choice and explain why you chose it.

Accept reasonable responses.

Dictionary:
 3, 6, 14, 15
Thesaurus:
 7, 16
Dictionary or Thesaurus:
 2
Encyclopedia:
 1, 8, 10, 13

Encyclopedia or Atlas:
 5
Atlas:
 4
Encyclopedia or Almanac:
 12
Almanac:
 9, 11

Name _____ Reading for Details

THE WILD WEST REPORTER

VOL. XXVI   Saturday, September 27, 2003   50¢

SHERIFF ROUNDS UP HORSE THIEVES!

The case of Mr. Shepard's missing horses has been solved! Last Saturday, Mr. Shepard reported that two of his prized stallions were missing. Sheriff Sam Goodbody, who immediately began investigating the case, said, "I had my suspicions about the horse-stealing scoundrels but had no proof."

Earlier in the week, Sheriff Goodbody spotted the three meanest horse thieves in the West, the notorious Basset brothers. He thought they looked up to no good, so he tailed them. While at Bald Ben's Barbershop, he overheard the brothers bragging about how easy it was to steal Mr. Shepard's stallions. Then he overheard their plan to swipe two more at high noon on Thursday, September 25.

Sheriff Goodbody was hiding in the tumbleweeds when the Basset brothers arrived at Mr. Shepard's farm. The brothers were quite surprised when the sheriff arrested them and hauled them off to jail. Mr. Shepard's horses were returned safe and sound.

THE NOTORIOUS BASSET BROTHERS

Directions: Carefully read the news article above. Then circle the correct answer for each question below.

1. When did Mr. Shepard report his horses missing?
   a. Thursday
   b. last Saturday
   c. September 25
   d. Tuesday

2. Who investigated the case?
   a. Sam Goody
   b. Mr. Shepard
   c. Sheriff Sam Goodbody
   d. Mr. Basset

3. Who did Sheriff Goodbody suspect had stolen the horses?
   a. Mr. Shepard
   b. the barber
   c. the Basset brothers
   d. the librarian

4. How did the sheriff find out about the Basset brothers' plan to steal more of Mr. Shepard's horses?
   a. He overheard the brothers talking at the saloon.
   b. The barber told him.
   c. Mr. Shepard told him.
   d. He overheard the brothers talking in the barbershop.

5. Why didn't the Basset brothers see the sheriff when they tried to steal horses a second time?
   a. The sheriff was hiding in a tree.
   b. The sheriff was watching in a plane.
   c. The sheriff was hiding in the tumbleweeds.
   d. The sheriff was disguised as a horse.

Bonus Box: On the back of this sheet, illustrate one of the scenes described in the news article above. Label each detail shown in the scene.

Answer Key

1. b
2. c
3. c
4. d
5. c

Name _____   Predicting Outcomes

Choose Your Own Ending

Directions: Read the story below. Then carefully think of several possible outcomes. Choose one outcome and write an ending for the story in the space provided. Then illustrate your ending in the picture frame.

The Strange Noise

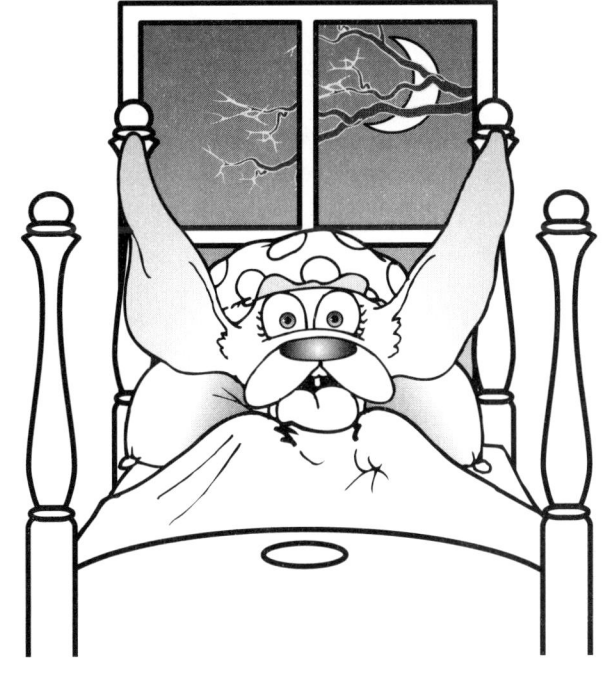

In the middle of the night, Pamela awoke to a strange noise coming from outside. Living out west in the desert, she was used to hearing strange noises late at night. But this was the eeriest noise Pamela had ever heard. This was no coyote or hoot owl sounding off in the night. As she listened, the sound seemed to be getting closer and closer. Now the strange noise appeared to be coming from right beneath her bedroom window! Pamela wanted to get out of her bed and look out the window to see what it was, but she was too scared. "What if it's a thief, or even worse, some kind of monster?" she thought. Finally, she decided to make a dash for the door and run downstairs to her parents' room. But just as she hopped out of bed, she heard the front door creak open. Pamela froze with fright and could not move. Her mind was racing. Should she run to her parents' room or remain in her room and hide under her bed?

Your Ending

_____
_____
_____
_____
_____
_____
_____
_____
_____

Draw a picture of your ending here.

Bonus Box: Write your own "Choose Your Own Ending" story on the back of this sheet. Then give it to a friend to write the story's ending.

How to Use Page 101

1. Ask your students if they've ever watched a movie that did not give an ending and the audience had to determine from events in the movie what might have happened. Allow several students to share their experiences.
2. Tell your students that this is known as a *cliffhanger*. Explain that sometimes a writer will end a story with a cliffhanger so that the reader has to use story details to help predict an ending.
3. Give each student one copy of page 101. Instruct each student to complete the page as directed.
4. Allow time for each student to share his story ending. Take a count to see how many different endings the class creates.

 Answer Key

There are numerous possible endings to the story, and students' endings will vary. Accept any reasonable ending.

Name _____ Sequencing

Cartoon Crazies

Directions: The cartoon below is out of order. Read each scene. Then carefully cut out each scene along the bold lines. Glue each scene in the correct order onto a sheet of construction paper.

Answer Key

Name _____   Drawing Conclusions

Dude Ranch Dream Vacation?

Duke and Daisy are spending two weeks at the Wild West Dude Ranch. It's been a week since they've seen their ma and pa, so they've decided to write home to tell about their stay.

Directions: Read each letter. Underline the clues in each letter that help explain how Duke and Daisy feel about their stay at the dude ranch. Use the underlined clues to help you conclude who is enjoying the dude ranch and who is not. Write your conclusions in the appropriate boxes at the bottom of the page.

Dear Ma and Pa,
   I know I didn't want to leave home at first. We've learned how to ride horses, use a lasso, and shoe a horse. We also get to help out when it's time to "rustle up some grub." (That's Western talk for eat.) I can't believe that a week has already passed. Gosh, before you know it, my stay at Wild West Dude Ranch will be over! See you soon.

Love,
Duke

Dear Ma and Pa,
   I can't believe that only a week has passed! Can you believe that they make us fix our own meals? I've had to climb up on a dirty horse and even clean out a dirty stall! I hope I survive another week here. I could have gone to Camp Pom-Pom. Just think, I could be wearing a cute costume and saying, "Go Team!" all day. Oh well, before you know it, my stay at Wild West Dude Ranch will be over. See you soon.

Love,
Daisy

I CONCLUDE THAT DUKE...

_____
_____
_____
_____

I CONCLUDE THAT DAISY...

_____
_____
_____
_____

Bonus Box: Think of the first time you spent the night away from home. Did you have a good time, or did you want to go back home? Write a brief paragraph giving details about how you felt.

Answer Key

Answers may vary. Accept reasonable responses.

Dear Ma and Pa,
  I know I didn't want to leave home at first. We've learned how to ride horses, use a lasso, and shoe a horse. We also get to help out when it's time to "rustle up some grub." (That's Western talk for eat.) I can't believe that a week has already passed. Gosh, before you know it, my stay at Wild West Dude Ranch will be over! See you soon.

  Love,
  Duke

Dear Ma and Pa,
  I can't believe that only a week has passed! Can you believe that they make us fix our own meals? I've had to climb up on a dirty horse and even clean out a dirty stall! I hope I survive another week here. I could have gone to Camp Pom-Pom. Just think, I could be wearing a cute costume and saying, "Go Team!" all day. Oh well, before you know it, my stay at Wild West Dude Ranch will be over. See you soon.

  Love,
  Daisy

I CONCLUDE THAT DUKE...
is having a dandy time at the dude ranch! He will probably want to go again next year.

I CONCLUDE THAT DAISY...
thinks the dude ranch is a dud! She would rather have gone to another camp.

Name _____ Main Idea

Horsing Around

Butch loves horses! He's in charge of five horses at Shady Grove Stables. Butch had to go out of town, so he wrote a note about each horse for his replacement. But Butch left in such a hurry that he forgot to write main idea sentences.

Directions: Match each main idea sentence with one of the five paragraphs below. Write the letter of each matching main idea sentence in the space provided on the appropriate cowboy hat.

Main Idea Sentences: **A.** Thunder is headstrong and quick to anger. **B.** Buttercup is very loving and like a mother to all the other horses. **C.** Bessie is a little lazy and has a sweet tooth. **D.** Peanut likes to eat and is a little overweight. **E.** Trevor is friendly but shy, especially around new people.	1. She likes to sleep late, so she often doesn't come out of her stall until 9:00 A.M. She doesn't like to exercise. Oh, and watch out. She'll raid the sugar bag. 
2. He likes to stay by himself in the pasture. He's not much for playing with the other horses. If he doesn't know you, it might take a day or two before he'll let you ride him. Be patient, though, and he'll become your friend.	3. He's very stubborn and will only respond if he gets a sugar cube. So keep a good supply on hand. Watch out for his temper! If he doesn't get what he wants, he may whack you with his head or charge at you.
4. Keep a close eye on her at mealtime. If you're not watching, she'll try to eat the other horses' food. She has gotten a little out of shape from not exercising.	5. She watches out for all the other horses, especially the little ones. If another horse is sick, she will stick by his side until he feels better. You can often see her helping new mothers take care of their offspring.

Bonus Box: Pets often have unique personalities. Think of your pet, a friend's pet, or a pet on TV. Then, on the back of this sheet, write a paragraph describing this pet. Be sure to include a main idea sentence and three detail sentences that support it.

Answer Key

1. C
2. E
3. A
4. D
5. B

Name _____   Main Idea

Passage to India

Now you're off to one of the world's most famous and beautiful buildings. You'll visit a tomb called the Taj Mahal in India. Read the paragraph below. The questions that follow will help you find the main idea.

> Long ago, an Indian ruler wanted a beautiful tomb built for his favorite wife. It took about 20,000 workers to build it between 1630 and 1650. The building is made of marble. It rests on a platform of red sandstone. A tall prayer tower stands at each corner of the platform. A dome covers the center of the building. The tomb is surrounded by a garden. There are also pools that reflect the beauty of the building. Indeed, the Indian ruler had made an everlasting monument to his beloved wife.

1. Circle the first and last sentences of the paragraph.
2. How are the two sentences alike? _____
   _____
3. Sometimes the main idea is written in the first sentence and repeated in the last sentence. Why do you think a writer would do that? _____
   _____
   _____

Armchair Assignment: Write a paragraph in which you repeat the main idea in the first and last sentences. Use the lines below, and the back of this sheet if necessary, to write your paragraph.

A building to honor me would be spectacular. _____
_____
_____
_____
_____
_____
_____

Bonus Box: Draw a picture of the building you described in your paragraph.

©The Education Center, Inc. • *Big Book of Skill Builders* • TEC60797

Answer Key

1. The following sentences should be circled: Long ago, an Indian ruler wanted a beautiful tomb built for his favorite wife. Indeed, the Indian ruler had made an everlasting monument to his beloved wife.
2. The two sentences relate the main idea of the paragraph.
3. Answers may vary. Possible answers include that a writer repeats the main idea to emphasize it.

Name _____ Series of Events

Try an Archaeological Experience!

Do Egyptian mummies spark your interest? If so, the Egyptian Museum in Cairo is the place to visit! The exhibit of King Tutankhamen is an example of how ancient Egyptian kings were buried. The paragraph below tells how King "Tut's" tomb was discovered. The paragraph tells a story through a series of events. Read the paragraph; then answer the questions that follow.

> Howard Carter was a British archaeologist with a dream. He wanted to solve a mystery: Where was Egyptian pharaoh Tutankhamen buried? During six stays in Egypt's Valley of the Kings, he had found nothing. He decided that a dig during the winter of 1922–1923 would be his last try. The place he chose was under some ancient grave-workers' huts. He and his team were excited to discover steps that led down to a sealed passageway. The passageway led to four rooms of a tomb. The rooms were filled with things that had belonged to King Tut. There were also three coffins—one of which was solid gold! Inside it lay the bandaged mummy of Tut. Its head and shoulders were covered with a solid-gold mask. The face on the mask showed Tut as a youthful and noble king. Unfortunately, Carter did not find any scrolls in the tomb that told the history of the king. That part of the mystery remains unsolved.

1. What is the main idea of the paragraph? _____
   _____

2. A series of events helps tell the story. List three of them.
   a. _____
   b. _____
   c. _____

3. Underline one detail sentence in the paragraph. How does this detail help make the paragraph interesting?

Armchair Assignment: Is there such a thing as a "mummy's curse"? Many people thought so after some unusual things happened to Carter and his crew. Write a paragraph that includes a series of events. Choose one of the following starters and write your paragraph on the back of this page.
- Howard Carter's partner discovered a mysterious insect bite on his cheek.
- A very odd thing happened to Howard Carter's pet canary.
- Officials in Egypt argued over who would visit the tomb first.

> **Bonus Box:** What were some of the items found in King Tut's tomb? Research to find out.

©The Education Center, Inc. • *Big Book of Skill Builders* • TEC60797

Answer Key

1. Howard Carter discovered the tomb of King Tutankhamen.
2. Answers may vary. Possible answers include that Carter chose a place to dig; he discovered steps that led down to a passageway; he found four rooms of a tomb.
3. Answers may vary. Accept reasonable answers.

Name _____ Drawing Conclusions

The Adventures of Roger Bag-It

The Looneyland Grocery Store has hired a new employee for the summer. And new and exciting adventures are about to begin!

Read the following sentences. Below each sentence are some conlusions. Circle the one that you think is best.

1. Roger turned on the lights, opened the blinds, and straightened up the grocery carts.
   a. Roger had shown a film.
   b. Roger was opening the store.
   c. Roger was closing the store.

2. Roger swept the aisles, cleaned the windows, and dusted the canned goods.
   a. Roger was in charge of the produce department.
   b. Roger was a clerk.
   c. Roger was assigned maintenance duty.

3. Roger helped Mrs. Lowe remove her items from the electric grocery cart and placed them on the checkout counter.
   a. Mrs. Lowe was lazy.
   b. Mrs. Lowe was an elderly lady.
   c. Mr. Lowe was still checking out the candy aisle.

4. Roger watched as cans of food rolled in all directions.
   a. Roger was trying to trip customers.
   b. Roger stacked the cans too high and they toppled over.
   c. Roger was trying a science experiment.

5. The store manager smiled and patted Roger on the back.
   a. Roger and the store manager were playing tag.
   b. The store manager was pleased with Roger's work.
   c. The store manager was unhappy with Roger's work.

6. Roger looked at the crowded parking lot, threw up his hands, and scowled.
   a. There were no customers anywhere.
   b. Roger had to gather all of the grocery carts.
   c. Roger was unhappy because it was raining.

7. Roger helped bag groceries at three different checkout counters.
   a. The grocery store was very busy.
   b. Roger liked to move around a lot.
   c. Roger went where the bags were.

8. Roger left the grocery store with his head hanging low and dragging his feet.
   a. Roger got a pay raise.
   b. Roger was tired.
   c. Roger had stepped on a wad of gum.

Bonus Box: Choose two of the situations above. Illustrate them on the back of this page.

Answer Key

Answers may vary.
1. b. Roger was opening the store.
2. c. Roger was assigned maintenance duty.
3. b. Mrs. Lowe was an elderly lady.
4. b. Roger stacked the cans too high and they toppled over.
5. b. The store manager was pleased with Roger's work.
6. b. Roger had to gather all of the grocery carts.
7. a. The grocery store was very busy.
8. b. Roger was tired.

Name _____   Drawing Conclusions

Camp Beverly "Hill-arious"

The kids and counselors at Camp Beverly "Hill-arious" are writing their first letters home. Help them finish the job before it's lights-out.

Read each letter and underline the facts that help explain how each person feels about camp. Think about the importance of the facts; then draw a conclusion for each letter. Complete each letter by writing three or four more sentences. Use the back of this page if you need more room.

Dear Mom and Dad,
  Camp is great! The bus ride here was long, but we stopped for snacks and bathroom breaks. Our counselor is really cool! He lets us go to the canteen when we want to.
  I bought a camp T-shirt…

Dear Mom and Dad,
  Well, here I am at camp. I guess it's okay, if you like bugs, heat, and camp food. I fell into the lake yesterday. But don't worry; I was rescued quickly. I've been to the infirmary…

Dear Mom and Dad,
  Wow! I can't believe it's summer again! I must be the luckiest college kid alive. Being a camp counselor is the world's greatest summer job.
  Let me tell you what's been going on…

Dear Mom and Dad,
  I told you I wouldn't like this job. Being a camp counselor is just not my cup of tea. This place should be named Brat City. Now I understand why parents send their kids to camp in the summertime.
  Here's how the first few days have gone…

Bonus Box: Think about a time when you spent a night away from home. Write your own letter home telling about your experiences.

©The Education Center, Inc. • Big Book of Skill Builders • TEC60797   115

Jean Craighead George—Children's Nature Author

Did you know a robin decorates her nest the day before laying her eggs? Or that dandelions are **edible?** Children's author Jean Craighead George includes such interesting facts in her stories. She has written over 80 books! Almost all of her books come from her own **experiences** with nature.

Jean's parents, both **entomologists,** instilled in her a deep love of the outdoors. Jean climbed trees to study owls. She made fishhooks from twigs. Her pets included opossums, lizards, and a turkey vulture. Jean and her twin brothers spent many weekends camping with their parents, exploring plant and animal life near their Washington, DC, home. In the third grade, Jean discovered another great love—writing. She would often return home from her family adventures and write about them.

Jean earned a degree in science and a degree in English from Pennsylvania State University. Following college, she worked as a reporter and an artist. Later Jean married, and she and her husband began to write children's nature books together. Her family grew. She and her husband had three children—Twig, Craig, and Luke.

Just as when she was a child, Jean and her children spent much of their time exploring the outdoors. Often they would come home with unusual pets—skunks, tarantulas, and even an owl who came to enjoy watching television and showering with family members. They eventually raised 173 wild pets, most of which were returned to nature.

After a while, Jean began writing books on her own. She wanted to tell about her experiences with nature. One of Jean's first novels, *My Side of the Mountain,* was based on her family camping trips. In the story, a young boy named Sam leaves his home in New York City to live in the wilderness. He begins his journey with only a few tools, including a small knife, a ball of string, and an ax. The book was a great success! It was a 1960 Newbery Honor Book and later became a movie.

Jean continued to be a student of nature. She visited Alaska. She watched scientists communicate with wolves. Jean used these experiences to write another successful novel, *Julie of the Wolves.* It is about a little girl who is lost on the **tundra.** She must talk to the wolves to survive. This book won the 1973 Newbery Medal. Jean was thrilled! She wrote two **sequels**—*Julie* and *Julie's Wolf Pack.*

For over 50 years, Jean has shared her love of nature with young people through her books. She has won many awards and helped children around the world learn to appreciate and protect the **environment.** Jean Craighead George has earned a lasting place in children's literature.

How to Use Pages 117–120

Duplicate pages 117 and 119 back-to-back. Distribute one copy to each student. Have each student read the biographical sketch and then complete items 1–7 and the Bonus Box. Discuss students' answers as a class.

Name _____   Jean C. George: Reading comprehension

Jean Craighead George—Children's Nature Author

Directions: Answer the following items. Use another sheet of paper if you need more space to write.

1. Define *edible, experiences, entomologists, tundra, sequels,* and *environment* as they are used in the article. _____
   _____
   _____
   _____
   _____
   _____
   _____

2. Write one word, such as *exciting,* that best describes Jean's early life. Explain why you chose this word. _____
   _____

3. What great love did Jean discover in the third grade? _____

4. How do you think owning unusual pets as a young girl influenced Jean's life? _____
   _____
   _____

5. Why is Jean described as being a "student of nature"? Why do you think she does this research? _____
   _____
   _____

6. What do you think Jean's stories teach her readers about the environment? _____
   _____
   _____

7. Choose an animal. Imagine this animal in its natural environment. Describe three things you might observe it doing. _____
   _____
   _____
   _____

Bonus Box: On another sheet of paper, design an award you would present to Ms. George. Explain why you would honor her.

Answer Key

Answers may vary. Accept reasonable responses.

1. In the article, *edible* means able to be eaten; *experiences* means events that happen to you; *entomologists* means scientists who study insects; *tundra* means a cold area of Northern Europe, North America, and Asia where the ground is permanently frozen; *sequels* means books or movies that continue the stories of earlier works; and *environment* means the natural world of the land, sea, and air.

2. Answers will vary. Accept reasonable responses.

3. The great love Jean discovered in the third grade was writing.

4. Answers may vary. Owning unusual pets as a young girl probably influenced Jean by teaching her to respect each animal's differences and uniqueness.

5. Jean is described as being a student of nature because she studies the environment. She probably does this research before writing her books so her writing will be accurate and her characters more real.

6. Answers may vary. Jean's stories probably teach her readers facts about plants and animals in the environment, how people interact with them, and how people should protect them.

7. Answers will vary.

Tiger Woods—Golf Champion

Earl ran excitedly into the house to get his wife, Tida. Their son had just swung a golf club with perfect form. The most amazing thing about it was that their son, Tiger, was less than one year old! Tiger's father decided that he would help his son develop this **natural** talent for golfing. By the age of two, Tiger was already playing the game amazingly well. Tiger even appeared on television, beating a famous comedian named Bob Hope in a putting contest. People around him began to recognize that young Tiger was a champion in the making.

Tiger's real name is Eldrick. He was born on December 30, 1975. Tiger was nicknamed in honor of a friend who saved his father's life during the Vietnam War. Tiger's mother, Tida, is from Thailand. She met Earl Woods, a Black American soldier, in Thailand, while he was serving in the Vietnam War. The couple married and then moved to America after Earl left the military.

When Tiger was four years old, his father took him to a golf course to practice. It was there that Tiger met the club pro, Rudy Duran, who coached him until he was about ten years old. Tiger loved golf more than anything else. Although Tiger's parents knew he had a great future in golf, they were determined that their son would also get a good education and learn to be a responsible person. Both Tida and Earl always insisted that their son finish his homework before going out to practice his game and that he display sportsmanlike behavior.

Tiger began to win many tournaments. At the age of eight, Tiger won his first junior world championship. He went on to win four more of these titles, in addition to three U.S. Junior **Amateur** titles and more than 100 local junior titles. Tiger was unstoppable! As his ability grew, Tiger's parents continued to encourage him to stay positive about himself and his game.

After graduating from high school with honors, Tiger attended Stanford University on a golf **scholarship.** In 1996, Tiger became the first golfer to win three **consecutive** U.S. Amateur Championships. That same year, Tiger made a very difficult decision. He left college in order to become a **professional** golfer. In 1997, Tiger achieved a **monumental** goal by winning the Masters Tournament and setting tournament records. Tiger is the youngest person ever to win the tournament and the first winner of African or Asian heritage.

Tiger Woods continues to work at being the best golfer and the best person he can be, proving himself a true champion.

How to Use Pages 121–124

Duplicate pages 121 and 123 back-to-back. Give one copy to each student. Have each student read the biographical sketch and then complete items 1–6 and the Bonus Box activity. Discuss students' answers together as a class.

Name _____ Tiger Woods: Reading comprehension

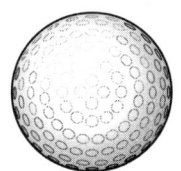 # Tiger Woods—Golf Champion

Directions: Answer the following items. Use another sheet of paper if you need more space to write.

1. Tiger was an extraordinary child. Support this opinion with a fact from the first paragraph.
   _____
   _____
   _____

2. Tiger was named after his father's friend from the Vietnam War. Do you think this proved to be a fitting nickname for Tiger? Why or why not? _____
   _____
   _____

3. How did Tiger's parents help him develop into a great champion? _____
   _____
   _____

4. Why do you think the decision to leave college was difficult for Tiger? _____
   _____
   _____

5. Write a sports headline describing Tiger's 1997 Masters victory. _____
   _____
   _____

6. Define *natural, amateur, scholarship, consecutive, professional,* and *monumental* as they are used in the article. _____
   _____
   _____
   _____
   _____

Bonus Box: Tiger Woods once said he would like to be the Michael Jordan of golf. What do you think he meant by this? Did he achieve his goal?

©The Education Center, Inc. • *Big Book of Skill Builders* • TEC60797

# Answer Key

Answers may vary. Accept reasonable responses.

1. Tiger was an extraordinary child because he was swinging a golf club when he was less than a year old, he played golf amazingly well by the age of two, and he beat an adult in a putting contest.

2. Students' answers will vary. Students may respond that Tiger's nickname is fitting because he is a fierce competitor and he is courageous.

3. Tiger's parents helped him develop into a great champion by helping him develop his natural talent, encouraging him to be positive about himself and his talent, and making sure he had a good education.

4. Students' answers will vary. Students may respond that the decision to leave college was probably difficult for Tiger because he would not earn his degree and he would have to earn a living playing golf.

5. Students' answers will vary.

6. In the article, *natural* means present from birth rather than being learned; *amateur* means someone who takes part in a sport or other activity for pleasure rather than for money; *scholarship* means a grant or a prize that pays you to go to college or to follow a course of study; *consecutive* means happening or following one after the other; *professional* means making money for something others do for fun; and *monumental* means very important.

Jane Goodall—Conservationist

"Happy birthday!" exclaimed Jane's parents. The lifelike chimpanzee toy did not frighten two-year-old Jane, as others warned her parents it might. Jane loved her new stuffed toy named Jubilee. This was the start of her fascination with animals. Little did Jane Goodall's parents know that one day their daughter would become an **expert** on chimpanzee behavior.

Born in England in 1934, Jane spent much of her time as a child observing the behavior of animals. Once, when Jane was four years old, she hid in a small, stuffy henhouse for about five hours. She wanted to find out how a hen laid an egg. By the time Jane was eight, she had decided that when she grew up, she would go to Africa to live with animals. Her mother told Jane that if she worked very hard, she would somehow find a way to live out her dream.

Jane was very determined. After attending secretarial school, she worked for a **documentary** film company. All the while Jane read and studied about Africa and its animal life. She went on nature walks and visited the Natural History Museum. Jane even worked as a waitress in order to save money. Finally, at age 23, she had earned enough for the trip!

Jane traveled by boat to Kenya, a country on Africa's east coast. It was there that she met Dr. Louis Leakey, a well-known scientist. Leakey was impressed with Jane's knowledge of animals and hired her as an assistant. Jane worked with Dr. Leakey digging up **fossils.** Although Jane was grateful for this experience, she wanted to study *living* animals. So Dr. Leakey arranged for Jane to begin a study of wild chimpanzees.

In July 1960, Jane arrived in Gombe National Park in Tanzania to begin her study. At first, she found it difficult to get near the animals because of their fear of her. Each day Jane patiently observed the **troop** of chimps from afar. Slowly, the chimpanzees got used to her being there. During her research, Jane discovered many new things. For example, she observed chimpanzees making and using tools, a skill once believed **exclusive** to humans.

Two years later, Jane returned to England and entered Cambridge University. In 1965, she received a **doctorate** degree in the study of animal behavior. Jane then returned to Africa. She established the Gombe Stream Research Centre. The research, which has now become the longest field study of any animal species in the wild, still continues at Gombe today.

Jane also founded The Jane Goodall Institute in 1977. This foundation provides ongoing support for chimpanzee research. Twenty-five years of Jane's research was published in 1985 and many of her scientific articles have appeared in *National Geographic.* Today Jane spends most of her time traveling around the world, spreading the news about the importance of wildlife conservation to life on this planet.

How to Use Pages 125–128

Duplicate pages 125 and 127 back-to-back. Give one copy to each student. Explain to students that the term *conservationist* means someone who protects natural resources, forests, and wildlife. Have each student read the biographical sketch and then complete items 1–6 and the Bonus Box. Discuss students' answers together as a class.

Name _____ Jane Goodall: Reading comprehension

Jane Goodall—Conservationist

Directions: Answer the following items. Use another sheet of paper if you need more space to write.

1. Explain the importance of the gift Jane received for her second birthday. _____
   _____
   _____

2. What interests and activities did Jane participate in that showed her strong interest in studying animals in the wild? _____
   _____
   _____
   _____

3. How did Jane's work with the chimpanzees differ from the work she did with Dr. Leakey?
   _____
   _____

4. What do you think was her greatest achievement? _____
   _____
   _____

5. Write one word that you think best describes Jane Goodall's life. Explain why you chose this word. _____
   _____
   _____

6. Define *expert, documentary, fossils, troop, exclusive,* and *doctorate* as they are used in this article. _____
   _____
   _____
   _____

Bonus Box: Jane Goodall's childhood dream was to watch free, wild animals living their own, undisturbed lives. Write about a dream that you have. What are some steps you can take to help make this dream come true?

Answer Key

Answers may vary. Accept reasonable responses.

1. Jane received a lifelike chimpanzee toy for her second birthday. It was important because it was the beginning of her fascination with animals.

2. As a child, Jane spent much of her time observing the behavior of animals. She hid in a henhouse to see how hens lay eggs. She took nature walks and visited the Natural History Museum. She read and studied about Africa and its animal life. She attended college and earned a doctorate degree in the study of animal behavior.

3. The work she did with Dr. Leakey dealt with dead animals. Her work with chimpanzees focused on living animals.

4. Answers will vary.

5. Answers will vary.

6. *Expert* means a person who knows a lot about a certain subject; *documentary* means a movie or television program made about real people or situations; *fossils* means the remains of animals or plants from millions of years ago, preserved as rocks; *troop* means a group of chimpanzees that live together; *exclusive* means limited to use by a single person or group; and *doctorate* means the degree, title, or rank of a doctor.

General Colin Powell—American Hero

"Trust me," said the general during one of his many newscasts. His manner was calm and confident. Throughout the Persian Gulf War, General Colin Powell appeared on television many times. He knew it was important for the American people to be well **informed** about the war's progress. After only 42 days, the fighting came to an end. The general's mission had been a success! Later that year, President George Bush awarded Colin the Medal of Freedom for leading our country through a difficult time.

Colin Luther Powell was born on April 5, 1937, in Harlem, a black community in New York City. His parents moved there from Jamaica in search of a better life. Colin's parents worked very hard to provide for their family, but still found time for him and his sister. Work and family were the two most important things to the Powells.

When Colin was five years old, his family moved to the Bronx, another area in New York City. There they lived in an apartment building with people from many different backgrounds—Irish, Jewish, and Italian. Colin attended school, although he wasn't a very good student. His parents urged him to study, but his lessons did not interest him.

When Colin graduated high school and began college, he did not know what he wanted to do with his life. Then one day he saw a marching drill team. As the **cadets** moved in unison in their crisp black uniforms, they caught Colin's attention. That was it! Colin would become a soldier. He joined the **ROTC** and eventually became the team's commander. He had direction—a goal. Colin's grades improved and he experienced a feeling of confidence and pride in his new successes.

After college, Colin joined the army and underwent **rugged** training courses where he learned things, such as how to parachute and how to survive in the wilderness. Colin's first assignment was in West Germany. His job was to protect Europe from the powerful Soviet Union. Colin also served in the war in Vietnam. He continued to do his best and prove himself to be a strong leader. He was **promoted** many times. He also married and began a family.

In 1972, after earning his master's degree in business administration, Colin was chosen to serve as a special assistant at the White House. People liked him. He was very organized and **dedicated.** Colin went on to become an assistant to the Secretary of Defense. In 1987, he became President Reagan's national security adviser. Two years later Colin became the first black chairman of the Joint Chiefs of Staff, supervising everyone in the **armed forces.**

General Colin Powell retired from the military in 1993. Through hard work and dedication, Colin accomplished many extraordinary things and earned many honors. He is truly an American hero.

How to Use Pages 129–132

Duplicate pages 129 and 131 back-to-back. Give one copy to each student. Have each student read the biographical sketch and then complete items 1–6 and the Bonus Box. Discuss students' answers together as a class.

Name _____   Colin Powell: Reading comprehension

General Colin Powell—American Hero

Directions: Answer the following items. Use another sheet of paper if you need more space to write.

1. Why did General Powell hold frequent newscasts during the Persian Gulf War? _____

2. How do you think Colin's life in the Bronx helped shape his character? _____

3. What do you think was the turning point in Colin's life? Explain. _____

4. Name two of Powell's achievements. Describe how he accomplished them. _____

5. Tell about a goal you have achieved. How did it make you feel? _____

6. Define *informed, cadets, ROTC, rugged, promoted, dedicated,* and *armed forces* as used in the article. _____

Bonus Box: Colin Powell gathered a set of rules to live by. One said, "It can be done!" Another said, "Have a vision." On another sheet of paper, write two of your own rules to live by. Explain why each one is important.

©The Education Center, Inc. • *Big Book of Skill Builders* • TEC60797

Answer Key

Answers may vary. Accept reasonable responses.

1. General Powell held frequent newscasts during the Persian Gulf War because he wanted Americans to know about what was happening.

2. Colin's life in the Bronx probably helped shape his character by helping him get along with people from many different backgrounds and understand that despite ethnic differences, all people are equal.

3. The turning point in Colin's life was probably when he joined the ROTC. It gave him a goal and helped him experience confidence and success.

4. Answers may vary. Possible achievements include: He helped our country achieve victory during the Persian Gulf War. He worked hard to become a good soldier. He continued his education, earning a master's degree. He rose to the highest position in the military. He was the first Black American to head the Joint Chiefs of Staff. He accomplished these achievements through hard work and dedication.

5. Answers will vary. Accept reasonable responses.

6. In the article, *informed* means having information, being educated about something; *cadets* means young people who are training to become members of the armed forces; *ROTC* means Reserved Officers' Training Corps; *rugged* means harsh or difficult; *promoted* means moved up to a more important job; *dedicated* means giving a lot of time and energy to something; and *armed forces* means all of the branches of a country's military, including the army, navy, air force, marine corps, and coast guard.

Name_____   The Lion, the Witch and the Wardrobe
Root Words

The Magic of Root Words

It doesn't take magic to understand the meaning of a word, just a little knowledge of its parts! Read Edmund's story below. Fill in the missing word parts using one of the root words shown. (Each root word may be used more than once.) Then, on the back of this sheet, write the meaning of each word.

capt, cept, ceiv, and cip = to take, seize, or hold

The Story of Narnia

While exploring the old professor's home, my sister Lucy found a passageway through a magical wardrobe. From there she entered Narnia, a land held _ _ _ _ive by an evil witch who claimed to be queen. She was greeted by a friendly faun who told her how the witch had cast a spell over the land so that it was always winter. When she returned home and told her story, we found her lie unac_ _ _ _able.

Then, one day, I found myself in the wardrobe. I, too, discovered my way into Narnia's icy world. My re _ _ _ _ion in Narnia was not like Lucy's. While there I met the queen. "Is this the one they call the White Witch?" I thought. The queen cleverly offered me some Turkish Delight. Little did I know it was enchanted food! I was _ _ _ _ivated by the queen and her offer to make me a crowned prince of Narnia. But, as I learned of the queen's cruelty, my per _ _ _ _ion of her changed. I finally understood my mistake. She wanted me, my brother, and my sisters dead! She had de_ _ _ _ _ ed me.

My brother and sisters met the great lion, Aslan, who helped weaken the magic of the White Witch. But the fight was not yet over. The witch reminded Aslan of my mistake and he willingly ac _ _ _ _ed my punishment. Then, with the help of Aslan and his loyal followers, we defeated the witch and eman_ _ _ ated the inhabitants from their frozen prison. Narnia was no longer sus _ _ _ _ ible to the witch's powers. We were crowned kings and queens of Narnia, but later returned to our world. What an ex_ _ _ _ional journey!

Edmund

Bonus Box: Find one new word for each of the above root words. Write the word and its meaning on the back of this sheet.

How to Use This Unit

Pages 133–138

The activities in this unit are designed to use with the book *The Lion, the Witch and the Wardrobe* by C. S. Lewis. Have students complete the activities during or after reading the story.

The Lion, the Witch and the Wardrobe

By C. S. Lewis

Four siblings—Lucy, Edmund, Susan, and Peter—step inside an old wardrobe and enter the enchanted Narnia. This once peaceful land of beasts, dwarfs, giants, and fauns is now one of endless winter, caused by a spell cast by the evil White Witch. Anyone daring to challenge the witch, who claims herself queen of Narnia, is turned into stone. Edmund is bewitched into betraying his older brother and his sisters, and joins the White Witch in her quest to keep Narnia in her icy grip. Edmund's treachery puts the children on the path to certain death until the great lion, Aslan, appears and weakens the magic of the White Witch. A great battle ensues, and with the help of Aslan and his friendly following, the children defeat the witch. Narnia is freed and the four are crowned kings and queens. In the end, the children leave the world of the wardrobe and return home, knowing that one day they will return to Narnia.

How to Use Page 133

1. After students have read the story, distribute page 133 to students.
2. Remind students that a root word is the main part of a word and knowing root words can help them understand the meanings of words.
3. Have each student complete the page as directed, using a dictionary for help as needed. If desired, use the key below to provide students with a word bank.
4. Discuss students' answers and the meaning of each word in relation to its root word.

 **Answer Key**

The answers below are listed in the order in which they appear in the story.

...From there she entered Narnia, a land held <u>c a p t</u> ive by an evil witch.
...When she returned home and told her story, we found her lie unac <u>c e p t</u> able.
...My re <u>c e p t</u> ion in Narnia was not like Lucy's.
...I was <u>c a p t</u> ivated by the queen and her offer to make me a crowned prince of Narnia.
...But, as I learned of the queen's cruelty, my per <u>c e p t</u> ion of her changed.
...She had de <u>c e i v</u> ed me.
...The witch reminded Aslan of my mistake and he willingly ac <u>c e p t</u> ed my punishment.
...Then, with the help of Aslan and his loyal followers, we defeated the witch and eman <u>c i p</u> ated the inhabitants from their frozen prison.
...Narnia was no longer sus <u>c e p t</u> ible to the witch's powers.
...What an ex <u>c e p t</u> ional journey!

Name_____   The Lion, the Witch and the Wardrobe
Character Traits

Statues With Character

Help! The White Witch has frozen Lucy, Edmund, Susan, and Peter into stone. Break this evil spell by matching each quote below to one of the characters. Write each quote number on the bottom of the correct statue. Beside each number, write a character trait that you think the quote shows. The first one is done for you.

Lucy
1–inquisitiveness

Edmund

Susan

Peter

1. "I can always get back if anything goes wrong."
2. "I think Lu ought to be the leader…Goodness knows she deserves it."
3. "Oh, surely not…It would be too awful for him. Think how you'd feel if you were he."
4. "Please, please…please couldn't I have just one piece of Turkish Delight to eat on the way home?"
5. "What is the matter? Aren't you well? Dear Mr. Tumnus, do tell me what is wrong."
6. "I'll pay you all out for this, you pack of stuck-up, self-satisfied prigs."
7. "I am sure nobody would mind…It isn't as if we wanted to take them out of the house; we shan't take them even out of the wardrobe."
8. "All the same…we'll still have to go and look for him. He is our brother after all…."
9. "She's not being silly at all…She's just making a story up for fun, aren't you, Lu?"
10. "We can't just go home, not after this. It is all on my account that the poor faun has got into this trouble."
11. "Do stop it…It won't make things any better having a row between you two. Let's go find Lucy."
12. "I'm sorry…."

Bonus Box: On the back of this sheet, draw another character statue, such as Aslan, Mr. Tumnus, or the White Witch. Below the statue, write three traits that describe the character. Support each trait with a quote from the story.

©The Education Center, Inc. • Big Book of Skill Builders • TEC60797

 **Answer Key**

Students' character trait answers may vary.

Lucy
1—inquisitiveness
5—caring
10—responsibility

Susan
3—consideration
7—sensibility
11—helpfulness

Edmund
4—greediness
6—vengefulness
12—repentance

Peter
2—fairness
8—bravery
9—kindness

Name _____

The Lion, the Witch and the Wardrobe
Story Elements

Into the Wardrobe

Enter the world of the wardrobe! Complete each section below. Then use crayons or colored pencils to color the wardrobe.

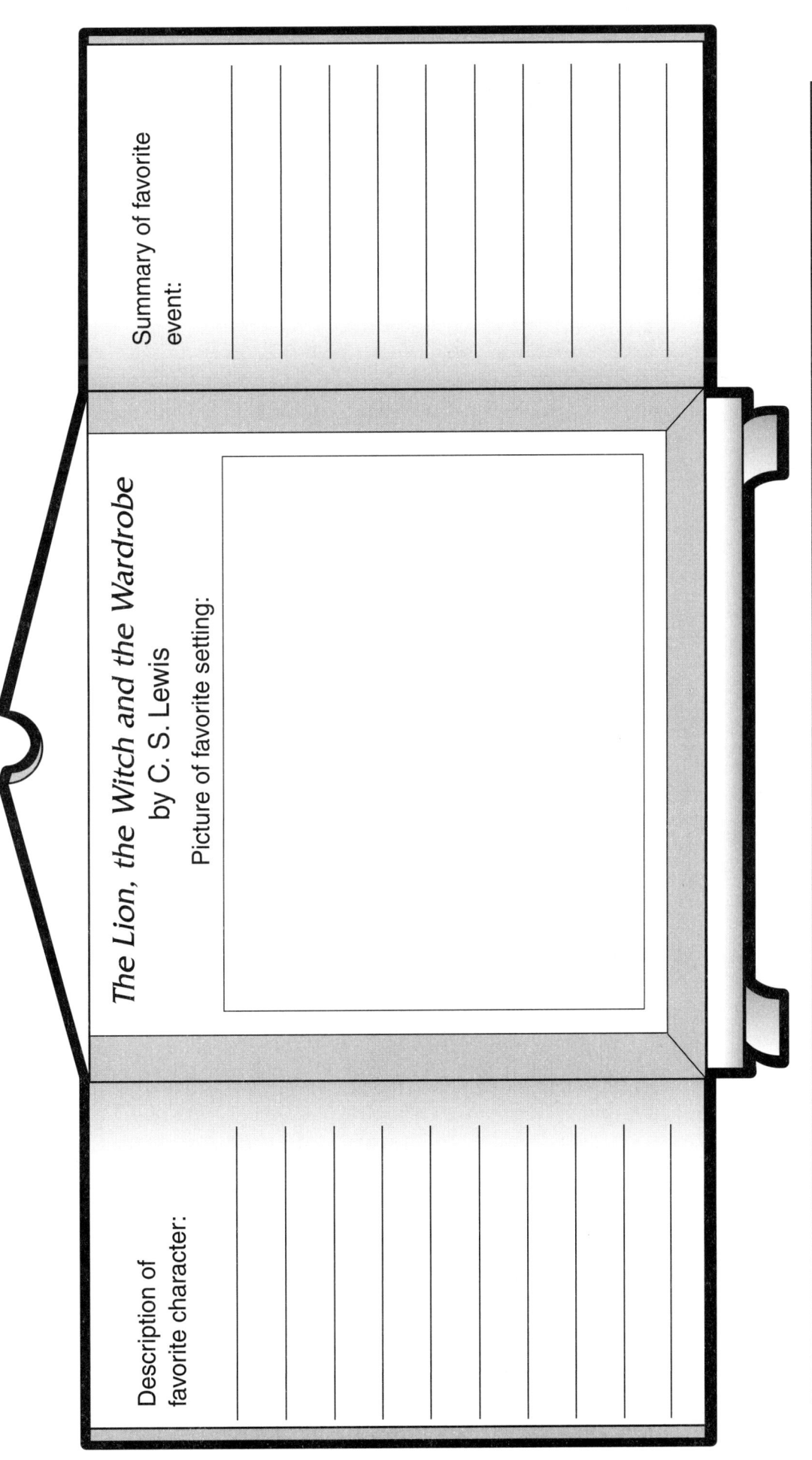

Summary of favorite event:

The Lion, the Witch and the Wardrobe
by C. S. Lewis

Picture of favorite setting:

Description of favorite character:

Bonus Box: Imagine that you walked through a wardrobe and entered a magical world. On another sheet of paper, write a description of this world's features, its inhabitants, and what life is like there.

©The Education Center, Inc. • *Big Book of Skill Builders* • TEC60797

How to Use Page 137

1. Give each student a copy of page 137 and crayons or colored pencils.
2. Instruct each student to complete the activity as directed.
3. If desired, have each student cut out the wardrobe along the bold lines and fold each door to close it. Direct the student to add decorative details and color the outside doors. Post students' completed work on a display titled "The World of the Wardrobe."

Name _____

Maniac Magee
Character Traits

Signs of Good Character

Maniac Magee spends a lot of time on the road. Along the way, he meets many people like himself who demonstrate good character.

Directions: Read the character traits listed on the signs below. On or near each sign, write the name of a character from the story who demonstrates this trait. In the blanks below the sign, describe the action that is the sign of this good behavior. The first one has been done for you.

> Good character is easy to find—just look for the signs!

Courage
Mars Bar

Sign: <u>He rescues Russell</u>
<u>McNab from the trestle</u>
<u>while a trolley is coming.</u>

Kindness

Sign: _____
_____
_____

Tolerance

Sign: _____
_____
_____

Resourcefulness

Sign: _____
_____
_____
_____

Determination

Sign: _____
_____
_____
_____

Caring

Sign: _____
_____
_____
_____

Honesty

Sign: _____
_____
_____
_____

Hardworking

Sign: _____
_____
_____
_____

Patience

Sign: _____
_____
_____
_____

Bonus Box: On the back of this sheet, write what you think are five of the most important character traits of a friend. Rank each one in order of importance.

How to Use This Unit

Pages 139–142

The activities in this unit reinforce critical and creative thinking using the novel *Maniac Magee* by Jerry Spinelli. Duplicate pages 139 and 141 for each student to use during or after reading the novel.

Maniac Magee

By Jerry Spinelli

In this Newbery Medal-winning tale, Jerry Spinelli introduces us to Jeffrey Lionel Magee, a 12-year-old homeless boy. One day Jeffrey stops in Two Mills, a town divided between the white-populated West End and the black-populated East End. While there, Jeffrey's legendary deeds, including winning a race running backwards and untying the famed Cobble's Knot, earn him the nickname "Maniac." But more importantly, through his search for a permanent home and loving family, Maniac helps break down the racial barriers and heal the division that has long plagued the town.

How to Use Page 139

Use the activity to explore the topic of character in the story.

1. Explain to students that the actions a person displays show the kind of person he or she is, or his or her *character*.
2. Give a copy of page 139 to each student. Point out the character traits listed on the page.
3. Have students define each trait and then describe the actions they would look for in a person who is said to display this trait.
4. Instruct each student to complete the activity as directed on the page.

 Answer Key

Answers will vary. Accept all reasonable responses. Possible answers include the following:

Courage
Mars Bar
Sign: He rescues Russell McNab from the trestle while a trolley is coming.

Kindness
Mrs. Beale
Sign: She buys Maniac a new pair of sneakers because his are worn out.

Tolerance
Maniac
Sign: He does not see a difference between the West End whites and the East End blacks.

Resourcefulness
Amanda Beale
Sign: She keeps her book collection from getting damaged by carrying it around with her in a suitcase.

Determination
Earl Grayson
Sign: It takes him over an hour to read his first book, *The Little Engine That Could*.

Caring
Amanda Beale
Sign: She sleeps with Hester and Lester in their room so Maniac can have a place to sleep.

Honesty
Maniac
Sign: He tells Mr. Beale that he doesn't have a home.

Hardworking
Mrs. Beale
Sign: She is always cleaning up Hester and Lester's messes.

Patience
Maniac
Sign: He keeps working on untying Cobble's Knot even after others have given up trying.

Name _____

Maniac Magee
Problem Resolution

Nailing Down Problems

While living in the community of Two Mills, Maniac faces many different problems. These include smaller problems like trying to untie Cobble's Knot, and bigger problems like finding a place to call home.

Directions: In the chart below, write five different problems from the story that Maniac faces. Write an event from the story that tells how he faces each one. Then color the nails to show how big you think the problem is. Use a scale from one to four, with four being the largest.

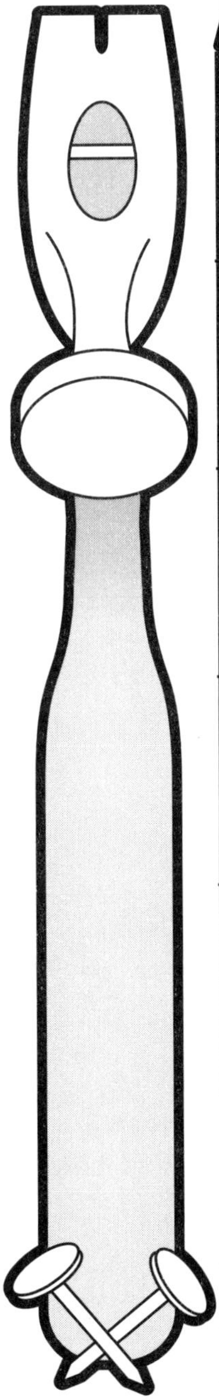

Problem	Story Event	Small Large
		1 2 3 4
		1 2 3 4
		1 2 3 4
		1 2 3 4
		1 2 3 4

Describe a problem you've had to face and explain how you dealt with it.

_____
_____
_____

Bonus Box: On the back of this sheet, trace the shape of your hand. On each finger, name a problem faced by students in your classroom, school, or neighborhood. Then list one way you can help solve each one.

©The Education Center, Inc. • *Big Book of Skill Builders* • TEC60797   141

How to Use Page 141

1. Duplicate page 141 for each student.
2. As a class, discuss some of the problems from the story that Maniac faces and how he deals with them. For example, Maniac wants Russell and Piper McNab to keep going to school, so he keeps offering them deals like showing them a shortcut to Mexico and feeding them pizza.
3. Instruct each student to complete the activity as directed on the page.
4. Discuss students' findings. Then have students explain how they may have helped solve some of Maniac's problems.

Shiloh
Vocabulary

Unleashing the Meaning

Each dog tag below contains a word from the story. As you read each chapter, match the word to its definition. (The item number matches the chapter in which each word is found.) Then use the word in a sentence, explaining how it relates to an event in the chapter. The first one is done for you.

1. cringe — **D** — Marty notices that Shiloh cringes and believes he has been mistreated.
2. concern — ___
3. earned — ___
4. protect — ___
5. problem — ___
6. lie — ___
7. ashamed — ___
8. secret — ___
9. trust — ___
10. right — ___
11. realize — ___
12. serious — ___
13. quarrel — ___
14. bargained — ___
15. choice — ___

A. thoughtful
B. embarrassed or guilty
C. received payment for work done
D. to shrink in fear
E. to make an untrue statement
F. to believe someone to be honest
G. good, fair, acceptable
H. a difficult situation
I. to become aware that something is true
J. an argument or disagreement
K. to keep safe from harm
L. discussing a price or an agreement
M. the chance to choose
N. personal business; responsibility
O. something kept hidden

How to Use This Unit

Pages 143–148

Use the creative activities in this unit to help your students understand the story elements of the Newbery Medal-winning novel *Shiloh* by Phyllis Reynolds Naylor. Duplicate pages 143, 145, and 147 for your students to complete during or after reading the novel.

Shiloh

By Phyllis Reynolds Naylor

Eleven-year-old Marty Preston loves roaming the solitary hills of his West Virginia home. But when a young beagle follows him home from the old Shiloh schoolhouse, his life is forever changed. Finding the animal mistreated, Marty refuses to return him to his cruel master. Marty vows he will do anything to save the dog he calls Shiloh, including keeping him a secret and sneaking him food from his struggling family's dinner table. But when Shiloh is viciously attacked by a neighboring dog, Marty must confront his decision and accept the consequences of his actions. Ultimately Marty learns that nothing is as simple as it seems and that nothing can break the bond between a boy and his dog.

 Answer Key

Students' sentences will vary.

1. cringe: D; Marty notices that Shiloh cringes and believes he has been mistreated.
2. concern: N; Mr. Preston tells Marty that Shiloh is not his concern.
3. earned: C; Marty earns money by collecting bottles and cans, in the hopes that he can buy Shiloh from Judd Travers.
4. protect: K; Marty builds a pen with a lean-to to protect Shiloh.
5. problem: H; Because Marty keeps Shiloh in a pen near his house, he has several problems to solve.
6. lie: E; Marty lies several times in order to protect Shiloh.
7. ashamed: B; Marty is ashamed when he asks a friend for extra food to feed Shiloh.
8. secret: O; Marty knows his secret can't go on forever.
9. trust: F; Marty's mother does not want to keep the secret about Shiloh from her husband because then he wouldn't trust her.
10. right: G; Marty asks his dad if it is right that he give Shiloh back to a man who mistreats him.
11. realize: I; Marty realizes the consequences of keeping the secret about Shiloh.
12. serious: A; Marty's father is serious when he talks to Judd about keeping Shiloh in his home.
13. quarrel: J; Marty understands that it is serious business to cause a quarrel with a neighbor.
14. bargained: L; Marty bargains with Judd about the purchase of Shiloh.
15. choice: M; Marty realizes he has no choice but to keep his part of the bargain in order to get Shiloh.

Name _____

Shiloh
Characterization

Shiloh Scrapbook

🐾 The happiest moment in Shiloh's life was when _____

🐾 The saddest moment in Shiloh's life was when _____

🐾 The scariest moment in Shiloh's life was when _____

A picture of Shiloh's favorite activity

A picture of Shiloh's favorite place to be

A picture of Shiloh

When Marty first met Shiloh, he was _____

Four favorite foods Shiloh likes to eat:
_____
_____

©The Education Center, Inc. • *Big Book of Skill Builders* • TEC60797

145

How to Use Page 145

1. Give each student a copy of page 145 and crayons or colored pencils.
2. Remind students that main characters do not have to be human, but can be animals as well. Ask students to describe Shiloh's character.
3. Discuss each section of the scrapbook page, pointing out to students that their responses may vary. Then have each student complete the activity.
4. Have students share their scrapbook pages.

Name _____

Shiloh
Summarizing

Build a Better Story Summary

1. Title of the book
2. Names of two main characters
3. Three words describing the setting
4. Four words stating the story's problem
5. Five words describing the beginning of the story
6. Six words describing the middle of the story
7. Seven words describing the ending of the story
8. Eight words describing a theme of the story

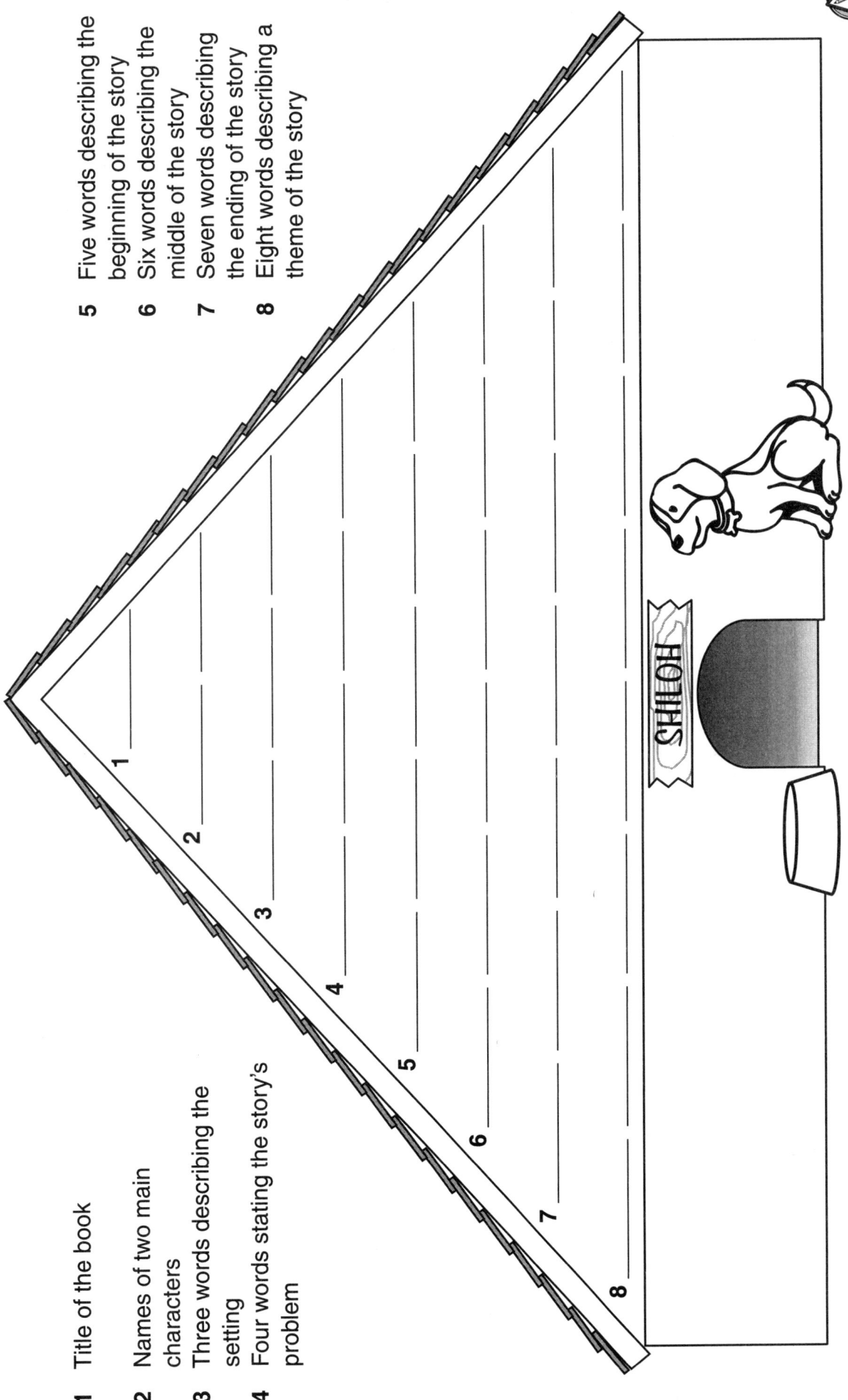

©The Education Center, Inc. • *Big Book of Skill Builders* • TEC60797

147

How to Use Page 147

1. Give each student a copy of page 147.
2. Remind students that a summary is like writing a paragraph. The first sentence states the main idea and is followed by supporting details. Explain that only the most important details about the characters, setting, plot, and theme of the story should be included.
3. Discuss the directions on the page. Encourage students to arrange their paragraphs in a logical order, using their blueprints as guides. Have each student complete the page as directed.
4. If desired, have students exchange papers and edit one another's summaries. Then have each student write a final copy on a sheet of loose-leaf paper.

 **Answer Key**

Students' answers and summaries will vary.

Name _____ The BFG
Vocabulary

WORDS FIT FOR A GIANT!

After feasting your eyes on the "langwitch" used by the BFG, try your own hand at some "wonder-rific" wordplay! Read the vocabulary words listed below. Choose ten pairs of words. Combine each word pair as shown in the examples. Write each word and its meaning on the menu.

Examples:
gigantic + enormous = *gigantous* (very, very big)
babble + argument = *babblement* (a babbling argument)

appetite beaming bottle
boy brute bubble cave cloak coarse colossal
country craggy crunching cunning desolate dim dream
ear forlorn frothy galloping giant girl guzzling horrid human
landscape lurking massive misty moody net peer petrified plan
ridiculous snitching squirming triumphant trumpet twit vast vegetable

Words	Meanings
1. _____	1. _____
2. _____	2. _____
3. _____	3. _____
4. _____	4. _____
5. _____	5. _____
6. _____	6. _____
7. _____	7. _____
8. _____	8. _____
9. _____	9. _____
10. _____	10. _____

©The Education Center, Inc. • Big Book of Skill Builders • TEC60797

How to Use This Unit

Pages 149–154

Use this creative collection of reproducibles to accompany the novel *The BFG* by Roald Dahl. Duplicate pages 149, 151, and 153 for your students to complete during or after reading the novel.

The BFG

By Roald Dahl

Snatched from her bed in the middle of the night by a big, friendly giant, young orphan Sophie begins the adventure of a lifetime. While in Giant Country, Sophie learns that there are giants who enjoy feasting upon "human beans"—especially little children. But Sophie soon learns that the BFG is not like the other giants. He spends his time collecting dreams and blowing the happy ones into the minds of sleeping children. Together with her new friend, Sophie devises a plan to rid the world of the nine nasty giants forever.

How to Use Page 149

1. Give each student a copy of page 149 and a dictionary, if necessary.
2. Discuss the directions and the examples on the page. Point out to students that the meanings of the new words are combinations of the original words' meanings.
3. Have each student complete the page as directed, using a dictionary for help as needed.
4. If desired, follow up the activity by having each student write a sentence for each of his combined words.

Students' words and meanings will vary.

Name _____

The BFG
Reading for Details

GIANT NEWS!

Imagine that you are one of the queen's royal reporters. Your new assignment is to cover the story of Sophie and the BFG! As any good reporter knows, you must gather the facts about the story—the who, what, where, when, and why or how.

Directions: Read each headline below. Complete the notes for the story by filling in the missing information.

Young Girl Kidnapped by Giant

Who: _____

What: _____

Where: _____

When: during the witching hour

Why/How: _____

Orphan Narrowly Escapes Being Eaten Alive

Who: _____

What: _____

Where: at the cave of the BFG

When: _____

Why/How: _____

Mystery Unfolds—Giant Tells About Dream Netting

Who: _____

What: catches dreams

Where: _____

When: _____

Why/How: _____

Secret Plan to Enlist Queen's Assistance

Who: Sophie and the BFG

What: _____

Where: _____

When: _____

Why/How: _____

Bonus Box: Choose another event from the story, such as the military helping capture the giants. On the back of this sheet, write a news article detailing the event, including the five Ws. Be sure to include a headline.

151

©The Education Center, Inc. • *Big Book of Skill Builders* • TEC60797

Students' answers may vary.

Young Girl Kidnapped by Giant
Who: Sophie
What: taken by force from her bed
Where: from the village orphanage
When: during the witching hour
Why/How: Sophie is snatched by the BFG through her bedroom window.

Orphan Narrowly Escapes Being Eaten Alive
Who: Sophie
What: giant called Bloodbottler starts to eat Sophie but spits her out
Where: at the cave of the BFG
When: shortly after she arrives in Giant Country
Why/How: Sophie is hiding in a snozzcumber that Bloodbottler tastes.

Mystery Unfolds—Giant Tells About Dream Netting
Who: BFG
What: catches dreams
Where: anywhere, especially in Dream Country
When: every day
Why/How: The BFG uses his big ears to listen for dreams, catches the dreams in his dream-catcher net, and then bottles the dreams in a jar.

Secret Plan to Enlist Queen's Assistance
Who: Sophie and the BFG
What: prepare a special dream for the queen
Where: the queen's palace in Hyde Park, England
When: after Sophie learns that the giants plan to eat girls and boys from their schools
Why/How: The BFG mixes a special dream and blows it into the sleeping queen while Sophie waits on the windowsill for the queen to awaken.

Name _____

The BFG
Creative Writing

MIXING UP THE PERFECT PHIZZWIZARD

The BFG is a master of mixing dreams, putting in just the right amounts from each bottle he chooses. If you could create the perfect dream, what would it be? Would you spend the day with the queen of England, or would you fly on a winged horse to a magical land?

Directions: Write a description of your dream on the jar below. Be sure to include the right ingredients—the characters involved, when and where the dream takes place, what happens in your dream, and how it ends.

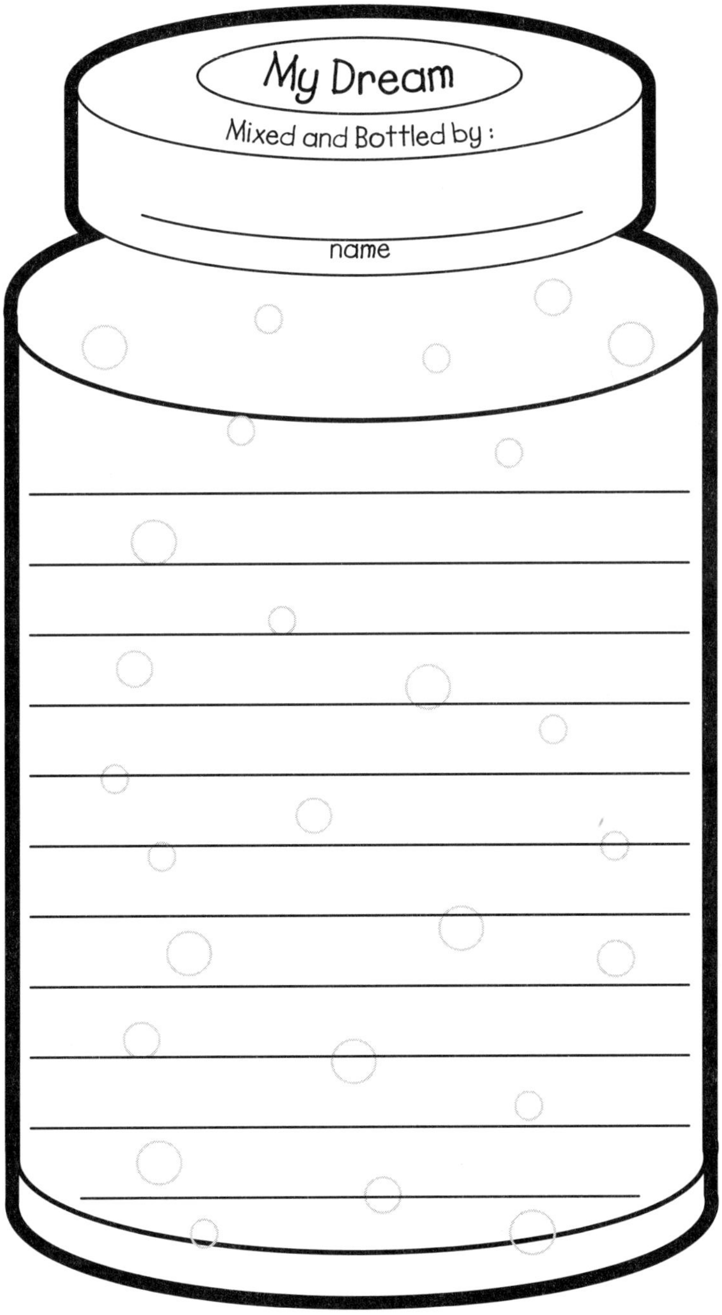

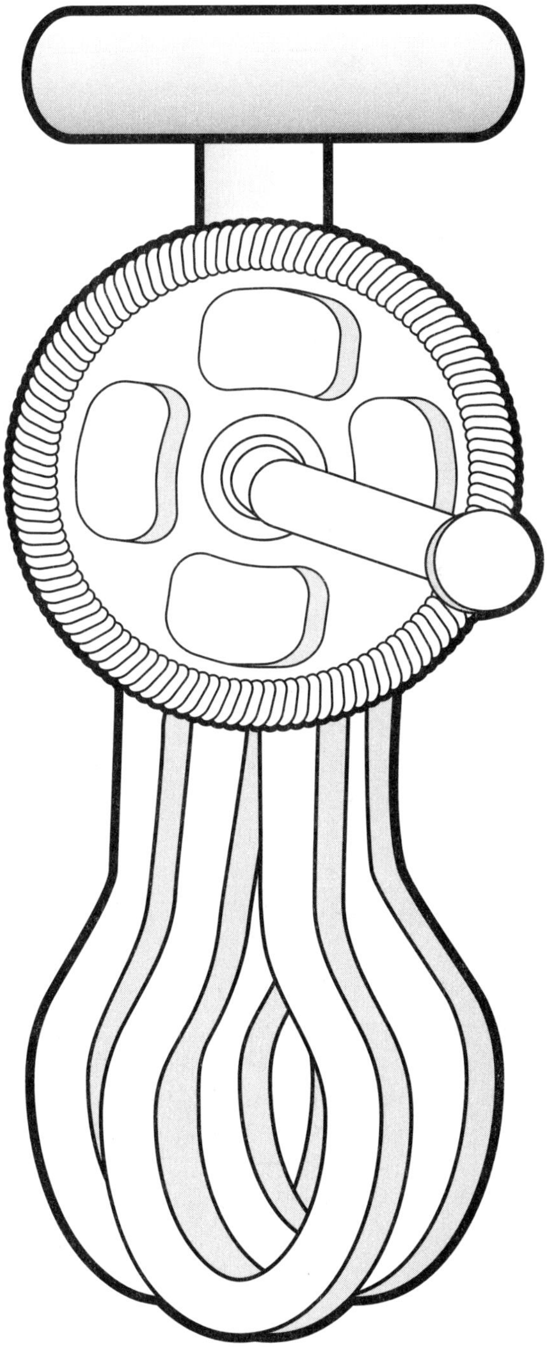

How to Use Page 153

1. Give each student a copy of page 153.
2. If desired, after students have completed the page, have each student cut out the jar. Post students' stories on a wall or bulletin board titled "Our Dreams—Mixed and Bottled by [teacher's name] Class."

Name _____   Number Forms

Mixed-Up Nuts

Sammy Squirrel has scrambled his acorns. Help him sort them out!

Directions: First find four nuts that contain different forms of the same number. Lightly color each set of matching nuts a different color. Then on the back of this sheet, make a labeled chart like the one shown below. Write each number in the correct column in the chart. The first one is done for you.

Acorns contain:
- 13,426
- thirteen thousand, four hundred twenty-six
- 1 thousand, 338
- 134,261
- 100,000 + 30,000 + 4,000 + 200 + 60 + 1
- 100,000 + 40,000 + 3,000 + 600 + 20 + 1
- thirteen thousand
- one hundred thirty-four thousand, two hundred sixty-one
- 10,000 + 3,000
- 13 thousand
- 10,000 + 3,000 + 400 + 20 + 6
- one hundred forty-three thousand, six hundred twenty-one
- 13 thousand, 426
- 134 thousand, 261
- 13,000
- 1,000 + 300 + 30 + 8
- 300,000 + 10,000 + 1,000 + 100
- 143 thousand, 621
- 311,100
- three hundred eleven thousand, one hundred
- 311 thousand, 100
- 1,338
- one thousand, three hundred thirty-eight
- 143,621

	Standard Form	Short Word Form	Word Form	Expanded Form
1.	13,426	13 thousand, 426	thirteen thousand, four hundred twenty-six	10,000 + 3,000 + 400 + 20 + 6

Bonus Box: Think of a secret code to show the value of each digit. For example, an apple can stand for a ten, a banana for one hundred, etc. Then, on the back of this sheet, rewrite three of the above numbers using your secret code.

Answer Key

The order of answers will vary.

	Standard Form	Short Word Form	Word Form	Expanded Form
1.	13,426	13 thousand, 426	thirteen thousand, four hundred twenty-six	10,000 + 3,000 + 400 + 20 + 6
2.	1,338	1 thousand, 338	one thousand, three hundred thirty-eight	1,000 + 300 + 30 + 8
3.	13,000	13 thousand	thirteen thousand	10,000 + 3,000
4.	143,621	143 thousand, 621	one hundred forty-three thousand, six hundred twenty-one	100,000 + 40,000 + 3,000 + 600 + 20 + 1
5.	134,261	134 thousand, 261	one hundred thirty-four thousand, two hundred sixty-one	100,000 + 30,000 + 4,000 + 200 + 60 + 1
6.	311,100	311 thousand, 100	three hundred eleven thousand, one hundred	300,000 + 10,000 + 1,000 + 100

Name _____   Comparing Whole Numbers

"Leaf-ing" Lots of Clues!

"Why should crazy chess players stay away from squirrels?" To solve this rodent riddle, follow the directions below.

Directions: Circle the letter beside the larger number on each leaf. Write the letter on the matching number's blank at the bottom of the page. Continue in the same manner until you solve the riddle.

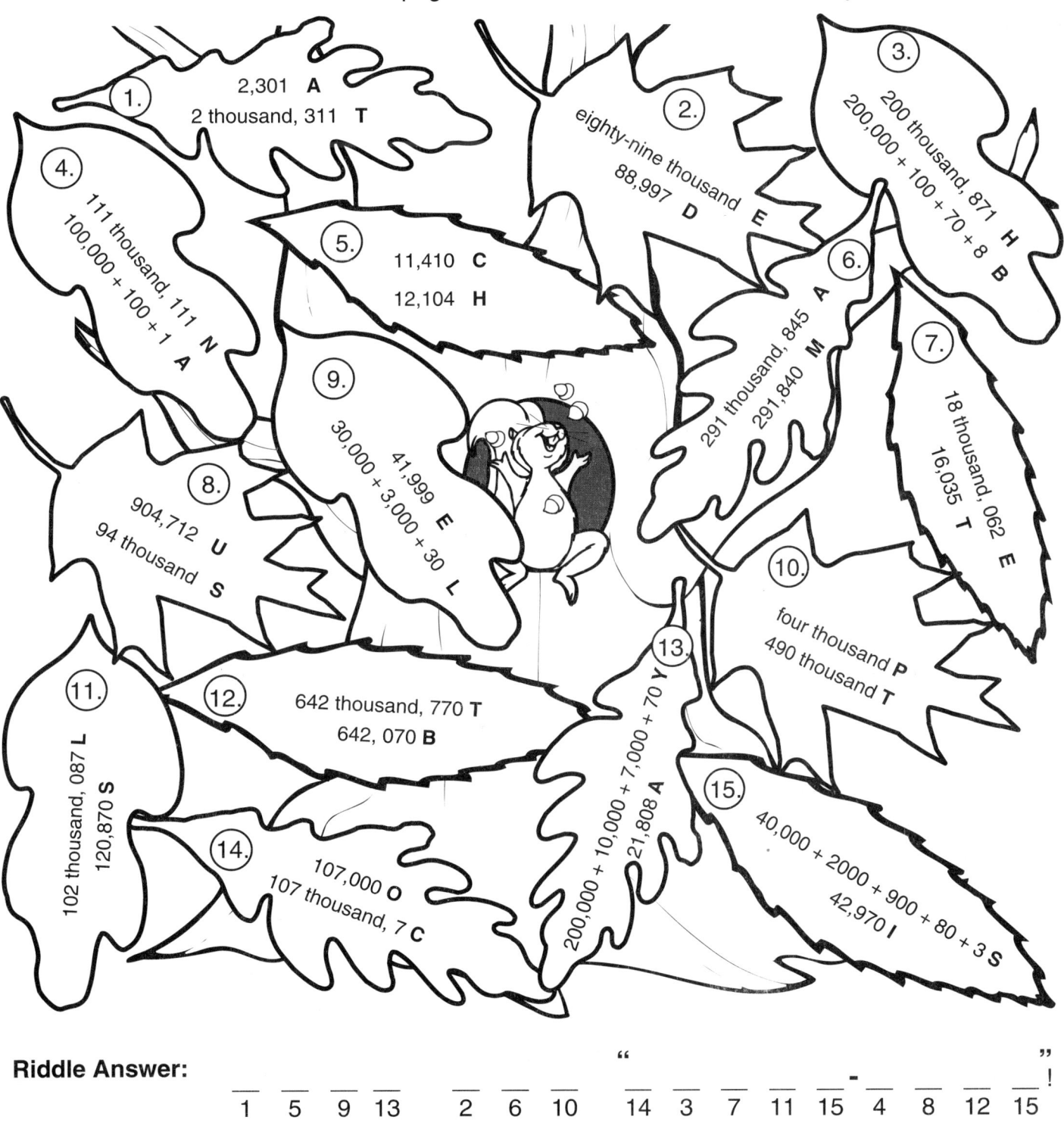

Riddle Answer: " __ __ __ __ __ __ __ __ __ __ __ __ - __ __ __ __ __ !"
  1 5 9 13 2 6 10 14 3 7 11 15 4 8 12 15

Bonus Box: Choose ten numbers from the leaves above. Then, on the back of this sheet, write the numbers in order from least to greatest.

Answer Key

1. T	6. A	11. S
2. E	7. E	12. T
3. H	8. U	13. Y
4. N	9. E	14. C
5. H	10. T	15. S

<u>T</u> <u>H</u> <u>E</u> <u>Y</u>   <u>E</u> <u>A</u> <u>T</u>   "<u>C</u> <u>H</u> <u>E</u> <u>S</u> <u>S</u>-<u>N</u> <u>U</u> <u>T</u> <u>S</u>"!
 1 5 9 13   2 6 10   14 3 7 11 15 4 8 12 15

Name _____ Place Value to 100 Millions

Place-Value Safari

See how many different kinds of African game you can spot below. First determine the value of the 3 in each number. Next look in the chart to tell what kind of animal this place value represents. Then identify the animal by writing its code and name on the lines provided.

Place Value of 3	Code	Animal
Ones	O	Elephant
Tens	T	Rhinoceros
Hundreds	H	Giraffe
Thousands	Th	Zebra
Ten Thousands	TTh	Lion
Hundred Thousands	HTh	Gnu
Millions	M	Leopard
Ten Millions	TM	Cape Buffalo
Hundred Millions	HM	Cheetah

1. 234,976,210 Code ____ Animal ____
2. 584,903,008 Code ____ Animal ____
3. 590,864,370 Code ____ Animal ____
4. 853,802,199 Code ____ Animal ____
5. 301,784,077 Code ____ Animal ____
6. 804,860,893 Code ____ Animal ____
7. 580,725,831 Code ____ Animal ____
8. 291,004,320 Code ____ Animal ____
9. 558,344,002 Code ____ Animal ____
10. 506,300,715 Code ____ Animal ____
11. 301,795,072 Code ____ Animal ____
12. 752,397,055 Code ____ Animal ____
13. 106,793,581 Code ____ Animal ____
14. 700,507,731 Code ____ Animal ____
15. 784,852,063 Code ____ Animal ____
16. 238,961,007 Code ____ Animal ____
17. 805,738,222 Code ____ Animal ____
18. 683,798,500 Code ____ Animal ____
19. 905,685,432 Code ____ Animal ____
20. 448,664,308 Code ____ Animal ____
21. 888,794,038 Code ____ Animal ____
22. 797,785,344 Code ____ Animal ____
23. 288,577,931 Code ____ Animal ____
24. 377,885,000 Code ____ Animal ____
25. 788,953,144 Code ____ Animal ____

Bonus Box: Which animal did you spot most often? Least often? Which animals were sighted only twice? Three times? Four times?

Answer Key

1. **2**34,976,210; TM; Cape Buffalo
2. 584,90**3**,008; Th; Zebra
3. 590,864,**3**70; H; Giraffe
4. 85**3**,802,199; M; Leopard
5. **3**01,784,077; HM; Cheetah
6. 804,860,89**3**; O; Elephant
7. 580,725,8**3**1; T; Rhinoceros
8. 291,004,**3**20; H; Giraffe
9. 558,**3**44,002; HTh; Gnu
10. 506,**3**00,715; HTh; Gnu
11. **3**01,795,072; HM; Cheetah
12. 752,**3**97,055; HTh; Gnu
13. 106,79**3**,581; Th; Zebra
14. 700,507,7**3**1; T; Rhinoceros
15. 784,852,06**3**; O; Elephant
16. 2**3**8,961,007; TM; Cape Buffalo
17. 805,7**3**8,222; TTh; Lion
18. 68**3**,798,500; M; Leopard
19. 905,685,4**3**2; T; Rhinoceros
20. 448,664,**3**08; H; Giraffe
21. 888,794,0**3**8; T; Rhinoceros
22. 797,785,**3**44; H; Giraffe
23. 288,577,9**3**1; T; Rhinoceros
24. **3**77,885,000; HM; Cheetah
25. 788,9**5**3,144; Th; Zebra

Bonus Box: The rhinoceros was spotted most often (five times). The lion was spotted only once. The Cape buffalo, leopard, and elephant were each spotted twice. The zebra, cheetah, and gnu were each spotted three times. The giraffe was spotted four times.

Names _____ Comparing Numbers Game

Place-Value Prowl

Directions: Choose a partner. Decide who will be the lion and who will be the leopard. Roll the die and write the number you roll in one of the six sections of your Round One box. Have your partner do the same. Continue taking turns—rolling the die and writing a number in a section of the game-box—until the boxes in Round One are filled. Then compare the number you made with the one created by your partner. The player with the larger number wins that round. Play five rounds.

Materials:
one die
a copy of this reproducible for each pair of students
a pencil for each student

Lion   Round One   Leopard

Round Two

Round Three

Round Four

Round Five

Rounds I won: _____   **Rounds I won:** _____

©The Education Center, Inc. • *Big Book of Skill Builders* • TEC60797

Name_____   Place Value to 100 Millions

MTV (Math Television) Presents...
"Squares of Fortune"

Give yourself a hand when you complete this puzzle! First cut out the column headings strip and glue it near the top of a sheet of construction paper. Then follow these steps:

1. Cut out the 24 boxes.
2. Arrange the boxes into six groups of four boxes each. Each group should have four different forms of the same number.
3. Find the group of boxes with the smallest number.
4. Arrange those four boxes on the sheet of construction paper, making sure that each form is in the correct column. Then arrange the remaining five groups in numerical order down to the largest number.
5. Beginning with the top-left box, read the words in each row from left to right.
6. If your sentence makes sense, glue all of the boxes onto the construction paper.

Column Headings:

Standard Form	Short Word Form	Word Form	Expanded Form
60,000,000 + 80,000 + 800 **times**	six million, six hundred eight thousand, eighty **been**	six hundred eight million, eighty thousand, eight hundred **one**	6,000,000 + 600,000 + 80,000 + 80 **Fortune"**
60,080,800 **her**	6 million, 608 thousand, 80 **has**	sixty million, eighty thousand, eight hundred **720**	6,608,080 **It**
60,000,000 + 800,000 + 80 **28,080**	60 million, 800 thousand, 80 **show,**	6,680,080 **that**	608,080,800 **times**
6 million, 680 thousand, 80 **"Wheel**	608 million, 80 thousand, 800 **in**	six million, six hundred eighty thousand, eight hundred **White**	60,800,080 **per**
600,000,000 + 8,000,000 + 80,000 + 800 **year.**	6,000,000 + 600,000 + 80,000 + 800 **claps**	sixty million, eight hundred thousand, eighty **or**	six million, six hundred eighty thousand, eighty **Of**
6 million, 680 thousand, 800 **Vanna**	60 million, 80 thousand, 800 **hands**	6,680,800 **hostess**	6,000,000 + 600,000 + 8,000 + 80 **estimated**

©The Education Center, Inc. • Big Book of Skill Builders • TEC60797

How to Use Page 163

Provide each student with a copy of page 163, a sheet of construction paper, scissors, and glue. Have each student cut out the column headings strip. With the sheet of construction paper turned vertically, have the student glue the headings strip near the top of the paper. Then direct students to follow steps 1–6 as outlined on the reproducible.

 Answer Key

Standard Form	Short Word Form	Word Form	Expanded Form
6,608,080 **It**	6 million, 608 thousand, 80 **has**	six million, six hundred eight thousand, eighty **been**	6,000,000 + 600,000 + 8,000 + 80 **estimated**
6,680,080 **that**	6 million, 680 thousand, 80 **"Wheel**	six million, six hundred eighty thousand, eighty **Of**	6,000,000 + 600,000 + 80,000 + 80 **Fortune"**
6,680,800 **hostess**	6 million, 680 thousand, 800 **Vanna**	six million, six hundred eighty thousand, eight hundred **White**	6,000,000 + 600,000 + 80,000 + 800 **claps**
60,080,800 **her**	60 million, 80 thousand, 800 **hands**	sixty million, eighty thousand, eight hundred **720**	60,000,000 + 80,000 + 800 **times**
60,800,080 **per**	60 million, 800 thousand, 80 **show,**	sixty million, eight hundred thousand, eighty **or**	60,000,000 + 800,000 + 80 **28,080**
608,080,800 **times**	608 million, 80 thousand, 800 **in**	six hundred eight million, eighty thousand, eight hundred **one**	600,000,000 + 8,000,000 + 80,000 + 800 **year.**

Name_____ Estimation and Addition Game

Adding at the Pad

Materials: spinner, scissors, paper clip, 2 sheets of loose-leaf paper, 2 pencils

Directions for Two Players:
1. Cut out each card along the bold lines.
2. Shuffle the cards and place them facedown in a pile.
3. Draw the top three cards and place them faceup in the center of the playing surface.
4. Player 1 chooses a faceup card, then spins the spinner twice to create a two-digit number. (For example, if the first spin shows an *8* and the second spin shows a *2*, then the two-digit number is *82*.)
5. Player 1 estimates a number that can be added to the two-digit number to produce a sum that falls within the range on the chosen card. (For example, if Player 1 chose the *350–380* card, then he could add *82 + 270* to get a sum of *352*, which falls within the range.)
6. Player 1 writes the two numbers on his paper, then adds them to check his estimate. If the estimate is correct (the sum falls within the range), he keeps that card. He then draws another facedown card to take its place on the playing surface. If the estimate is incorrect, he puts the card back on the playing surface.
7. Player 2 takes his turn in the same manner.
8. After all cards are claimed, both players add the total number of points on their cards. The player with the most points is the winner.

1 point	1 point	1 point	1 point
200–230	230–260	260–290	290–320
2 points	**2 points**	**2 points**	**2 points**
320–350	350–380	380–410	410–440
3 points	**3 points**	**3 points**	**3 points**
440–470	470–500	500–530	530–560
4 points	**4 points**	**4 points**	**4 points**
560–590	590–620	620–650	650–680
5 points	**5 points**	**5 points**	**5 points**
680–710	710–740	740–770	770–800
6 points	**6 points**	**6 points**	**6 points**
800–830	830–860	860–890	890–920

How to Use Page 165

Have your students give their estimation and addition skills a workout with this two-player game. Distribute one copy of page 165 and the materials listed there to each pair of students. Demonstrate to students how to assemble and use the spinner (see the illustration on this page). Then have each pair play the game as directed.

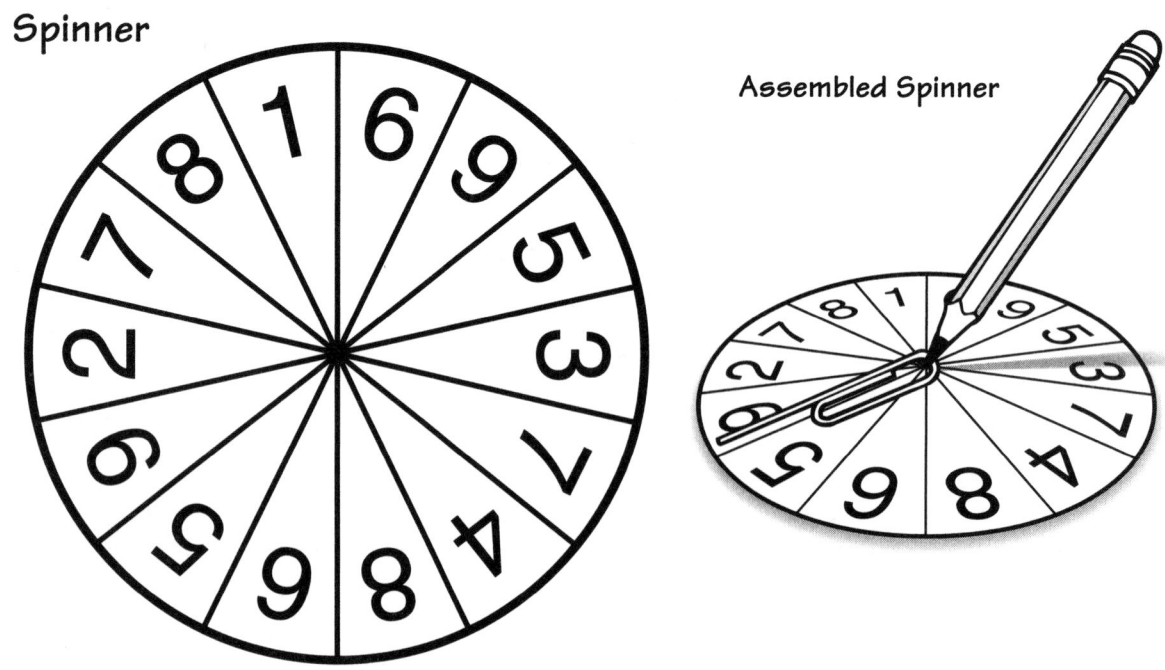

Spinner

Assembled Spinner

Name _____ Subtraction Game

Lily-Pad Leap

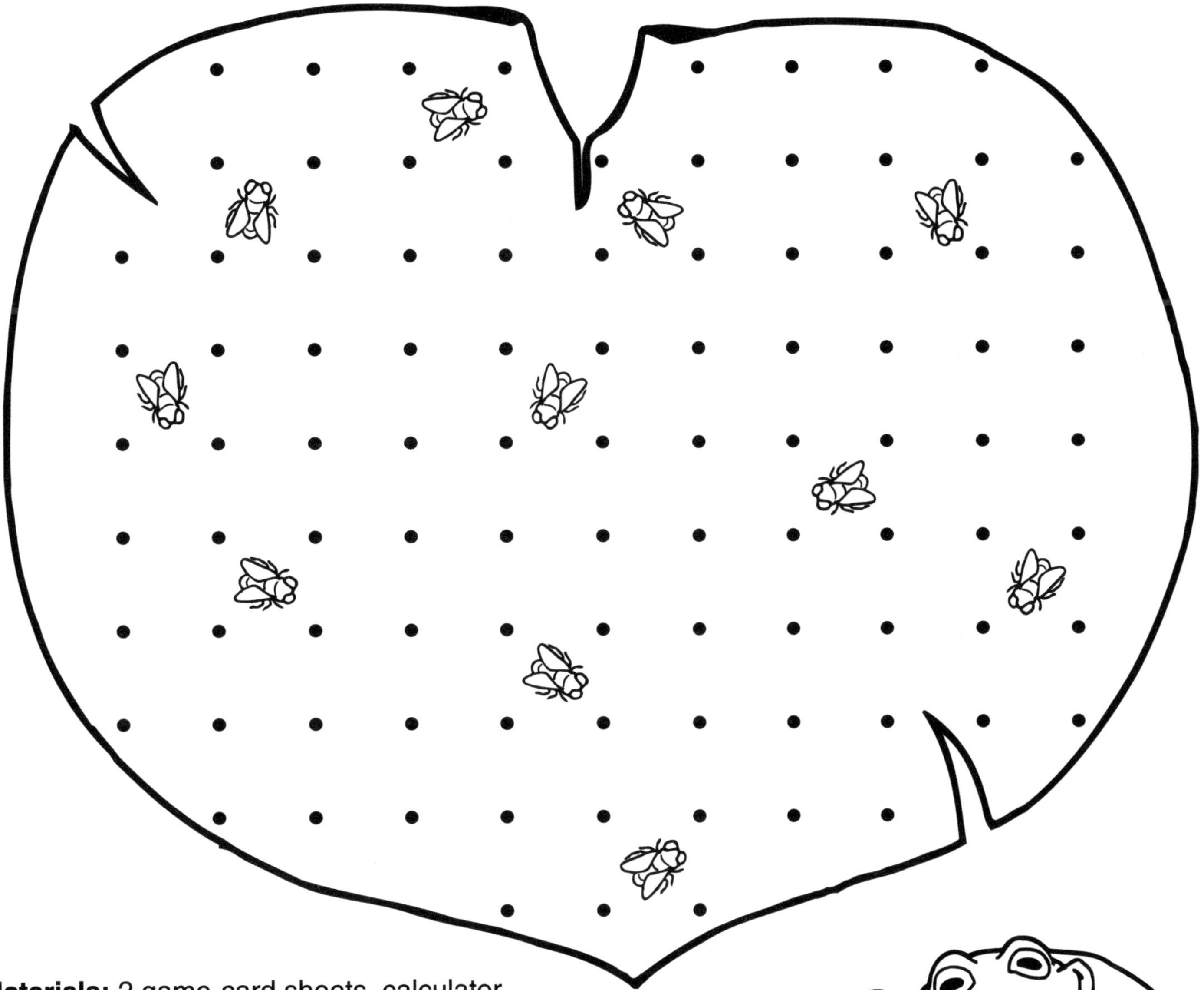

Materials: 2 game-card sheets, calculator, scissors, 2 sheets of loose-leaf paper, 2 pencils

Directions for Two Players:
1. Cut out the cards. Place them facedown in a pile.
2. Player 1 draws a card and works the subtraction problem on her paper.
3. Player 2 uses the calculator to check Player 1's work. If the answer is correct, Player 1 draws a line segment to leap from one dot to another. If the answer is not correct, a line is not drawn.
4. Player 2 takes a turn in the same manner.
5. Continue play. The player who draws a line that encloses a box writes her initials in that box. This player also draws another line segment on the gameboard.
6. Each box is worth one point. Each box with a fly inside is worth two points. The player with the most points at the end of the game wins.

©The Education Center, Inc. • Big Book of Skill Builders • TEC60797

167

How to Use Page 167

Make two copies of the game-card sheet below. Program each card with a different subtraction problem (for a total of 48 different problems). Distribute one copy of both game-card sheets, a copy of page 167, and the materials listed on page 167 to each pair of students. Direct the pairs to follow the directions on the sheet to play the game.

Program more copies of the cards with different or more challenging problems as desired.

Open Game Cards

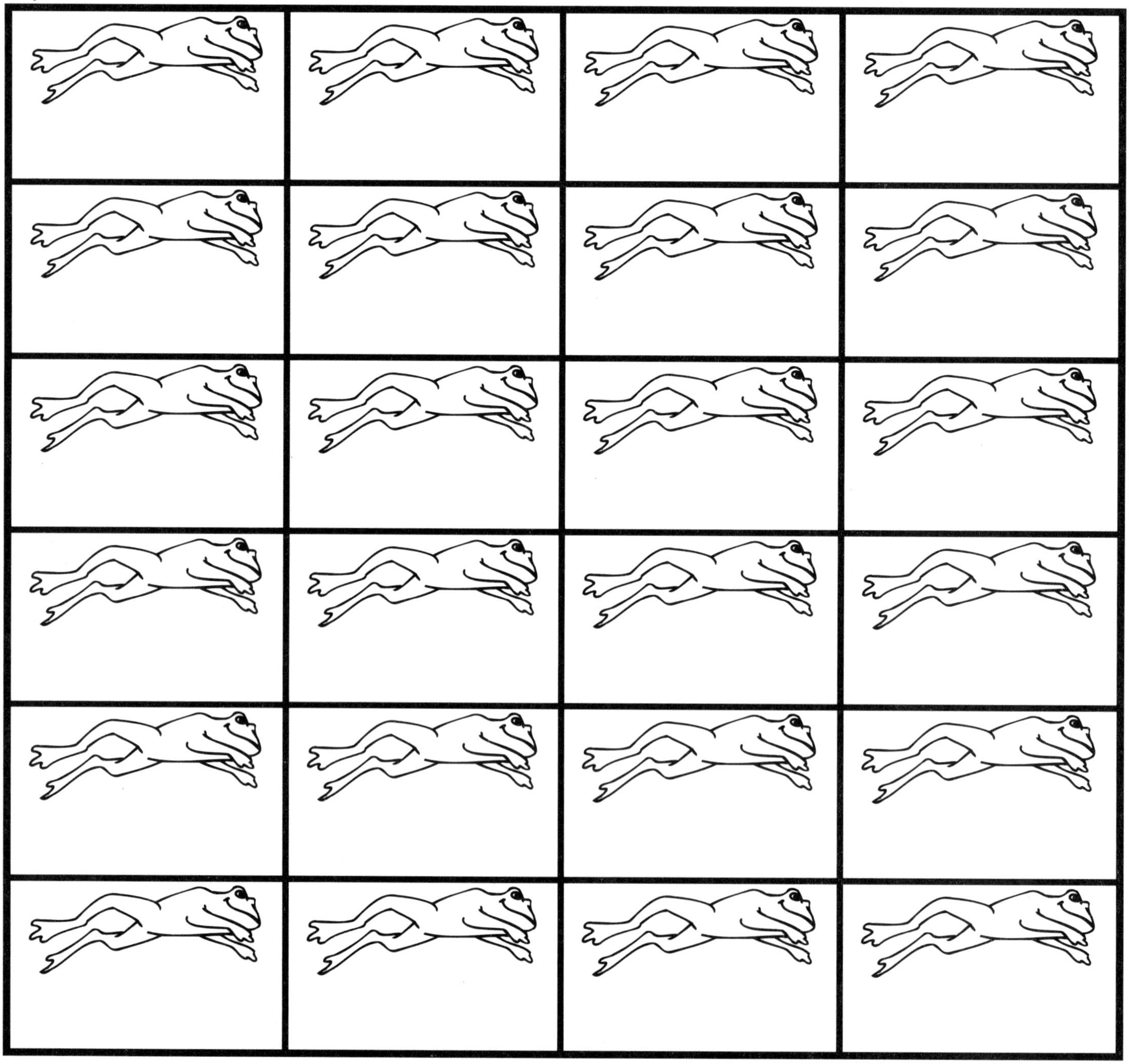

Multiplication-Facts Game

Name _____

Multiplication Spin

Directions for Two Players:
1. Player 1 chooses and colors a square on the gameboard, then spins the spinner.
2. Player 1 multiplies the number on the colored square by the number shown on the spinner.
3. Player 2 uses the calculator to check Player 1's answer.
4. If the answer is correct, Player 1 records the point value at the beginning of the row containing the colored square on the sheet of paper.
5. Player 2 takes a turn in the same manner.
6. Continue play until all squares are colored or until time is up. The player with the most points at the end of the game wins.

Materials: spinner, paper clip, pencil, calculator, sheet of loose-leaf paper, crayon

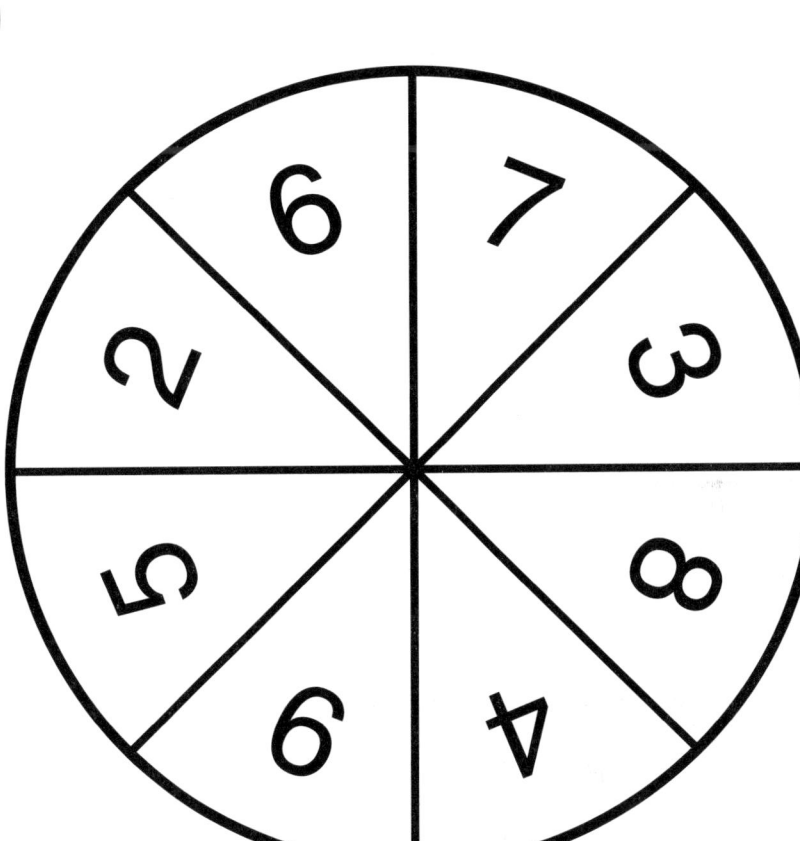

1 point	1	1	1	1	1	1
1 point	2	2	2	2	2	2
2 points	3	3	3	3	3	3
2 points	4	4	4	4	4	4
2 points	5	5	5	5	5	5
3 points	6	6	6	6	6	6
3 points	7	7	7	7	7	7
4 points	8	8	8	8	8	8
4 points	9	9	9	9	9	9
5 points	10	10	10	10	10	10
5 points	11	11	11	11	11	11
6 points	12	12	12	12	12	12

©The Education Center, Inc. • Big Book of Skill Builders • TEC60797

How to Use Page 169

Distribute one copy of page 169 and the materials listed on that page to each pair of students. Demonstrate how to assemble and use the spinner (see page 166). Then have each pair play the game as directed.

Increase the difficulty of the game by programming the open gameboard below with two-digit or three-digit numbers. Make a copy of page 169, glue the new gameboard over the old one, and duplicate the desired number of copies.

Open Gameboard

1 point						
1 point						
2 points						
2 points						
2 points						
3 points						
3 points						
4 points						
4 points						
5 points						
5 points						
6 points						

Name _____ Division Game

"Ribbit-ing" Remainders!

Materials: pair of dice, 2 game markers, 2 sheets of loose-leaf paper, 2 pencils

Directions for Two Players:
1. Players 1 and 2 place their markers on Start.
2. Player 1 rolls each die separately to make a two-digit number. (For example, if the first die rolled shows a *5* and the second die rolled shows a *3*, then the two-digit number is *53*.)
3. Player 1 divides that number by the number shown on his space. (For example, *53 ÷ 3 = 17* with a remainder of *2*.)
4. Player 1 then moves his marker the number of spaces equal to the remainder in the division problem. (For example, move *2* spaces with a remainder of *2*.)
5. Player 2 takes a turn in the same manner.
6. Continue to play. The first player to reach Finish is the winner.

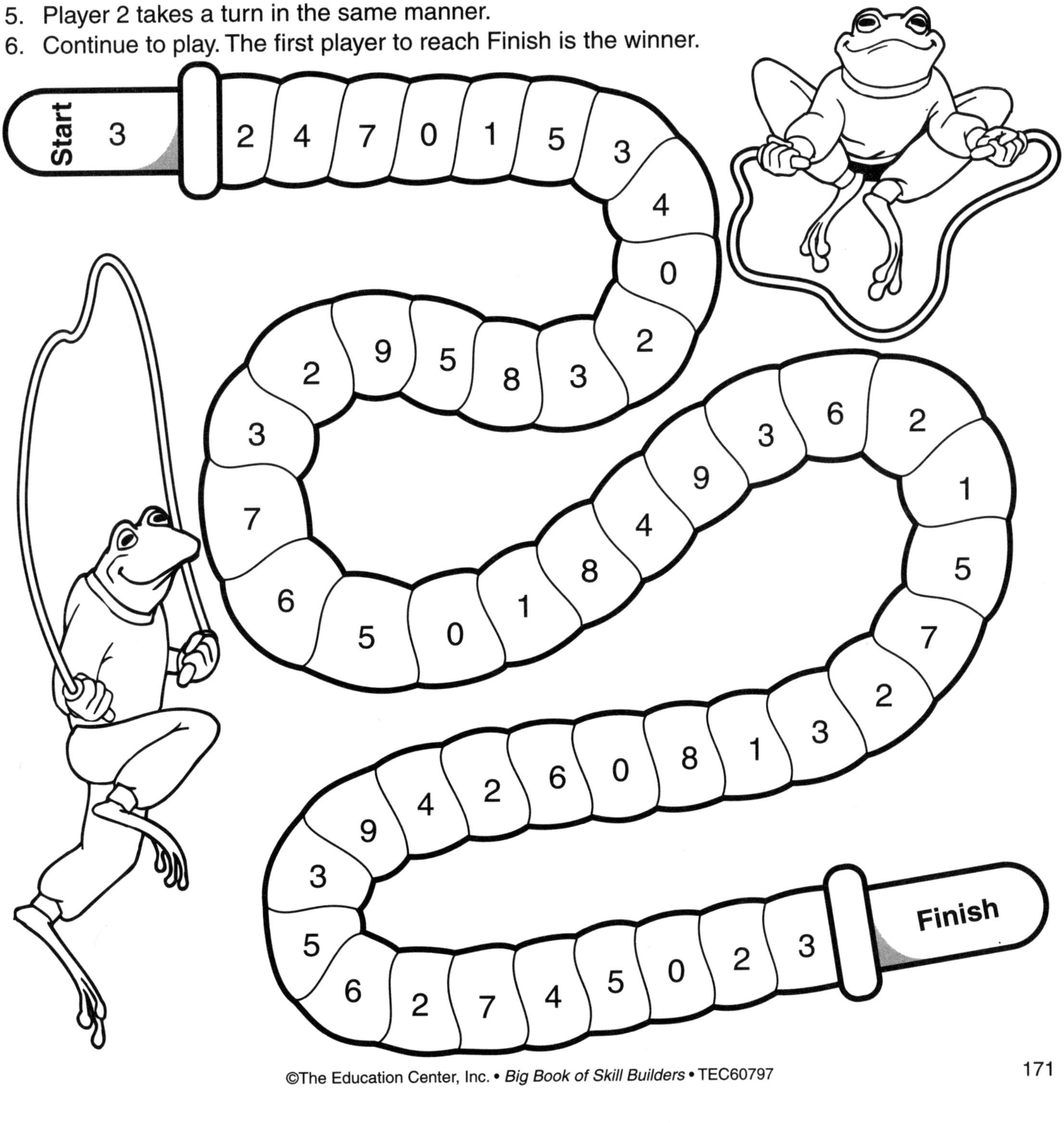

©The Education Center, Inc. • *Big Book of Skill Builders* • TEC60797

How to Use Page 171

Distribute one copy of page 171 and the materials listed on that page to each pair of students. Instruct each pair to play the game as directed on the sheet. Have each player show his work on a sheet of loose-leaf paper.

Increase the level of difficulty by giving each pair an extra die to create a three-digit number.

Name _____ Multiplying by a One-Digit Number

Having a Ball!

Mort, owner of Mort's Sports Store, accidentally bumped into a display and sent sports balls spilling to the floor! Help Mort put his display back together by following the directions below.

375 × 2	4,369 × 7	106 × 3
1,092 × 5	535 × 9	935 × 3
12,952 × 2	236 × 3	94 × 5
351 × 7	453 × 3	1,441 × 2
896 × 2	487 × 5	224 × 7
43 × 9	98 × 6	10,043 × 5

Directions:
1. Solve the multiplication problems in the sports balls at the right.
2. Cut out the 18 balls along the bold lines.
3. Arrange the balls in six rows of three each. Use the clues below to help you determine which balls belong in each row.
4. Check your work. Then glue the balls in the correct arrangement onto another sheet of paper.

Clues:
1. The first row (bottom row) has the three smallest products.
2. There are no 2s in the second row products.
3. The third row products each have three digits and are each greater than 500.
4. Each product in the fourth row has the digit 4 in the hundreds place.
5. The fifth row has the three largest products.
6. The three remaining balls belong in the sixth row.

Bonus Box: Make up three multiplication problems that would belong on the display's seventh row. Write a clue that explains how the three problems are alike, yet different from those on the other six rows.

©The Education Center, Inc. • Big Book of Skill Builders • TEC60797

Answer Key

Row 6	935 × 3 = 2,805	896 × 2 = 1,792	1,441 × 2 = 2,882
Row 5	12,952 × 2 = 25,904	10,043 × 5 = 50,215	4,369 × 7 = 30,583
Row 4	1,092 × 5 = 5,460	487 × 5 = 2,435	351 × 7 = 2,457
Row 3	236 × 3 = 708	375 × 2 = 750	98 × 6 = 588
Row 2	535 × 9 = 4,815	453 × 3 = 1,359	224 × 7 = 1,568
Row 1	106 × 3 = 318	94 × 5 = 470	43 × 9 = 387

Name _____

Estimation Game

Music to My Ears

Are you a good estimator when you're shopping? Play this game with a partner to help fine-tune your estimation skills!

Materials:
2 copies of the game sheet and price tags
game chips (popcorn, paper squares, etc.)
die
scissors
container (bowl, basket, shoebox, etc.)
paper and pencils

Before you play:
1. Cut out the price tags at the right of the page.
2. Place both players' price tags in a container.

To play:
1. Player 1 rolls the die and selects a price tag from the container. Player 1 then estimates a product by rounding the price to the nearest dollar and then multiplying that price by the number showing on the die. (If a one is rolled, multiply by ten.)
2. Player 1 finds on his gameboard the range in which the estimated product fits and places a game chip on the square.
3. Player 2 checks the estimate.
4. If the estimate is within the chosen range, the game chip remains; if not, the chip is removed.
5. Player 1 returns the price tag to the container.
6. Players switch roles and continue play.
7. The first player to cover five squares in any row, column, or diagonal wins the round.

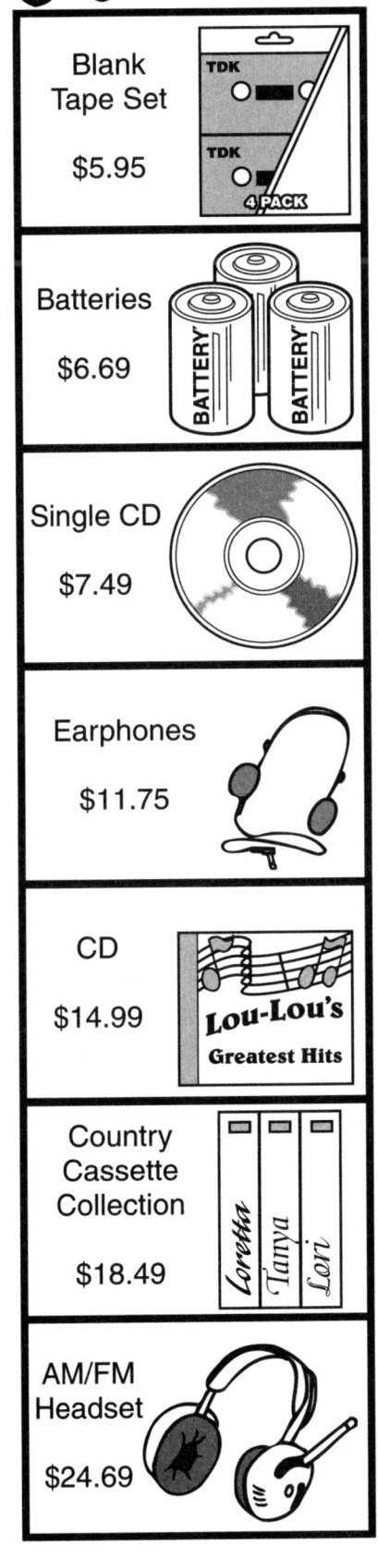

$40–$49	$150–$159	$10–$19	$200–$209	$130–$139
$80–$89	$120–$129	$230–$239	$50–$59	$240–$249
$160–$169	$90–$99	$190–$199	$70–$79	$30–$39
$100–$109	$140–$149	$170–$179	$210–$219	$60–$69
$250–$259	$180–$189	$20–$29	$220–$229	$110–$119

©The Education Center, Inc. • Big Book of Skill Builders • TEC60797

Name _____   Multiplication of Larger Numbers

Boning Up on Multiplication

Pete's job at the Pet Parade is feeding and washing the puppies. Work each problem below on the back of this sheet. Write the product in the dog bowl. Use a ruler to draw a line between each bowl and bone that contain the same product. Then answer the riddle at the bottom of the page by writing the letters that the lines cross in the correct spaces.

1. 542 x 342 =
2. 567 x 754 =
3. 679 x 268 =
4. 789 x 973 =
5. 985 x 875 =
6. 454 x 357 =
7. 780 x 864 =
8. 689 x 207 =
9. 512 x 893 =
10. 264 x 374 =

Bones:
- 185,364
- 861,875
- 162,078
- 181,972
- 427,518
- 142,623
- 98,736
- 767,697
- 673,920
- 457,216

Paw print letters: S, E, C, X, P, A, O, H, N, M, L, D, O, E, S, W, L

What kind of soap does Pete use on the puppies' fur?

___ ___ ___ ___ - ___ ___ ___ ___ ___ ___
 1   2   3   4   5   6   7   8   9 10

Answer Key

1. 185,364
2. 427,518
3. 181,972
4. 767,697
5. 861,875

6. 162,078
7. 673,920
8. 142,623
9. 457,216
10. 98,736

Riddle:

$\underset{1}{S}\ \underset{2}{H}\ \underset{3}{A}\ \underset{4}{M}\ -\ \underset{5}{P}\ \underset{6}{O}\ \underset{7}{O}\ \underset{8}{D}\ \underset{9}{L}\ \underset{10}{E}$

Name _____ Division

Dr. Division's Dilemma

The students in Dr. Division's math class have rearranged the desks in her classroom. Help Dr. Division find the desk that does not belong in each group.

Directions: Solve each division problem. Show your work on another sheet of paper. Find the problem in each group whose answer is different from the others. Cross out that desk.

Group 1: 49÷7, 72÷8, 54÷6, 81÷9
Group 2: 48÷8, 36÷6, 63÷7, 30÷5
Group 3: 31÷7, 39÷9, 19÷4, 45÷6
Group 4: 49÷5, 85÷9, 58÷6, 64÷7
Group 5: 77÷8, 86÷9, 68÷7, 58÷6
Group 6: 80÷5, 51÷3, 96÷6, 48÷3

Bonus Box: On the back of this sheet, create a seating chart for your classroom—the way you'd like for it to be arranged!

✓ Answer Key ✓

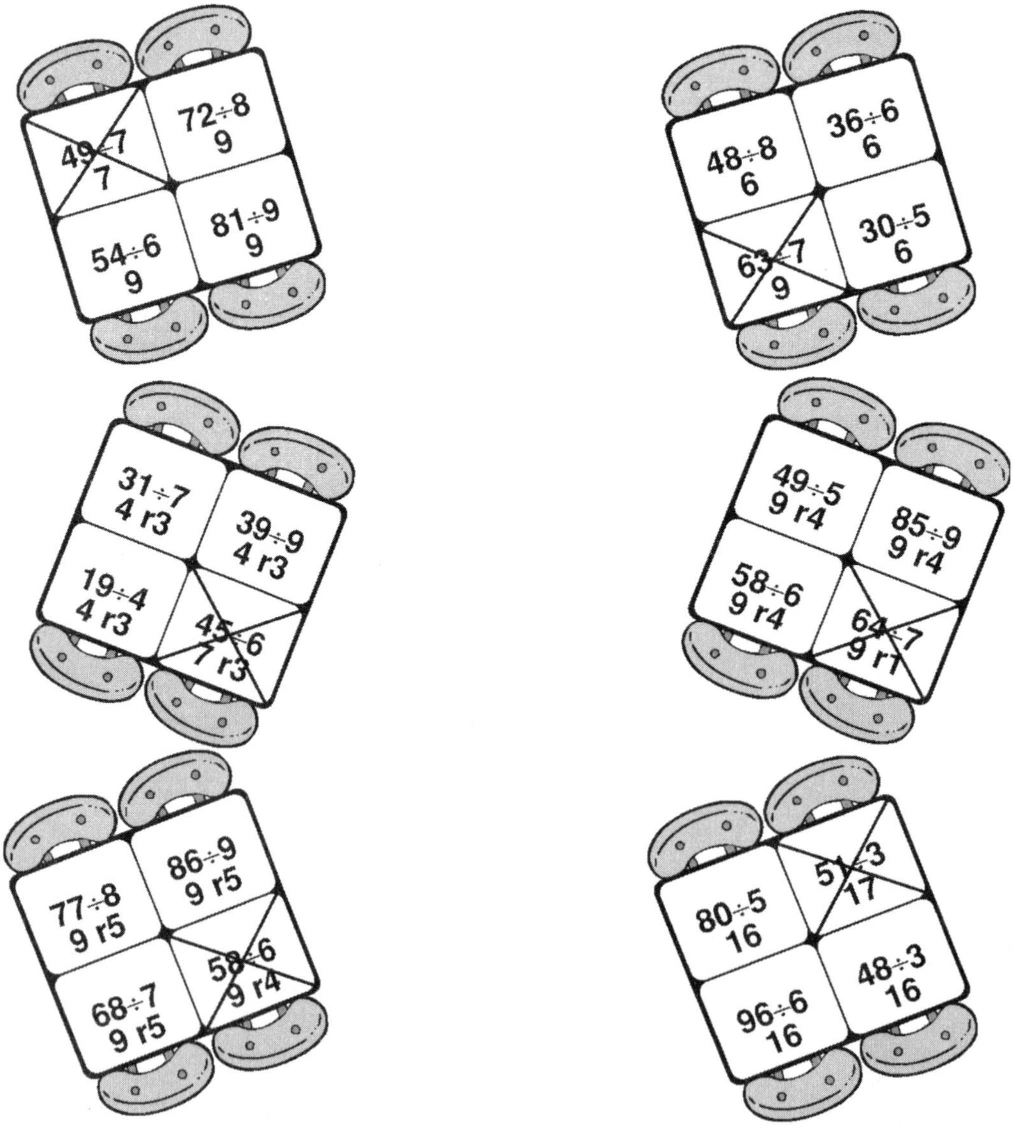

Group 1 (top-left):
- 49÷7 = 7
- 72÷8 = 9
- 54÷6 = 9
- 81÷9 = 9

Group 2 (top-right):
- 48÷8 = 6
- 36÷6 = 6
- 63÷7 = 9
- 30÷5 = 6

Group 3 (middle-left):
- 31÷7 = 4 r3
- 39÷9 = 4 r3
- 19÷4 = 4 r3
- 45÷6 = 7 r3

Group 4 (middle-right):
- 49÷5 = 9 r4
- 85÷9 = 9 r4
- 58÷6 = 9 r4
- 64÷7 = 9 r1

Group 5 (bottom-left):
- 77÷8 = 9 r5
- 86÷9 = 9 r5
- 68÷7 = 9 r5
- 58÷6 = 9 r4

Group 6 (bottom-right):
- 80÷5 = 16
- 51÷3 = 17
- 96÷6 = 16
- 48÷3 = 16

Name _____ Unit Pricing

Baseball Bargains

Two vendors—Barry and Bebe—are each opening a snack and souvenir stand at a baseball stadium. So who offers the better buys? To find out, use the formula below to calculate the *unit price* of each vendor's products. Then color the baseball next to the item that is the better bargain. The first one is done for you.

Unit Price = Total Price ÷ Total Items *Or* Total Ounces

Barry's Bargains
- Hotdogs .... 3 for $5.25
- Lemonade .... 10 oz. for $.60
- Ice-Cream Cones ..... 10 oz. for $1.20
- Candy Apples .... 2 for $2.50
- Roasted Peanuts .... 12 oz. for $.60
- Baseball Cards .... 40 for $9.60
- Pennants .... 1 for $3.75
- Baseballs .... 2 for $8.60

Bebe's Bargains
- Hotdogs .... 1 for $1.85
- Lemonade .... 25 oz. for $1.00
- Ice-Cream Cones .... 5 oz. for $.70
- Candy Apples .... 1 for $1.50
- Roasted Peanuts .... 20 oz. for $.80
- Baseball Cards .... 20 for $5.00
- Pennants .... 2 for $5.50
- Baseballs .... 3 for $12.75

Item	Barry's Unit Price		Bebe's Unit Price	
1. hot dogs	$5.25 ÷ 3 = $1.75	●	$1.85 ÷ 1 = $1.85	○
2. lemonade		○		○
3. ice-cream cones		○		○
4. candy apples		○		○
5. roasted peanuts		○		○
6. baseball cards		○		○
7. pennants		○		○
8. baseballs		○		○

Bonus Box: If a third vendor named Betty wanted to set her prices between those of her two competitors, what would the price be for each item?

Answer Key

Item	Barry's Unit Price		Bebe's Unit Price	
1. hot dogs	$5.25 ÷ 3 = $1.75		$1.85 ÷ 1 = $1.85	
2. lemonade	$.60 ÷ 10 = $.06		$1.00 ÷ 25 = $.04	
3. ice-cream cones	$1.20 ÷ 10 = $.12		$.70 ÷ 5 = $.14	
4. candy apples	$2.50 ÷ 2 = $1.25		$1.50 ÷ 1 = $1.50	
5. roasted peanuts	$.60 ÷ 12 = $.05		$.80 ÷ 20 = $.04	
6. baseball cards	$9.60 ÷ 40 = $.24		$5.00 ÷ 20 = $.25	
7. pennants	$3.75 ÷ 1 = $3.75		$5.50 ÷ 2 = $2.75	
8. baseballs	$8.60 ÷ 2 = $4.30		$12.75 ÷ 3 = $4.25	

Bonus Box: Accept reasonable answers.
Some answers are rounded to the nearest cent.

1. $1.80
2. $.05
3. $.13
4. $1.38
5. either $.04 or $.05
6. either $.24 or $.25
7. $3.25
8. $4.28

Dino's Dinner

Decimals to Thousandths

On what do delightful dinosaurs like Dino dine? To find out, look at each underlined digit below. Use a crayon to color its place value in the chart. If you correctly identify each place value, you'll see the path that leads you to Dino's favorite dish. The first one is done for you.

Note: The place values on the chart are **not** written in order!

1. <u>3</u>.0 1 4
2. 0.2 5 <u>9</u>
3. 0.0 <u>5</u>
4. 2 <u>5</u>.1 8 3
5. 0.0 <u>0</u> 2
6. 9.<u>3</u> 8 4
7. 0.1 9 <u>5</u>
8. 1.9 <u>1</u>
9. 0.<u>2</u> 4 1
10. 5.0 6 <u>8</u>
11. 4 <u>2</u>.3 5
12. <u>7</u>.1 1
13. 1 3.2 <u>6</u> 4
14. 0.<u>9</u>
15. 0.2 3 <u>7</u>

ones	hundredths	thousandths	tenths
tenths	thousandths	ones	hundredths
hundredths	thousandths	ones	tenths
thousandths	ones	tenths	hundredths
ones	thousandths	hundredths	tenths
hundredths	tenths	ones	thousandths
thousandths	ones	tenths	hundredths
hundredths	ones	thousandths	tenths
ones	tenths	hundredths	thousandths
tenths	hundredths	thousandths	ones
thousandths	tenths	hundredths	ones
hundredths	thousandths	ones	tenths
tenths	thousandths	ones	hundredths
thousandths	ones	tenths	hundredths
ones	tenths	hundredths	thousandths

Brontosaurus Burgers

Tyrannosaurus Tacos

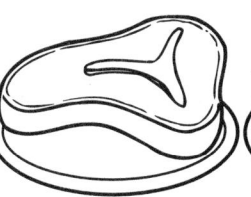
Stegosaurus Steaks

Pentaceratops Pasta

Bonus Box: Circle five numerals above. On the back of this page, write each numeral in word form.

©The Education Center, Inc. • Big Book of Skill Builders • TEC60797

Answer Key

#	Number				
1.	3.014	ones	hundredths	thousandths	tenths
2.	0.259	tenths	thousandths	ones	hundredths
3.	0.05	hundredths	thousandths	ones	tenths
4.	25.183	thousandths	ones	tenths	hundredths
5.	0.002	ones	thousandths	hundredths	tenths
6.	9.384	hundredths	tenths	ones	thousandths
7.	0.195	thousandths	ones	tenths	hundredths
8.	1.91	hundredths	ones	thousandths	tenths
9.	0.241	ones	tenths	hundredths	thousandths
10.	5.068	tenths	hundredths	thousandths	ones
11.	42.35	thousandths	tenths	hundredths	ones
12.	7.11	hundredths	thousandths	ones	tenths
13.	13.264	tenths	thousandths	ones	hundredths
14.	0.9	thousandths	ones	tenths	hundredths
15.	0.237	ones	tenths	hundredths	thousandths

Dino's favorite dish is Pentaceratops Pasta.

Standard Form and Word Names of Decimals

6.78	three and fifteen hundredths	five hundred forty-six thousandths	three hundred fifteen thousandths
0.315	5.046	five and forty-six hundredths	0.067
forty-nine hundredths	six and seventy-eight hundredths	0.409	5.46
0.546	3.015	four and nine hundredths	3.15
four hundred nine thousandths	three and fifteen thousandths	0.678	five and forty-six thousandths
six hundred seventy-eight thousandths	4.09	sixty-seven thousandths	0.49

©The Education Center, Inc. • Big Book of Skill Builders • TEC60797

How to Use Page 185

1. Remind students how to read a decimal.
2. Pair students. Give each pair a copy of page 185 and scissors.
3. Direct the pair to cut apart the 24 boxes on the reproducible and then place them facedown in a 4 x 6 grid on a desktop.
4. Tell students that there are 12 different numbers represented in the game, with each number written in *standard form* and *word-name form*.
5. Share the rules below for playing the game.

Directions for Playing the Game:

1. Player 1 turns over two cards.
2. If the two cards name the same number, Player 1 keeps them and takes another turn.
3. If the two cards don't match, they are returned, facedown, to the playing surface. Then Player 2 takes a turn.
4. Play continues until 12 matches have been formed. The winner is the player with more matches.

Answer Key

0.067	sixty-seven thousandths
0.678	six hundred seventy-eight thousandths
6.78	six and seventy-eight hundredths
0.409	four hundred nine thousandths
0.49	forty-nine hundredths
4.09	four and nine hundredths
0.315	three hundred fifteen thousandths
3.015	three and fifteen thousandths
3.15	three and fifteen hundredths
0.546	five hundred forty-six thousandths
5.046	five and forty-six thousandths
5.46	five and forty-six hundredths

Name_____   Comparing and Ordering Decimals

Just How Big?

Just like dinosaurs, numbers can be large or small. Read each number sentence below. Then decide which numeral will make each sentence true. Lightly color the dinosaur egg beside the correct numeral. The first one is done for you.

1. 1.4   <   (R) 1.34   (S) 1.82
2. 0.56   >   (E) 0.78   (U) 0.049
3. 4.82   >   (G) 4.08   (N) 4.824
4. 0.02   <   (P.) 0.003   (A) 3.0
5. 8.4   >   (M) 8.04   (I) 8.404
6. 6.5   >   (O) 6.52   (U) 6.25
7. 2.407 >   (K) 2.7   (H) 2.047
8. 0.264 >   (N) 0.252   (L) 0.268
9. 5.72   <   (R) 4.6   (T) 9.04
10. 0.23   <   (U) 0.20   (E) 0.24
11. 4.196 >   (C) 4.063   (B) 4.209
12. 0.400 <   (P) 0.466   (W) 0.312
13. 12.609 <   (A) 12.07   (O) 12.7

The smallest adult dinosaur was about the size of a chicken (28 inches long). Find out its name by writing the letter that you colored above for each numeral shown below.

___ ___ ___ ___ ___ ___ ___ ___ ___ ___ ___ ___ ___
11 13 5   12 1   13 3   8   4   9   7   6   1

Bonus Box: Choose any five numerals from the columns above. On the back of this sheet, write the five numerals in order from least to greatest.

©The Education Center, Inc. • *Big Book of Skill Builders* • TEC60797

Answer Key

1. 1.4 < 1.82 (S)
2. 0.56 > 0.049 (U)
3. 4.82 > 4.08 (G)
4. 0.02 < 3.0 (A)
5. 8.4 > 8.04 (M)
6. 6.5 > 6.25 (U)
7. 2.407 > 2.047 (H)
8. 0.264 > 0.252 (N)
9. 5.72 < 9.04 (T)
10. 0.23 < 0.24 (E)
11. 4.196 > 4.063 (C)
12. 0.400 < 0.466 (P)
13. 12.609 < 12.7 (O)

C	O	M	P	S	O	G	N	A	T	H	U	S
11	13	5	12	1	13	3	8	4	9	7	6	1

Name _____   Rounding Decimals

Stomping Round With Decimals

Materials: 1 die, 2 game markers

Directions for Two Players:
1. Players 1 and 2 place their markers on Start.
2. Player 1 rolls the die and finds the matching place value in the chart below. (For example, if a 1 is rolled, the matching place value is tenths.)
3. Player 1 rounds the numeral shown on his space to the place value that he rolled. (For example, 3.456 rounded to the nearest tenth is 3.5.)
4. If correct, Player 1 moves his marker the number of spaces shown in the chart. (For example, move 1 space if a 1 is rolled.)
5. Player 2 takes a turn in the same manner.
6. Continue to play. The first player to reach Finish is the winner.

Roll	Round to the nearest	Move
1	tenth	1 space
2	whole number	2 spaces
3	hundredth	3 spaces
4	whole number	1 space
5	hundredth	2 spaces
6	tenth	3 spaces

START: 1.353, 8.508, 4.912, 0.763, 3.467, 0.409, 13.085

Bottom row: 1.501, 3.579, 4.683, 3.095, 2.316, 8.652

Right column (bottom to top): 0.305, 9.513, 0.884, 7.238, 12.057, 7.123

Right inner column (bottom to top): 0.876, 8.218, 0.026, 9.072, 5.063, 6.469

FINISH: 8.006, 3.145, 1.352

©The Education Center, Inc. • Big Book of Skill Builders • TEC60797

How to Use Page 189

1. Give one copy of page 189 and the materials listed on that page to each pair of students. Use the rules below to remind students how to round numbers.
   - Find the place to which you are rounding.
   - Look at the digit to the right of that place.
   - If the digit is 5 or greater, round up. If it is less than 5, round down.
2. Instruct each pair to play the game as directed on the sheet.
3. After they finish the game, give each pair of students scissors, glue, and a sheet of construction paper. Have the pair cut out each game space and arrange the numerals in order from smallest to largest. Then direct the pair to glue the numerals in order on the construction paper. Award each pair who correctly orders the numerals with a special treat.

Name _____ Fractions

Spin the Wheel!

Welcome to Wheel of Fractions! Follow the steps below to find out how to play the game.

Directions:
1. Write a fraction beside each letter to tell what part of the region or group is shaded.
2. Write each letter in the box above its matching fraction in the puzzles at the bottom of the page. Some letters are used more than once.
3. Four boxes won't have matching letters. Leave those boxes empty.

Remember:

A fraction may name **part of a region.**
1 shaded part → 1 ← numerator
4 parts in all → 4 ← denominator
$\frac{1}{4}$ of the square is shaded.

A fraction may name **part of a group.**
3 shaded stars → 3 ← numerator
5 stars in the group → 5 ← denominator
$\frac{3}{5}$ of the stars are shaded.

___ = T	___ = P	___ = R	___ = B
___ = E	___ = D	___ = O	___ = C
___ = G	___ = M	___ = F	___ = L
___ = N	___ = S	___ = I	___ = H

Singer

| $\frac{5}{6}$ | $\frac{3}{5}$ | $\frac{3}{8}$ | $\frac{5}{8}$ | $\frac{2}{3}$ | $\frac{3}{5}$ | $\frac{7}{12}$ | $\frac{1}{5}$ | $\frac{5}{8}$ | $\frac{1}{6}$ | $\frac{2}{3}$ |

U.S. History

| $\frac{7}{10}$ | $\frac{5}{8}$ | $\frac{3}{8}$ | $\frac{3}{8}$ | $\frac{3}{2}$ | $\frac{1}{6}$ | $\frac{1}{8}$ | $\frac{4}{5}$ | $\frac{1}{4}$ | $\frac{5}{8}$ | $\frac{2}{5}$ | $\frac{7}{8}$ | $\frac{1}{2}$ | $\frac{1}{3}$ |

Television

| $\frac{7}{8}$ | $\frac{1}{6}$ | $\frac{3}{10}$ | $\frac{3}{5}$ | $\frac{1}{4}$ | $\frac{8}{7}$ | $\frac{1}{3}$ | $\frac{5}{8}$ | $\frac{3}{10}$ | $\frac{3}{4}$ | $\frac{1}{3}$ | $\frac{1}{6}$ | $\frac{2}{3}$ |

©The Education Center, Inc. • Big Book of Skill Builders • TEC60797

Answer Key

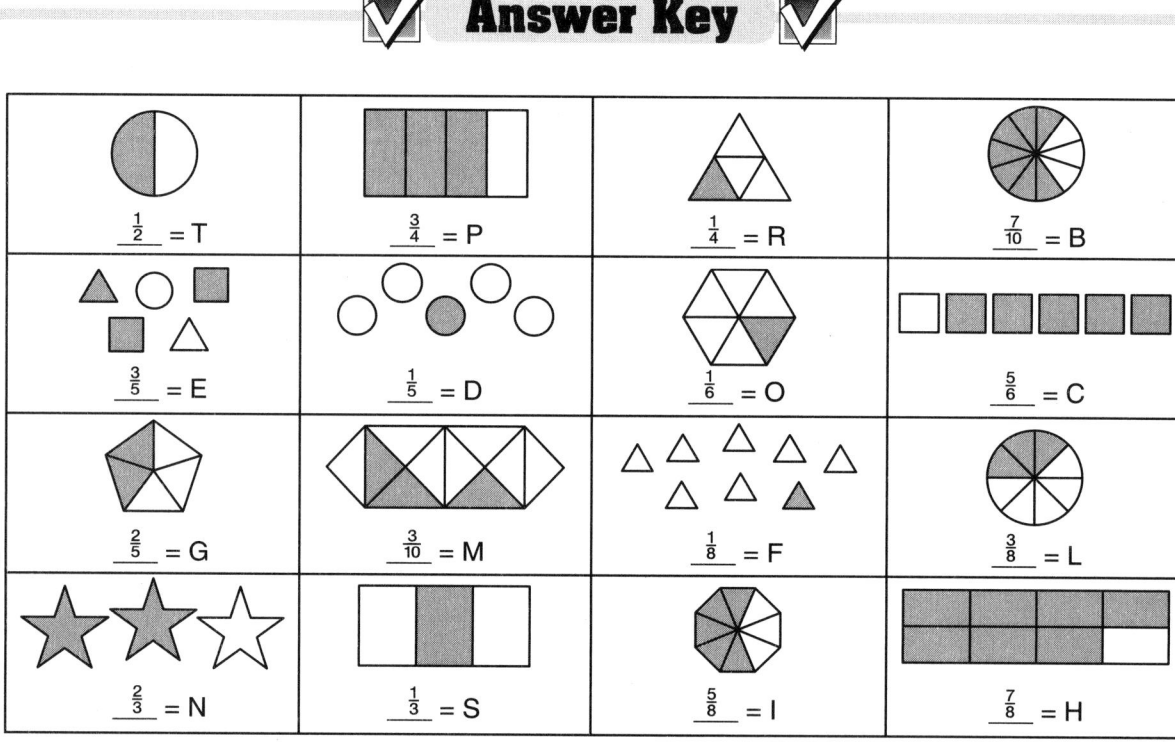

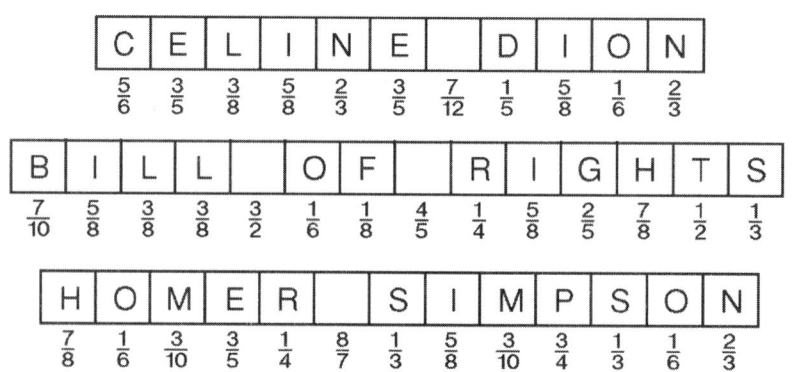

Name_____ Equivalent Fractions

Fraction Jeopardy

"I bet a gazillion dollars, Alex!!"

$ GAZILLION

Directions: In this game of Fraction Jeopardy, every fraction in a column is equivalent to the fraction listed at the top of the column. To play, write an equivalent fraction for the clue in each box. Show how you find each answer. Three examples have been done for you.

Remember: To find an equivalent fraction, multiply the numerator and denominator by the same number. For example:

$$\frac{1}{2} = \frac{1 \times 2}{2 \times 2} = \frac{2}{4}$$

($\frac{2}{2}$ is another name for **1**, so you're multiplying $\frac{1}{2}$ by **1**.)

$\frac{1}{2}$	$\frac{3}{4}$	$\frac{2}{3}$	$\frac{4}{5}$	$\frac{1}{6}$	$\frac{1}{4}$
My denominator is 10. $\frac{1 \times 5}{2 \times 5} = \frac{5}{10}$	My denominator is 8.	My numerator is 4.	My denominator is 10.	My numerator is 2.	My denominator is 12.
My denominator is 4.	My denominator is 12.	My denominator is 9.	My denominator is 50.	My numerator is 3.	My numerator is 5.
My numerator is 3.	My numerator is 12.	My denominator is 15.	My numerator is 16. $\frac{4 \times 4}{5 \times 4} = \frac{16}{20}$	My numerator is 6.	My denominator is 8.
My denominator is 8.	My numerator is 15.	My numerator is 20.	My denominator is 30.	My denominator is 24.	My denominator is 16.
My denominator is 16.	My denominator is 40.	My denominator is 12.	My denominator is 40.	My numerator is 5.	My numerator is 8.
My numerator is 10.	My numerator is 18.	My numerator is 12.	My numerator is 48.	My numerator is 7.	My denominator is 40. $\frac{1 \times 10}{4 \times 10} = \frac{10}{40}$

Answer Key

$\frac{1}{2}$	$\frac{3}{4}$	$\frac{2}{3}$	$\frac{4}{5}$	$\frac{1}{6}$	$\frac{1}{4}$
My denominator is 10. $\frac{1 \times 5}{2 \times 5} = \frac{5}{10}$	My denominator is 8. $\frac{3 \times 2}{4 \times 2} = \frac{6}{8}$	My numerator is 4. $\frac{2 \times 2}{3 \times 2} = \frac{4}{6}$	My denominator is 10. $\frac{4 \times 2}{5 \times 2} = \frac{8}{10}$	My numerator is 2. $\frac{1 \times 2}{6 \times 2} = \frac{2}{12}$	My denominator is 12. $\frac{1 \times 3}{4 \times 3} = \frac{3}{12}$
My denominator is 4. $\frac{1 \times 2}{2 \times 2} = \frac{2}{4}$	My denominator is 12. $\frac{3 \times 3}{4 \times 3} = \frac{9}{12}$	My denominator is 9. $\frac{2 \times 3}{3 \times 3} = \frac{6}{9}$	My denominator is 50. $\frac{4 \times 10}{5 \times 10} = \frac{40}{50}$	My numerator is 3. $\frac{1 \times 3}{6 \times 3} = \frac{3}{18}$	My numerator is 5. $\frac{1 \times 5}{4 \times 5} = \frac{5}{20}$
My numerator is 3. $\frac{1 \times 3}{2 \times 3} = \frac{3}{6}$	My numerator is 12. $\frac{3 \times 4}{4 \times 4} = \frac{12}{16}$	My denominator is 15. $\frac{2 \times 5}{3 \times 5} = \frac{10}{15}$	My numerator is 16. $\frac{4 \times 4}{5 \times 4} = \frac{16}{20}$	My numerator is 6. $\frac{1 \times 6}{6 \times 6} = \frac{6}{36}$	My denominator is 8. $\frac{1 \times 2}{4 \times 2} = \frac{2}{8}$
My denominator is 8. $\frac{1 \times 4}{2 \times 4} = \frac{4}{8}$	My numerator is 15. $\frac{3 \times 5}{4 \times 5} = \frac{15}{20}$	My numerator is 20. $\frac{2 \times 10}{3 \times 10} = \frac{20}{30}$	My denominator is 30. $\frac{4 \times 6}{5 \times 6} = \frac{24}{30}$	My denominator is 24. $\frac{1 \times 4}{6 \times 4} = \frac{4}{24}$	My denominator is 16. $\frac{1 \times 4}{4 \times 4} = \frac{4}{16}$
My denominator is 16. $\frac{1 \times 8}{2 \times 8} = \frac{8}{16}$	My denominator is 40. $\frac{3 \times 10}{4 \times 10} = \frac{30}{40}$	My denominator is 12. $\frac{2 \times 4}{3 \times 4} = \frac{8}{12}$	My denominator is 40. $\frac{4 \times 8}{5 \times 8} = \frac{32}{40}$	My numerator is 5. $\frac{1 \times 5}{6 \times 5} = \frac{5}{30}$	My numerator is 8. $\frac{1 \times 8}{4 \times 8} = \frac{8}{32}$
My numerator is 10. $\frac{1 \times 10}{2 \times 10} = \frac{10}{20}$	My numerator is 18. $\frac{3 \times 6}{4 \times 6} = \frac{18}{24}$	My numerator is 12. $\frac{2 \times 6}{3 \times 6} = \frac{12}{18}$	My numerator is 48. $\frac{4 \times 12}{5 \times 12} = \frac{48}{60}$	My numerator is 7. $\frac{1 \times 7}{6 \times 7} = \frac{7}{42}$	My denominator is 40. $\frac{1 \times 10}{4 \times 10} = \frac{10}{40}$

Name _____   Simplifying Fractions

Hollywood Fraction Squares

How do you win big on Hollywood Fraction Squares? By getting a three-in-a-row match!

Directions: In each game, simplify each fraction to its lowest terms. Some fractions are already in lowest terms, so you won't have to simplify them. After all the fractions have been simplified in a game, circle three fractions in a row (vertical, horizontal, or diagonal) that are the same. Game 1 has been started for you.

Remember: To simplify a fraction to its lowest terms, divide the numerator and denominator by their greatest common factor. For example, simplify $\frac{20}{24}$ to lowest terms:

factors of 20: 1, 2, **4**, 5, 10, 20   factors of 24: 1, 2, 3, **4**, 6, 8, 12, 24
greatest common factor: **4**

$$\frac{20 \div 4}{24 \div 4} = \frac{5}{6}$$

$\frac{20}{24}$ in lowest terms is $\frac{5}{6}$.

Game 1

$\frac{5 \div 5}{10 \div 5} = \frac{1}{2}$	$\frac{9}{12}$	$\frac{1}{2}$
$\frac{4}{6}$	$\frac{3}{6}$	$\frac{6}{8}$
$\frac{6}{12}$	$\frac{2}{5}$	$\frac{6}{10}$

Game 2

$\frac{7}{14}$	$\frac{2}{6}$	$\frac{6}{15}$
$\frac{5}{15}$	$\frac{4}{12}$	$\frac{8}{10}$
$\frac{12}{16}$	$\frac{1}{3}$	$\frac{6}{18}$

Game 3

$\frac{4}{8}$	$\frac{10}{20}$	$\frac{3}{9}$
$\frac{15}{20}$	$\frac{9}{12}$	$\frac{3}{4}$
$\frac{9}{18}$	$\frac{10}{12}$	$\frac{3}{5}$

Game 4

$\frac{8}{20}$	$\frac{2}{4}$	$\frac{2}{3}$
$\frac{8}{16}$	$\frac{10}{14}$	$\frac{21}{28}$
$\frac{2}{5}$	$\frac{12}{30}$	$\frac{4}{10}$

Answer Key

Game 1

$\frac{5 \div 5}{10 \div 5} = \frac{1}{2}$	$\frac{9 \div 3}{12 \div 3} = \frac{3}{4}$	$\frac{1}{2}$
$\frac{4 \div 2}{6 \div 2} = \frac{2}{3}$	$\frac{3 \div 3}{6 \div 3} = \frac{1}{2}$	$\frac{6 \div 2}{8 \div 2} = \frac{3}{4}$
$\frac{6 \div 6}{12 \div 6} = \frac{1}{2}$	$\frac{2}{5}$	$\frac{6 \div 2}{10 \div 2} = \frac{3}{5}$

Game 2

$\frac{7 \div 7}{14 \div 7} = \frac{1}{2}$	$\frac{2 \div 2}{6 \div 2} = \frac{1}{3}$	$\frac{6 \div 3}{15 \div 3} = \frac{2}{5}$
$\frac{5 \div 5}{15 \div 5} = \frac{1}{3}$	$\frac{4 \div 4}{12 \div 4} = \frac{1}{3}$	$\frac{8 \div 2}{10 \div 2} = \frac{4}{5}$
$\frac{12 \div 4}{16 \div 4} = \frac{3}{4}$	$\frac{1}{3}$	$\frac{6 \div 6}{18 \div 6} = \frac{1}{3}$

Game 3

$\frac{4 \div 4}{8 \div 4} = \frac{1}{2}$	$\frac{10 \div 10}{20 \div 10} = \frac{1}{2}$	$\frac{3 \div 3}{9 \div 3} = \frac{1}{3}$
$\frac{15 \div 5}{20 \div 5} = \frac{3}{4}$	$\frac{9 \div 3}{12 \div 3} = \frac{3}{4}$	$\frac{3}{4}$
$\frac{9 \div 9}{18 \div 9} = \frac{1}{2}$	$\frac{10 \div 2}{12 \div 2} = \frac{5}{6}$	$\frac{3}{5}$

Game 4

$\frac{8 \div 4}{20 \div 4} = \frac{2}{5}$	$\frac{2 \div 2}{4 \div 2} = \frac{1}{2}$	$\frac{2}{3}$
$\frac{8 \div 8}{16 \div 8} = \frac{1}{2}$	$\frac{10 \div 2}{14 \div 2} = \frac{5}{7}$	$\frac{21 \div 7}{28 \div 7} = \frac{3}{4}$
$\frac{2}{5}$	$\frac{12 \div 6}{30 \div 6} = \frac{2}{5}$	$\frac{4 \div 2}{10 \div 2} = \frac{2}{5}$

Name_____ Comparing Fractions

Let's Make a Deal!

Which curtain will it be—#1, #2, or #3? You have the chance to win the grand prize behind one of three curtains!

Directions:
1. Circle one of the three curtains at the top of the chart.
2. Compare the fractions in each row.
3. Write <, >, or = in the circle between the fractions in each pair. Two examples are done for you.
4. Then follow the directions at the bottom of the page to find out which prize you won.

Remember:

To compare like fractions, compare the numerators. Compare $\frac{2}{5}$ and $\frac{4}{5}$:
$\frac{2}{5} < \frac{4}{5}$ because 2 is less than 4.

To compare unlike fractions, rename them as like fractions. Compare $\frac{2}{3}$ and $\frac{3}{4}$:

First, rename $\frac{2}{3}$ and $\frac{3}{4}$ as like fractions: Then compare numerators.

$\frac{2}{3} \times \frac{4}{4} = \frac{8}{12}$
$\frac{3}{4} \times \frac{3}{3} = \frac{9}{12}$

8 < 9
So $\frac{8}{12} < \frac{9}{12}$ and $\frac{2}{3} < \frac{3}{4}$.

									Curtain 1 <	Curtain 2 =	Curtain 3 >
B	$\frac{2}{5}$	⊙>	$\frac{1}{5}$	C	$\frac{1}{3}$ ⊙< $\frac{1}{2}$; $\frac{2}{6}$ $\frac{3}{6}$		U	$\frac{4}{6}$ ○ $\frac{2}{3}$			
I	$\frac{3}{5}$ ○ $\frac{3}{10}$			M	$\frac{2}{4}$ ○ $\frac{1}{2}$		O	$\frac{2}{3}$ ○ $\frac{5}{6}$			
B	$\frac{5}{10}$ ○ $\frac{1}{2}$			M	$\frac{3}{10}$ ○ $\frac{7}{10}$		C	$\frac{1}{2}$ ○ $\frac{3}{8}$			
P	$\frac{3}{8}$ ○ $\frac{7}{16}$			R	$\frac{2}{5}$ ○ $\frac{4}{10}$		Y	$\frac{5}{6}$ ○ $\frac{1}{3}$			
U	$\frac{1}{5}$ ○ $\frac{4}{15}$			C	$\frac{7}{8}$ ○ $\frac{5}{8}$		E	$\frac{1}{2}$ ○ $\frac{6}{12}$			
L	$\frac{6}{8}$ ○ $\frac{3}{4}$			T	$\frac{5}{8}$ ○ $\frac{7}{8}$		L	$\frac{5}{12}$ ○ $\frac{1}{4}$			
E	$\frac{9}{16}$ ○ $\frac{1}{2}$			E	$\frac{2}{3}$ ○ $\frac{3}{4}$		L	$\frac{4}{5}$ ○ $\frac{8}{10}$			
S	$\frac{3}{4}$ ○ $\frac{1}{4}$			A	$\frac{7}{8}$ ○ $\frac{14}{16}$		R	$\frac{3}{5}$ ○ $\frac{3}{4}$			

To determine your prize, write each letter in its matching column:
• If the letter is beside a < sign, write the letter in the box under the < curtain.
• If the letter is beside a > sign, write the letter in the box under the > curtain.
• If the letter is beside an = sign, write the letter in the box under the = curtain.

Now read the letters from top to bottom under the curtain you chose to find out your prize!

©The Education Center, Inc. • Big Book of Skill Builders • TEC60797

Answer Key

							Curtain 1 <	Curtain 2 =	Curtain 3 >
B	$\frac{2}{5} > \frac{1}{5}$	**C**	$\frac{1}{3} < \frac{1}{2}$ $\frac{2}{6}\ \ \frac{3}{6}$	**U**	$\frac{4}{6} = \frac{2}{3}$ $\frac{4}{6}\ \ \frac{4}{6}$		C	U	B
I	$\frac{3}{5} > \frac{3}{10}$ $\frac{6}{10}\ \ \frac{3}{10}$	**M**	$\frac{2}{4} = \frac{1}{2}$ $\frac{2}{4}\ \ \frac{2}{4}$	**O**	$\frac{2}{3} < \frac{5}{6}$ $\frac{4}{6}\ \ \frac{5}{6}$		O	M	I
B	$\frac{5}{10} = \frac{1}{2}$ $\frac{5}{10}\ \ \frac{5}{10}$	**M**	$\frac{3}{10} < \frac{7}{10}$	**C**	$\frac{1}{2} > \frac{3}{8}$ $\frac{4}{8}\ \ \frac{3}{8}$		M	B	C
P	$\frac{3}{8} < \frac{7}{16}$ $\frac{6}{16}\ \ \frac{7}{16}$	**R**	$\frac{2}{5} = \frac{4}{10}$ $\frac{4}{10}\ \ \frac{4}{10}$	**Y**	$\frac{5}{6} > \frac{1}{3}$ $\frac{5}{6}\ \ \frac{2}{6}$		P	R	Y
U	$\frac{1}{5} < \frac{4}{15}$ $\frac{3}{15}\ \ \frac{4}{15}$	**C**	$\frac{7}{8} > \frac{5}{8}$	**E**	$\frac{1}{2} = \frac{6}{12}$ $\frac{6}{12}\ \ \frac{6}{12}$		U	E	C
L	$\frac{6}{8} = \frac{3}{4}$ $\frac{6}{8}\ \ \frac{6}{8}$	**T**	$\frac{5}{8} < \frac{7}{8}$	**L**	$\frac{5}{12} > \frac{1}{4}$ $\frac{5}{12}\ \ \frac{3}{12}$		T	L	L
E	$\frac{9}{16} > \frac{1}{2}$ $\frac{9}{16}\ \ \frac{8}{16}$	**E**	$\frac{2}{3} < \frac{3}{4}$ $\frac{8}{12}\ \ \frac{9}{12}$	**L**	$\frac{4}{5} = \frac{8}{10}$ $\frac{8}{10}\ \ \frac{8}{10}$		E	L	E
S	$\frac{3}{4} > \frac{1}{4}$	**A**	$\frac{7}{8} = \frac{14}{16}$ $\frac{14}{16}\ \ \frac{14}{16}$	**R**	$\frac{3}{5} < \frac{3}{4}$ $\frac{12}{20}\ \ \frac{15}{20}$		R	A	S

Name _____ Improper Fractions and Mixed Numbers

One Scoop or Two?

Did you know that Americans eat more ice cream than people in any other country—an average of 15 quarts per person a year?

Directions: Add to solve each fraction problem below. Change each answer to a mixed number or whole number. Check your answers by completing the dot-to-dot puzzle. First check to see if the mixed number beside "Start" matches your answer for number 1. Then find the answer for number 2 on the puzzle and connect the two answers. Continue this process with numbers 3–14 to complete the puzzle.

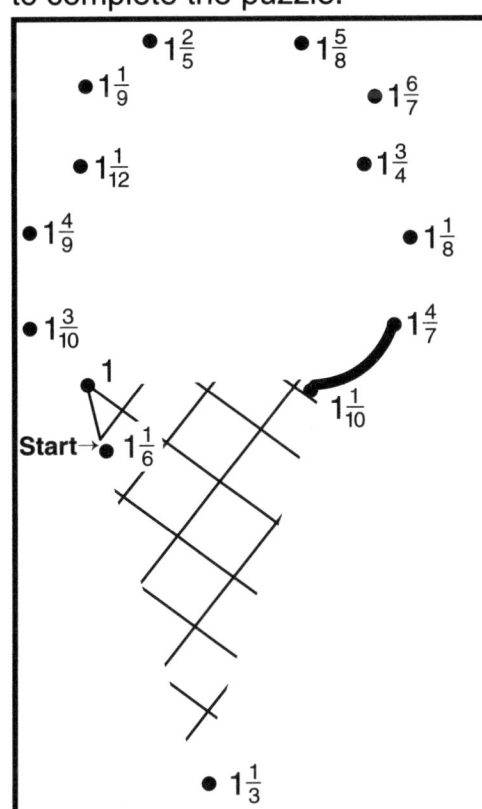

1. $\frac{4}{6} + \frac{3}{6} = \Box = \Box$

2. $\frac{2}{3} + \frac{2}{3} = \Box = \Box$

3. $\frac{9}{10} + \frac{2}{10} = \Box = \Box$

4. $\frac{6}{8} + \frac{2}{8} = \Box = \Box$

5. $\frac{8}{10} + \frac{5}{10} = \Box = \Box$

6. $\frac{6}{9} + \frac{7}{9} = \Box = \Box$

7. $\frac{11}{12} + \frac{2}{12} = \Box = \Box$

8. $\frac{4}{9} + \frac{6}{9} = \Box = \Box$

9. $\frac{3}{5} + \frac{4}{5} = \Box = \Box$

10. $\frac{6}{8} + \frac{7}{8} = \Box = \Box$

11. $\frac{5}{7} + \frac{8}{7} = \Box = \Box$

12. $\frac{3}{4} + \frac{1}{4} + \frac{3}{4} = \Box = \Box$

13. $\frac{1}{8} + \frac{3}{8} + \frac{5}{8} = \Box = \Box$

14. $\frac{2}{7} + \frac{3}{7} + \frac{6}{7} = \Box = \Box$

15. Debra and Stephanie brought ice cream to a party. Debra brought $\frac{3}{4}$ gallon of chocolate ice cream. Stephanie brought $1\frac{3}{4}$ gallons of strawberry ice cream. How many total gallons of ice cream did the two girls bring to the party? Write your answer in simplest form.

_____

16. Liz loves lots of toppings on her ice-cream sundae. She put $\frac{1}{8}$ tablespoon of sprinkles, $\frac{2}{8}$ tablespoon of nuts, $\frac{4}{8}$ tablespoon of cookie crumbs, 1 tablespoon of chocolate syrup, and $1\frac{7}{8}$ tablespoons of whipped cream on a sundae. How many total tablespoons of toppings did Liz put on her sundae? Write your answer in simplest form. _____

Bonus Box:

1. I'm an improper fraction. My numerator and denominator are both multiples of two. My numerator is four times my denominator. My denominator is the greatest common factor of 16 and 20. What am I? _____

2. I'm a mixed number. My denominator is the sixth prime number. My numerator is one less than my denominator. I am greater than five but less than six. What am I? _____

©The Education Center, Inc. • Big Book of Skill Builders • TEC60797

Answer Key

1. $\frac{7}{6} = 1\frac{1}{6}$
2. $\frac{4}{3} = 1\frac{1}{3}$
3. $\frac{11}{10} = 1\frac{1}{10}$
4. $\frac{8}{8} = 1$
5. $\frac{13}{10} = 1\frac{3}{10}$
6. $\frac{13}{9} = 1\frac{4}{9}$
7. $\frac{13}{12} = 1\frac{1}{12}$
8. $\frac{10}{9} = 1\frac{1}{9}$
9. $\frac{7}{5} = 1\frac{2}{5}$
10. $\frac{13}{8} = 1\frac{5}{8}$
11. $\frac{13}{7} = 1\frac{6}{7}$
12. $\frac{7}{4} = 1\frac{3}{4}$
13. $\frac{9}{8} = 1\frac{1}{8}$
14. $\frac{11}{7} = 1\frac{4}{7}$
15. $1\frac{6}{4} = 2\frac{2}{4} = 2\frac{1}{2}$ gallons
16. $2\frac{14}{8} = 3\frac{6}{8} = 3\frac{3}{4}$ tablespoons

Bonus Box:
1. $\frac{16}{4}$
2. $5\frac{12}{13}$

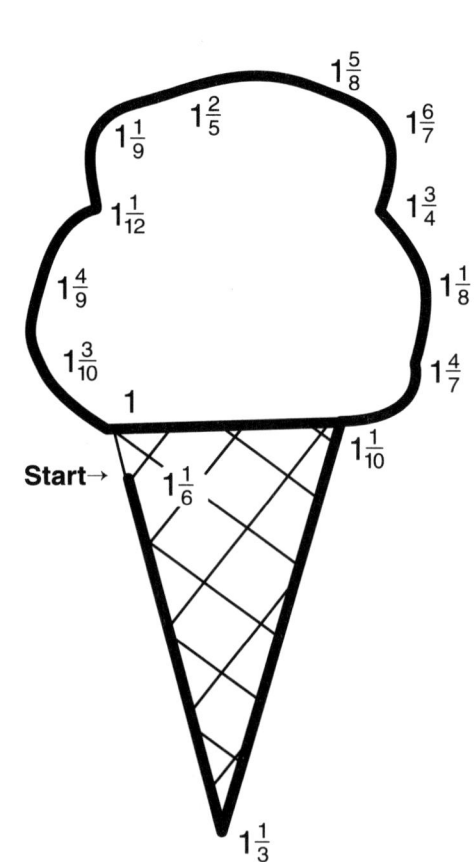

200

Name _____

Addition and Subtraction of Fractions

Have a Slice!

Sal's Unusual Pizza Parlor gets its name from the unusually sized and colored pizza slices it serves.

Directions: Add or subtract to solve each problem below. Write each answer in lowest terms. Find each matching pizza slice and color it as directed.

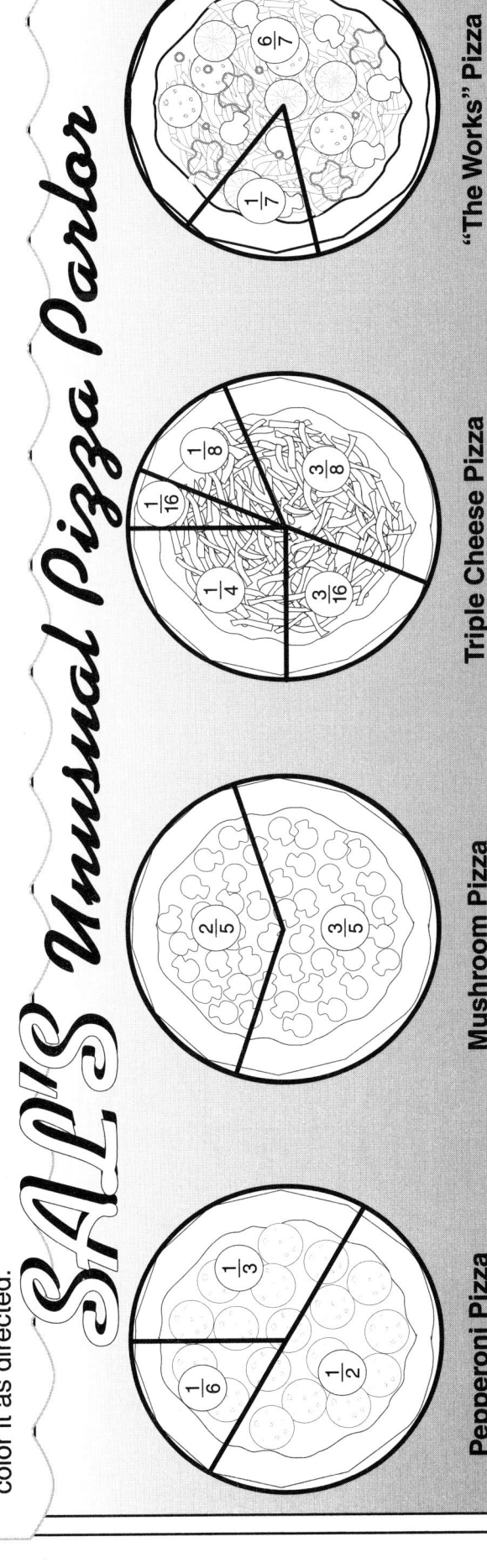

Pepperoni Pizza   **Mushroom Pizza**   **Triple Cheese Pizza**   **"The Works" Pizza**

1. $\frac{1}{24} + \frac{3}{24} =$ ☐
(Color this slice dark blue.)

2. $\frac{15}{25} - \frac{5}{25} =$ ☐
(Color this slice red.)

3. $\frac{4}{16} + \frac{2}{16} =$ ☐
(Color this slice yellow.)

4. $\frac{12}{32} - \frac{6}{32} =$ ☐
(Color this slice green.)

5. $\frac{7}{21} + \frac{11}{21} =$ ☐
(Color this slice brown.)

6. $\frac{12}{15} - \frac{7}{15} =$ ☐
(Color this slice orange.)

7. $\frac{3}{28} + \frac{1}{28} =$ ☐
(Color this slice purple.)

8. $\frac{9}{10} - \frac{3}{10} =$ ☐
(Color this slice black.)

5. $\frac{2}{16} + \frac{2}{16} =$ ☐
(Color this slice light blue.)

10. $\frac{7}{24} - \frac{4}{24} =$ ☐
(Color this slice gray.)

11. $\frac{3}{10} + \frac{2}{10} =$ ☐
(Color this slice pink.)

12. $\frac{8}{48} - \frac{5}{48} =$ ☐
(Color this slice white.)

Bonus Box: Create your own unique pizza on the back of this page.

©The Education Center, Inc. • *Big Book of Skill Builders* • TEC60797

201

Answer Key

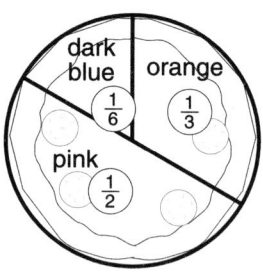 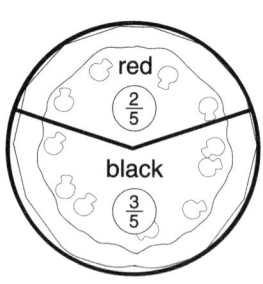 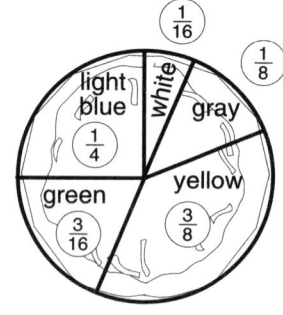 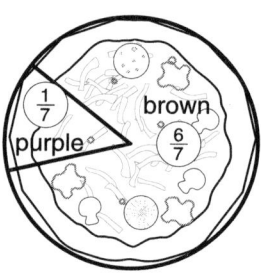

1. $\frac{4}{24} = \frac{1}{6}$ (dark blue)   2. $\frac{10}{25} = \frac{2}{5}$ (red)   3. $\frac{6}{16} = \frac{3}{8}$ (yellow)   4. $\frac{6}{32} = \frac{3}{16}$ (green)

5. $\frac{18}{21} = \frac{6}{7}$ (brown)   6. $\frac{5}{15} = \frac{1}{3}$ (orange)   7. $\frac{4}{28} = \frac{1}{7}$ (purple)   8. $\frac{6}{10} = \frac{3}{5}$ (black)

9. $\frac{4}{16} = \frac{1}{4}$ (light blue)   10. $\frac{3}{24} = \frac{1}{8}$ (gray)   11. $\frac{5}{10} = \frac{1}{2}$ (pink)   12. $\frac{3}{48} = \frac{1}{16}$ (white)

Name _____

Changing Fractions to Percents

Go Fish!

Mario is working at the local marina this summer. Hanging out at the dock during his morning break, Mario discovered a "reel-y" good way to catch up on his percent practice. Follow the directions below to help Mario complete the activities on this page.

Directions: Look at the fish on each line below. Match each fraction with its equivalent percent by coloring the fish the same color. Use a different color for each pair of matching fish. Show your work on the back of this sheet.

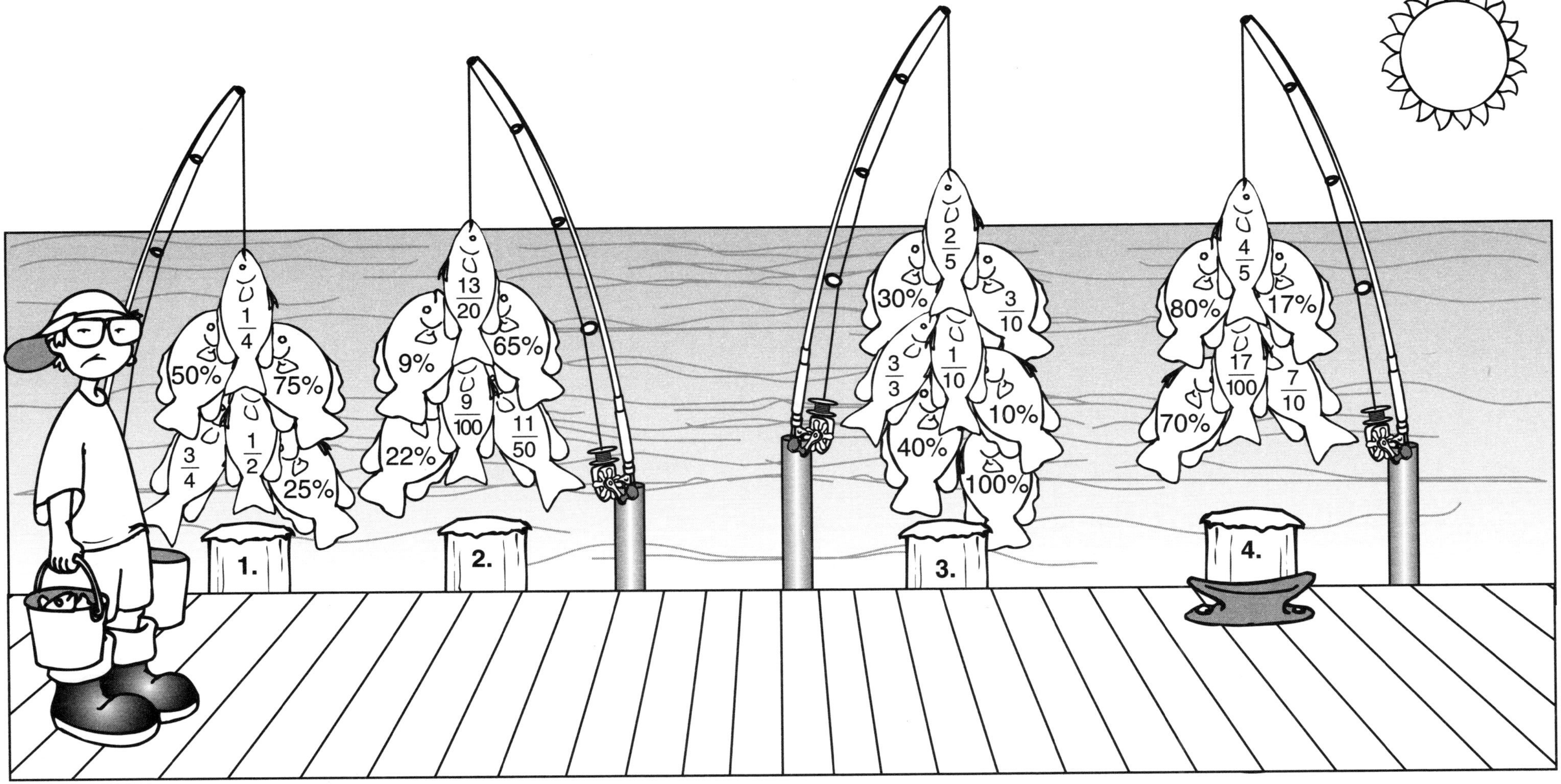

1. 50%, 3/4, 1/4, 75%, 1/2, 25%

2. 9%, 13/20, 65%, 9/100, 11/50, 22%

3. 30%, 2/5, 3/3, 3/10, 1/10, 10%, 40%, 100%

4. 80%, 4/5, 17%, 5/100 (17/100), 7/10, 70%

©The Education Center, Inc. • *Big Book of Skill Builders* • TEC60797

203

Answer Key

1. $\frac{1}{4} = 25\%$

   $\frac{1}{2} = 50\%$

   $\frac{3}{4} = 75\%$

3. $\frac{1}{10} = 10\%$

   $\frac{3}{3} = 100\%$

   $\frac{2}{5} = 40\%$

   $\frac{3}{10} = 30\%$

2. $\frac{13}{20} = 65\%$

   $\frac{11}{50} = 22\%$

   $\frac{9}{100} = 9\%$

4. $\frac{4}{5} = 80\%$

   $\frac{7}{10} = 70\%$

   $\frac{17}{100} = 17\%$

Name _____

Metric Units of Length Game

Racin' Rabbits

On your mark! Get set! Go! Follow the directions below to find out which racin' rabbit will make it to the finish line first.

Directions:
1. Cut out the ruler from the bottom of this page.
2. Each player, using a colored pencil, colors a rabbit at the starting line.
3. Each player spins the spinner; the higher spin goes first.
4. To begin play, Player 1 spins the spinner. Using the code, Player 1 begins at the starting line and measures the distance for his spin. He then marks an X on the spot where his rabbit hopped.
5. Player 2 then takes a turn in the same manner.
6. The first rabbit to reach the finish line is the winner. Continue play with Races 2 and 3.

Materials:
2 colored pencils
spinner
paper clip
scissors

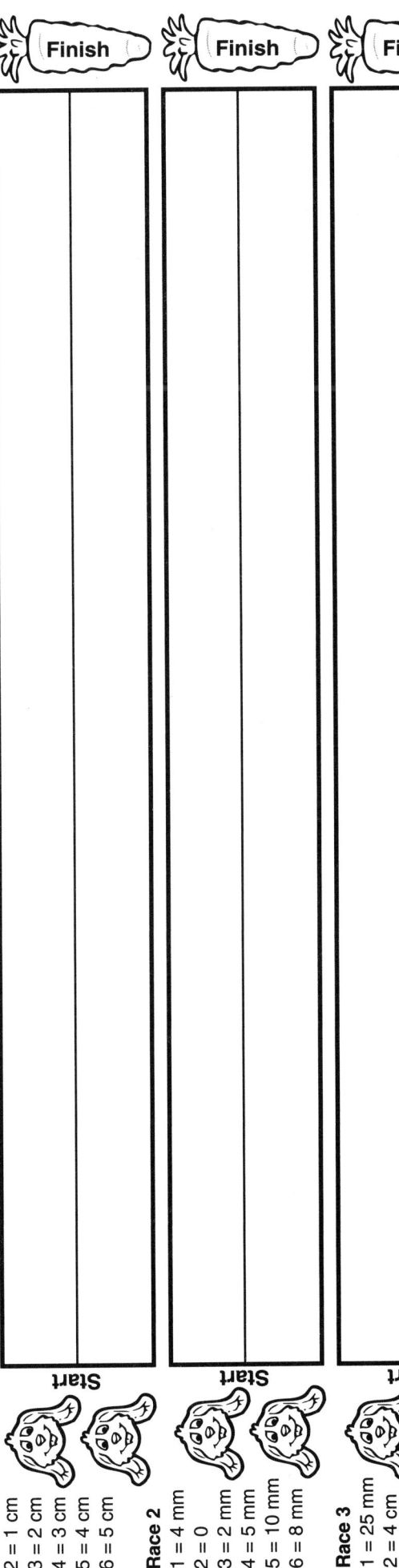

Race 1
1 = 0
2 = 1 cm
3 = 2 cm
4 = 3 cm
5 = 4 cm
6 = 5 cm

Race 2
1 = 4 mm
2 = 0
3 = 2 mm
4 = 5 mm
5 = 10 mm
6 = 8 mm

Race 3
1 = 25 mm
2 = 4 cm
3 = 1 cm
4 = 3 cm
5 = 15 mm
6 = 8 cm

©The Education Center, Inc. • *Big Book of Skill Builders* • TEC60797

205

How to Use Page 205

1. Give one copy of page 205 and the materials listed on that page to each pair of students.
2. Demonstrate to students how to assemble and use the spinner (see the illustration on this page).
3. Then have each pair play the game as directed.

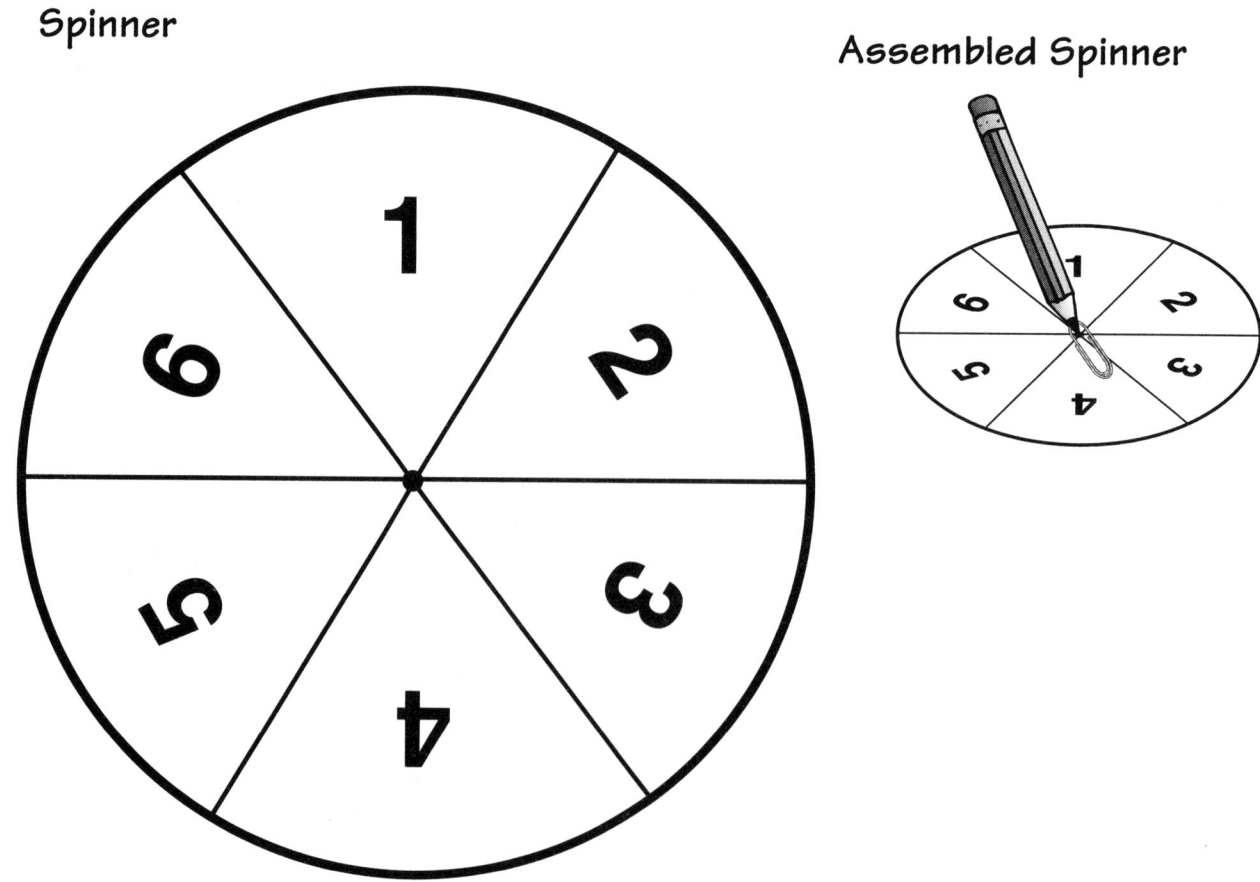

Spinner

Assembled Spinner

Name _____ Customary Units of Length

A Ravenous (Very Hungry!) Rabbit

Roscoe the ravenous rabbit has lost his stash of carrots! Lead Roscoe down the path to his stash by following the directions below.

Directions: Each object below needs a measurement. For each one, lightly shade the measurement that makes the most sense. If you make the correct choice, you'll discover the path to Roscoe's carrots. The first one is done for you.

1.	the height of a ten-year-old	**4 ft.**	4 in.	4 yd.	4 mi.
2.	the width of a television screen	21 yd.	21 in.	21 ft.	21 mi.
3.	the length of a shoelace	20 yd.	20 mi.	20 in.	20 ft.
4.	the distance from California to New York	2,500 in.	2,500 ft.	2,500 mi.	2,500 yd.
5.	the width of a textbook	2 mi.	2 ft.	2 yd.	2 in.
6.	the length of pencil	6 mi.	6 ft.	6 in.	6 yd.
7.	the diameter of a beach ball	2 mi.	2 ft.	2 yd.	2 in.
8.	the height of a flagpole	10 yd.	10 ft.	10 in.	10 mi.
9.	the height of a mountain	5,000 mi.	5,000 ft.	5,000 yd.	5,000 in.
10.	the distance of a marathon race	26 mi.	26 yd.	26 in.	26 ft.
11.	the height of a table	3 in.	3 ft.	3 yd.	3 mi.
12.	the length of a bed	6 mi.	6 yd.	6 ft.	6 in.
13.	the length of a stapler	5 mi.	5 ft.	5 in.	5 yd.
14.	the height of a door	$2\frac{1}{2}$ in.	$2\frac{1}{2}$ ft.	$2\frac{1}{2}$ mi.	$2\frac{1}{2}$ yd.

Cottontail Carol's Cabbage Patch   **Harold Hare's Hollow**   **Aunt Viola's Vegetable Bin**   **Uncle Wally's Wheelbarrow**

Bonus Box: Choose a student whose desk is about six feet from your desk. Measure to see if your estimate is correct.

Answer Key

#	Answer				
1.	4 ft.	**4 ft.**	4 in.	4 yd.	4 mi.
2.	21 in.	21 yd.	**21 in.**	21 ft.	21 mi.
3.	20 in.	20 yd.	20 mi.	**20 in.**	20 ft.
4.	2,500 mi.	2,500 in.	2,500 ft.	**2,500 mi.**	2,500 yd.
5.	2 in.	2 mi.	2 ft.	2 yd.	**2 in.**
6.	6 in.	6 mi.	6 ft.	**6 in.**	6 yd.
7.	2 ft.	2 mi.	**2 ft.**	2 yd.	2 in.
8.	10 yd.	**10 yd.**	10 ft.	10 in.	10 mi.
9.	5,000 ft.	5,000 mi.	**5,000 ft.**	5,000 yd.	5,000 in.
10.	26 mi.	**26 mi.**	26 yd.	26 in.	26 ft.
11.	3 ft.	3 in.	**3 ft.**	3 yd.	3 mi.
12.	6 ft.	6 mi.	6 yd.	**6 ft.**	6 in.
13.	5 in.	5 mi.	5 ft.	**5 in.**	5 yd.
14.	$2\frac{1}{2}$ yd.	$2\frac{1}{2}$ in.	$2\frac{1}{2}$ ft.	$2\frac{1}{2}$ mi.	**$2\frac{1}{2}$ yd.**

Roscoe hid his stash of carrots in Uncle Wally's wheelbarrow.

Name _____   Customary Units of Length

Carrot Conversions

Candy Cottontail, a student at Cottontail Academy, loves to learn about measurement. Follow the directions to help Candy complete the measurement tasks below.

Directions: Each length is given in one unit. Change each length to the other two units.

Remember:
12 in. = 1 ft.   3 ft. = 1 yd.   36 in. = 1 yd.

To change a larger unit to a smaller unit, **multiply**.
4 ft. = ___?___ in.
1 ft. = 12 in.
4 x 12 = 48
4 ft. = **48** in.

To change a smaller unit to a larger unit, **divide**.
(Remember that you may have a remainder.)
13 ft. = ___?___ yd.
3 ft. = 1 yd.
13 ÷ 3 = 4 R1
12 ft. = **4** yd. **1** ft.

1. 3 yd.
a. _____ in.   b. _____ ft.

6. 64 ft.
a. _____ in.   b. _____ yd. _____ ft.

2. 60 in.
a. _____ ft.   b. _____ yd. _____ ft.

7. 20 yd.
a. _____ in.   b. _____ ft.

3. 3 ft.
a. _____ in.   b. _____ yd.

8. 7 ft.
a. _____ in.   b. _____ yd. _____ ft.

4. 396 in.
a. _____ ft.   b. _____ yd.

9. 252 in.
a. _____ ft.   b. _____ yd.

5. 10 yd.
a. _____ in.   b. _____ ft.

10. 100 ft.
a. _____ in.   b. _____ yd. _____ ft.

Bonus Box: Order the ten carrots above from shortest to longest.

Answer Key

1. a. 108 in.   b. 9 ft.
2. a. 5 ft.   b. 1 yd. 2 ft.
3. a. 36 in.   b. 1 yd.
4. a. 33 ft.   b. 11 yd.
5. a. 360 in.   b. 30 ft.
6. a. 768 in.   b. 21 yd. 1 ft.
7. a. 720 in.   b. 60 ft.
8. a. 84 in.   b. 2 yd. 1 ft.
9. a. 21 ft.   b. 7 yd.
10. a. 1,200 in. b. 33 yd. 1 ft.

Bonus Box: 3, 2, 8, 1, 9, 5, 4, 7, 6, 10

Name _____ Metric Units of Length

Hoppin' Through Hareville

Use the kilometer scale provided and a centimeter ruler to help you hop through Hareville and answer the questions below.

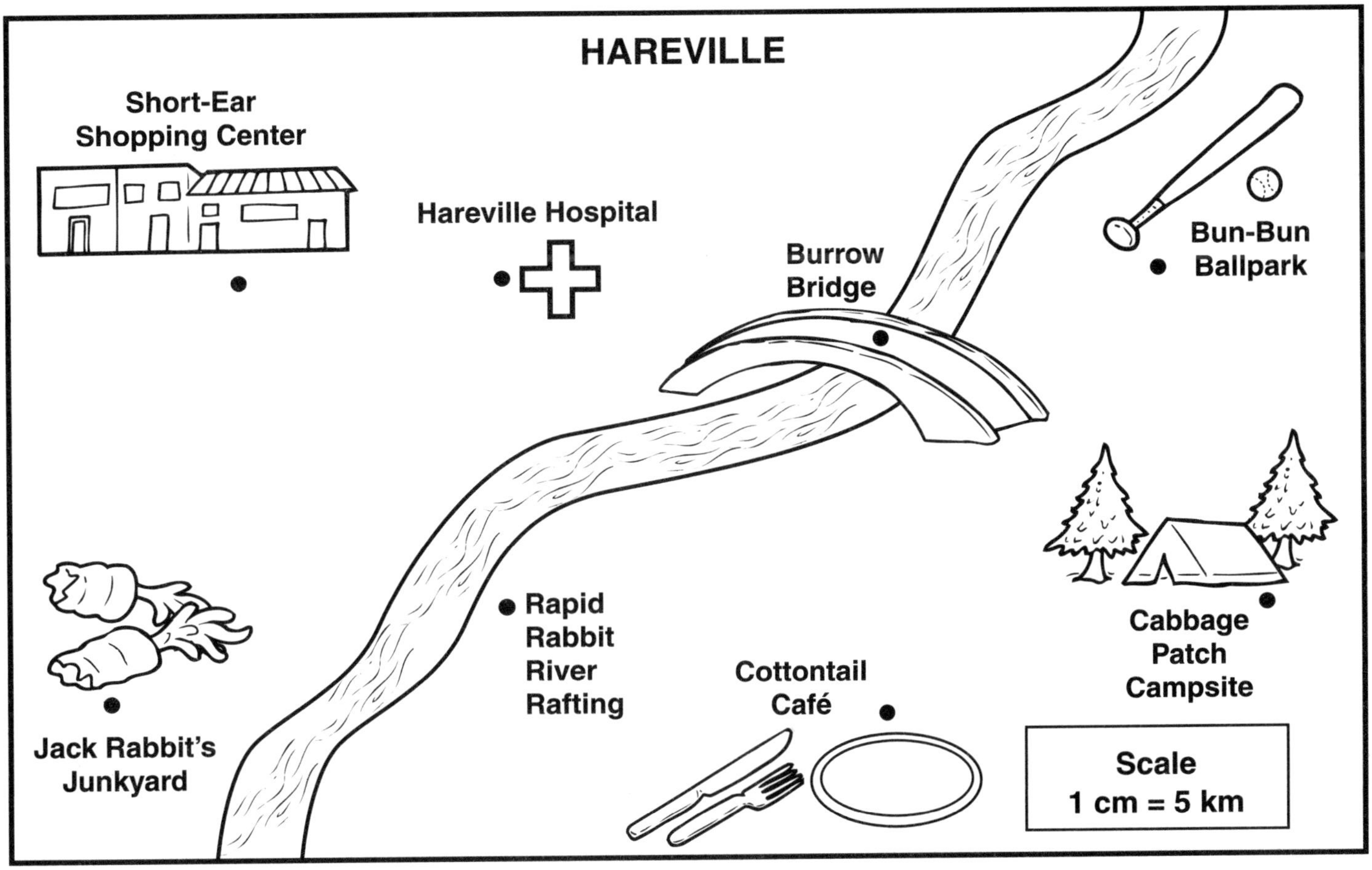

HAREVILLE

(Map showing: Short-Ear Shopping Center, Hareville Hospital, Burrow Bridge, Bun-Bun Ballpark, Jack Rabbit's Junkyard, Rapid Rabbit River Rafting, Cottontail Café, Cabbage Patch Campsite)

Scale: 1 cm = 5 km

1. How far is it from the campsite to the café? _____ kilometers
2. How far is it from the ballpark to Rapid Rabbit River Rafting? _____ kilometers
3. If you hopped from the hospital to the shopping center, then to the junkyard, how many kilometers have you hopped? _____ kilometers
4. How far is Cottontail Café from Burrow Bridge? _____ kilometers
5. If you began at the ballpark and hopped across the bridge to the hospital, then back across the bridge to the ballpark, how far did you travel? _____ kilometers
6. Which is longer, hopping from the junkyard to the shopping center or from the junkyard to the hospital? _____
7. What is the hopping distance between the bridge and the junkyard? _____ kilometers
8. You are helping coach Bunny Baseball this season. The coach needs you to hop over to the shopping center to pick up the team's uniforms and then come straight back to practice. How far will you travel? _____ kilometers
9. After baseball practice you hop to the Cottontail Café for some carrot soufflé. How far did you hop? _____ kilometers

Bonus Box: On the back of this sheet, write a word problem that can be solved by using the map above. Exchange papers with another student and solve each other's problems.

©The Education Center, Inc. • Big Book of Skill Builders • TEC60797

Answer Key

1. 27½ km
2. 50 km
3. 47½ km
4. 25 km
5. 90 km
6. from the junkyard to the hospital
7. 57½ km
8. 125 km
9. 35 km

Name _____ Metric Units of Weight and Capacity

But Can It Shoot Free Throws?

Did you know that the world's tallest animal may grow nearly 18 feet tall? Follow the directions to name this mystery animal.

Directions: Read each sentence below. If a sentence seems *unreasonable,* circle the information that you think is wrong and correct it right above the circle. Then cross out the matching square at the bottom of the page. If the sentence seems *reasonable,* leave it as is. The remaining letters in the grid will spell the name of the world's tallest animal!

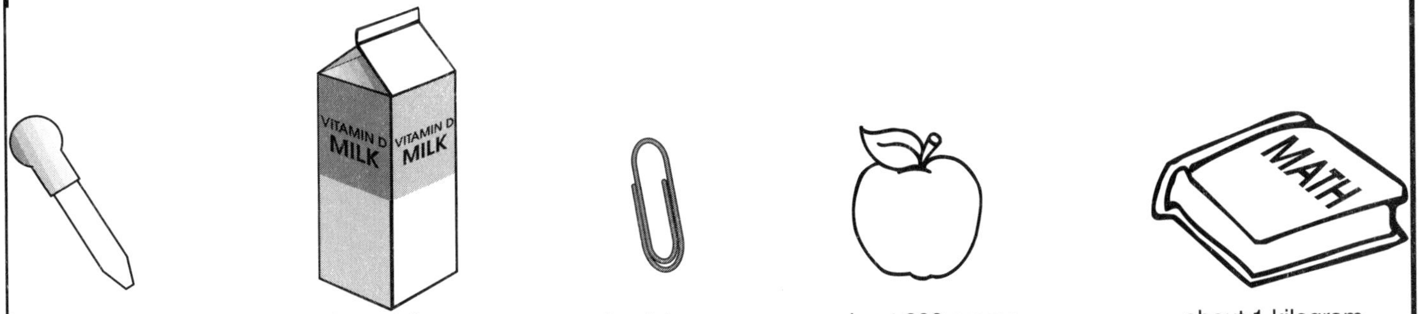

about 1 milliliter (ml)	about 1 liter (l)	about 1 gram (g)	about 200 grams (g)	about 1 kilogram (kg)

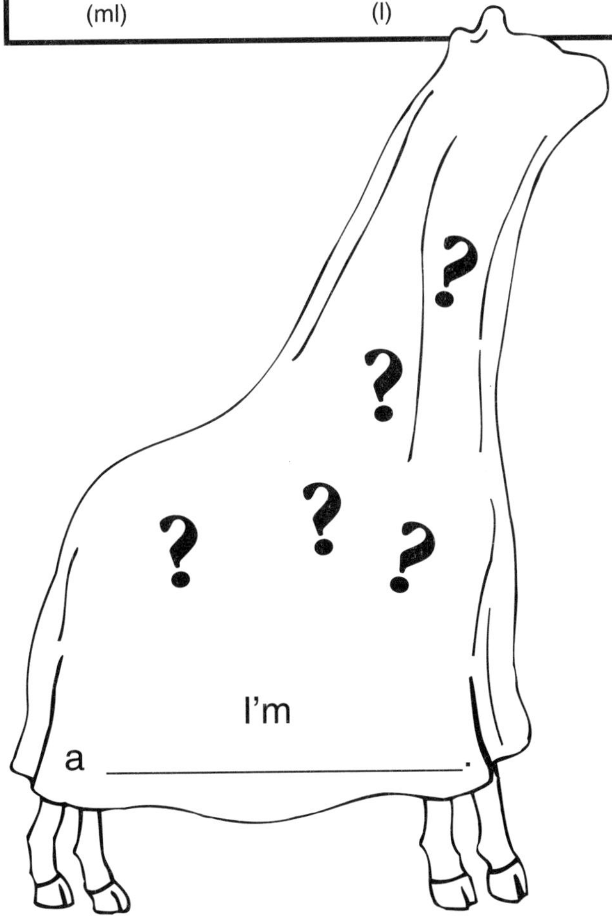

1. An average-size man has a mass of about 75 kg.
2. A milk jug holds approximately 20 ml.
3. The capacity of a soup bowl is about 250 ml.
4. An elephant has a mass of about 2,000 g.
5. A mouse weighs about 20 kg.
6. If you mix 1.6 l of blue paint with 0.55 l of yellow paint, you'll have 2.15 l of green paint.
7. The blue whale, the largest known animal on earth, weighs about 1,000,000 g.
8. The mass of a car is about 1,500 kg.
9. A teapot holds about 700 ml.
10. A bathtub can hold 14 l of water.
11. A box of cereal has a mass of about 444 kg.
12. A Saint Bernard dog can weigh 800 kg.
13. 0.65 kg is the same as 6,500 g.
14. 25 ml is equal to 0.025 l.
15. 8,604 mg is the same as 86.04 g.

I'm a _____.

1	2	3	4	5	6	7	8	9	10	11	12	13	14	15
G	S	I	T	R	R	N	A	F	F	E	H	U	E	S

Bonus Box: What do you think is the second tallest animal in the world? Research to find out.

©The Education Center, Inc. • *Big Book of Skill Builders* • TEC60797

Answer Key

1. G: reasonable
2. S: unreasonable (2 l)
3. I: reasonable
4. T: unreasonable (2,000 kg)
5. R: unreasonable (20 g)
6. R: reasonable
7. N: unreasonable (1 metric ton = 1,000 kg = 1,000,000 g; the blue whale weighs approximately 91 metric tons, or 91,000,000 g.)
8. A: reasonable
9. F: reasonable
10. F: reasonable
11. E: unreasonable (444 g)
12. H: unreasonable (80 kg)
13. U: unreasonable (650 g)
14. E: reasonable
15. S: unreasonable (8.604 g)

Solution: I'm a *giraffe*.

Bonus Box: The world's second tallest animal is the African elephant.

Name _____   Customary Units of Weight

Over the River and Through the Woods

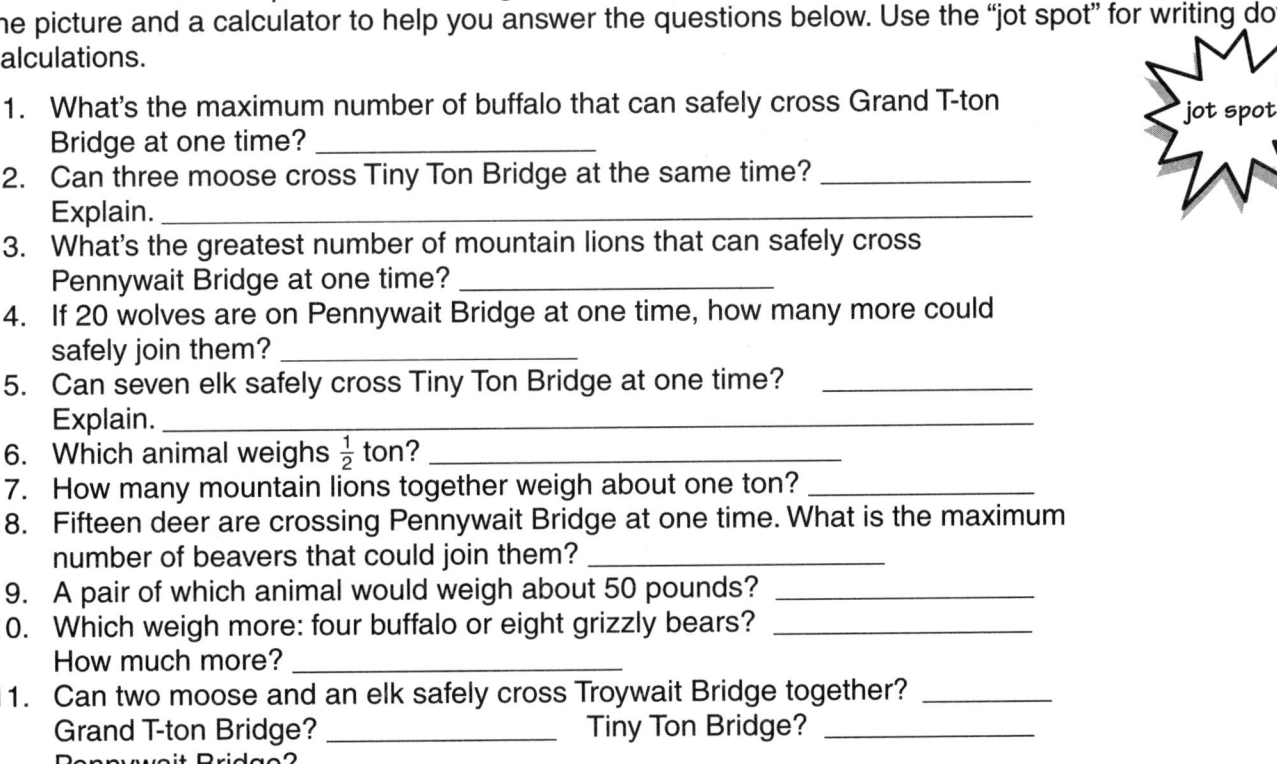

The animals in the picture cross bridges to move from one place to another. Use the information in the picture and a calculator to help you answer the questions below. Use the "jot spot" for writing down calculations.

1. What's the maximum number of buffalo that can safely cross Grand T-ton Bridge at one time? _____
2. Can three moose cross Tiny Ton Bridge at the same time? _____
   Explain. _____
3. What's the greatest number of mountain lions that can safely cross Pennywait Bridge at one time? _____
4. If 20 wolves are on Pennywait Bridge at one time, how many more could safely join them? _____
5. Can seven elk safely cross Tiny Ton Bridge at one time? _____
   Explain. _____
6. Which animal weighs $\frac{1}{2}$ ton? _____
7. How many mountain lions together weigh about one ton? _____
8. Fifteen deer are crossing Pennywait Bridge at one time. What is the maximum number of beavers that could join them? _____
9. A pair of which animal would weigh about 50 pounds? _____
10. Which weigh more: four buffalo or eight grizzly bears? _____
    How much more? _____
11. Can two moose and an elk safely cross Troywait Bridge together? _____
    Grand T-ton Bridge? _____ Tiny Ton Bridge? _____
    Pennywait Bridge? _____
12. Could one of each of the nine animals safely cross Troywait Bridge together? _____
    Explain. _____

Bonus Box: Make a list of five combinations of four animals each that could safely cross Pennywait Bridge at one time. For example: one moose, one grizzly bear, and two wolves (2,700 lb.).

©The Education Center, Inc. • Big Book of Skill Builders • TEC60797

Answer Key

1. two (Two buffalo weigh 3,600 pounds. The weight limit of the Grand T-ton Bridge is 2 tons or 4,000 pounds.)
2. yes (Three moose weigh 4,500 pounds. The weight limit of the Tiny Ton Bridge is 2.5 tons or 5,000 pounds.)
3. 13 (13 x 220 = 2,860 pounds. The weight limit of the Pennywait Bridge is $1\frac{1}{2}$ tons or 3,000 pounds.)
4. ten (Twenty wolves weigh 2,000 pounds. The weight limit of the Pennywait Bridge is $1\frac{1}{2}$ tons or 3,000 pounds. The bridge could hold 1,000 more pounds, or ten wolves.)
5. no (Seven elk weigh 5,600 pounds. The weight limit of the Tiny Ton Bridge is 2.5 tons or 5,000 pounds.)
6. grizzly bear ($\frac{1}{2}$ ton is equal to 1,000 pounds)
7. nine (9 x 220 = 1,980 pounds; a ton is 2,000 pounds)
8. four (15 deer weigh 2,850 pounds; The weight limit of the Pennywait Bridge is $1\frac{1}{2}$ tons or 3,000 pounds. The bridge can hold 150 more pounds. Four beavers weigh 140 pounds.)
9. raccoon (2 x 25 = 50 pounds)
10. eight grizzly bears; 800 pounds more (Four buffalo weigh 7,200 pounds. Eight grizzly bears weigh 8,000 pounds. 8,000 − 7,200 = 800 pounds)
11. Troywait: yes; Grand T-ton: yes; Tiny Ton: yes; Pennywait: no (Two moose and an elk weigh 3,800 pounds. The weight limit of each bridge in pounds is 6,000; 4,000; 5,000; and 3,000 respectively.)
12. yes (The total weight of one each of the nine animals is 5,670 pounds. The weight limit of the Troywait Bridge is 3 tons or 6,000 pounds.)

Bonus Box: Accept combinations that meet the criteria: four animals whose combined weight must be 3,000 pounds or less. Examples:
    one buffalo and three raccoons (1,875 lb.)
    two grizzly bears and two wolves (2,200 lb.)
    three elk and a deer (2,590 lb.)

Name_____   Customary Units of Length, Weight, and Capacity

Let's Make a Guess!

How good are you at guesstimating? Make an estimate of the customary measure that you think will complete each sentence below. Be sure that your estimates are reasonable.

When you're finished, exchange papers with a classmate. As you read your classmate's response for each sentence, draw a smiley face in the circle if you think the estimate is *reasonable*. Draw a frown if you think the estimate is *unreasonable*.

Return the paper to your partner and explain to him or her why you drew each frown.

◯ 1. The total weight of all of my classmates is about _____ _____.

◯ 2. I drink about _____ _____ of soda each week.

◯ 3. My pencil is about _____ _____ long.

◯ 4. I eat about _____ _____ of food each day.

◯ 5. The distance from my desk to the nearest water fountain is about _____ _____.

◯ 6. I live about _____ _____ from school.

◯ 7. My favorite hat (or cap) has a mass of about _____ _____.

◯ 8. I usually drink about _____ _____ of water from the school fountain each day.

◯ 9. My math book has a mass of about _____ _____.

◯ 10. The distance from our classroom to the playground is about _____ _____.

◯ 11. The largest thing in our classroom—_____—has a mass of about _____ _____.

◯ 12. The smallest container in our classroom—_____—holds about _____ _____ of liquid.

◯ 13. On the back of this sheet, draw a picture of something that has a mass of about five pounds.

◯ 14. On the back of this sheet, draw a picture of something that has a capacity of about four ounces of liquid.

◯ 15. On the back of this sheet, draw a picture of something that is about 30 inches tall or long.

Bonus Box: Write a letter to your representative in Congress. Express your views on whether or not the United States should convert to the metric system.

©The Education Center, Inc. • *Big Book of Skill Builders* • TEC60797   217

Name_____ Customary Units of Weight and Capacity

Making Comparisons

An analogy is a way of comparing things. Comparing is looking for likenesses between two things—even though the two things might not at first appear to be alike at all.

Example: *wing* is to *fly* as *foot* is to *run*

Determine how the first two measurements in each analogy are related. Then circle the answer that completes the analogy.

1. quart is to capacity as pound is to
   a. length   b. ton   c. weight

2. cup is to quart as quart is to
   a. pound   b. gallon   c. fluid ounce

3. 16 ounces is to 1 pound as 2,000 pounds is to
   a. 4 tons   b. 1 gallon   c. 1 ton

4. $\frac{1}{2}$ gallon is to 2 quarts as $\frac{1}{2}$ ton is to
   a. 1,000 pounds   b. 2,000 pounds   c. 3,000 pounds

5. 3 cups is to 24 fluid ounces as 3 pounds is to
   a. 24 ounces   b. 48 ounces   c. 16 ounces

6. $\frac{3}{4}$ ton is to 1,500 pounds as $\frac{3}{4}$ pound is to
   a. 18 ounces   b. 12 ounces   c. 24 ounces

7. cup is to pint as pint is to
   a. gallon   b. pound   c. quart

8. 8 pints is to 4 quarts as 8 quarts is to
   a. 2 gallons   b. 12 pints   c. 4 gallons

Write your own answers to the following analogies:

9. 1 cup is to 8 fluid ounces as 4 cups is to _____

10. gallon is to pint as ton is to _____

11. $\frac{1}{2}$ cup is to 4 fluid ounces as $\frac{1}{2}$ gallon is to _____

12. 4 quarts is to 1 gallon as 8 fluid ounces is to _____

Bonus Box: On the back of this sheet, write two analogies about customary weight and capacity. Leave one part of each analogy blank. Exchange papers with a classmate and complete each other's analogies.

©The Education Center, Inc. • *Big Book of Skill Builders* • TEC60797

Answer Key

1. c. weight
2. b. gallon
3. c. 1 ton
4. a. 1,000 pounds
5. b. 48 ounces
6. b. 12 ounces
7. c. quart
8. a. 2 gallons
9. 32 fluid ounces
10. 250 pounds
11. 2 quarts (or 4 pints or 8 cups)
12. 1 cup

Name _____ Area

And the Area Is...

What is *area* anyway? Area is the size of a flat surface in square units. Color and then cut out each pattern block at the bottom of this page. Then use the cutouts to complete items 2–5 on a sheet of notebook paper and item 6 on a sheet of drawing paper.

1. Suppose the area of the triangle is 1 square unit. What is the area of the rhombus? _____ The square? _____
   The trapezoid? _____ The hexagon? _____

2. Put two pattern blocks together to make a *parallelogram* with an area of 4 square units. Trace and color your figure.

3. Put two pattern blocks together to make a *trapezoid* with an area of 3 square units. Trace and color your figure.

4. Put three pattern blocks together to make a *regular hexagon* with an area of 6 square units. Trace and color your figure.

5. Trace and color a shape with an area of 20 square units. Use each pattern block as many times as you want.

6. Trace and color a design on a sheet of drawing paper using each pattern block as many times as you want. Then fill in the information below to determine the area of your picture. Use the information from item 1 to help you. Finally, use the total area in the title of your design.

_____ (number of triangles in your design) x __1__ (area of triangle) = _____ square units

_____ (number of rhombuses in your design) x _____ (area of rhombus) = _____ square units

_____ (number of squares in your design) x _____ (area of square) = _____ square units

_____ (number of trapezoids in your design) x _____ (area of trapezoid) = _____ square units

_____ (number of hexagons in your design) x _____ (area of hexagon) = _____ square units

Total area = _____ **square units**

©The Education Center, Inc. • *Big Book of Skill Builders* • TEC60797

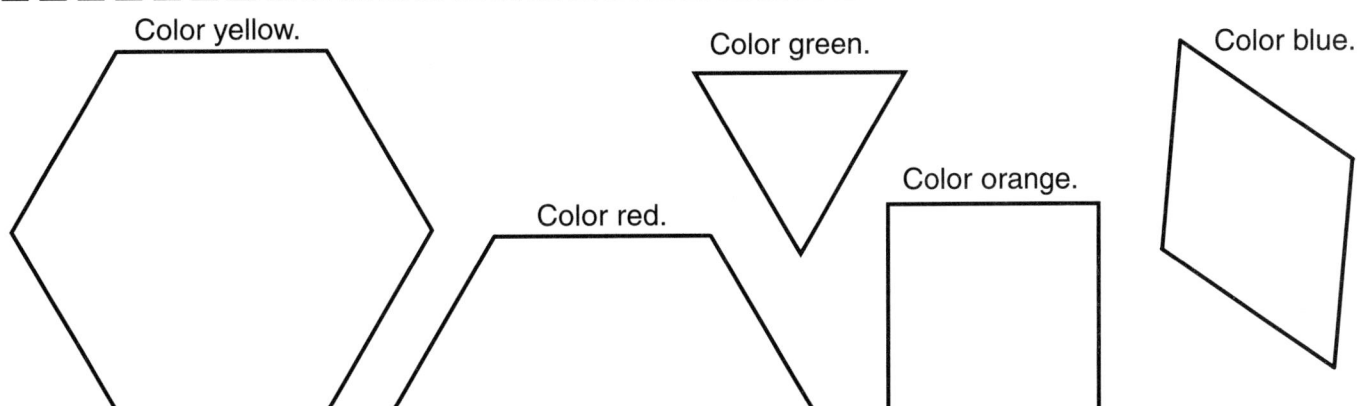

How to Use Page 221

Remind students that *perimeter* is the distance around a figure. Explain that the *area* is the size of a flat surface in square units. Provide each student with a copy of page 221, colored pencils, scissors, and a sheet of drawing paper. Then have each student complete the page as directed. Allow each student to share his design and catchy title. If desired, bind the pages in a class design book or post them on a classroom wall.

 Answer Key

1. 2 square units, 2 square units, 3 square units, and 6 square units
2. Placement of blocks may vary.

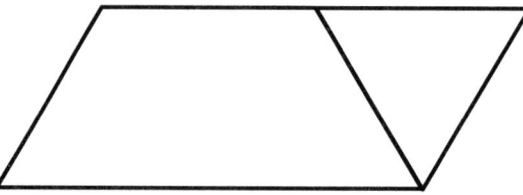

3. Placement of blocks may vary.

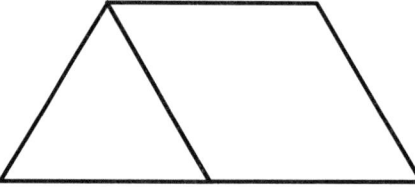

4. Placement of blocks may vary.

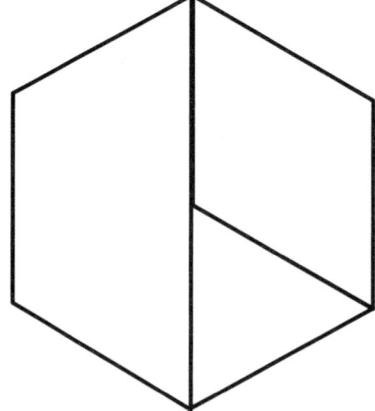

5. Answers will vary.
6. Answers will vary.

Name_____   Area and Perimeter

I've Been Framed!

Frames 'R' Us is known far and wide for the beautiful work its employees do. The total cost of framing an item includes the **backing,** which is placed behind a photograph or print that is to be framed; the **molding,** which extends completely around the photograph or print; and **protective glass,** which completely covers a framed item.

Study the charts below that show the costs of framing materials. These costs also include labor and tax.

Protective Glass			Backing
area	regular	nonglare	
less than 40 sq. in.	$4.00	$6.00	$2.50
40 sq. in.–79 sq. in	8.00	12.00	4.00
80 sq. in.–119 sq. in.	12.00	18.00	5.50
120 sq. in.–179 sq. in.	16.00	24.00	7.00
180 sq. in.–239 sq. in.	20.00	30.00	8.50
240 sq. in.–360 sq. in.	28.00	40.00	10.00

Molding	
perimeter	
up to 24"	$15.00
24"–35"	$20.00
36"–45"	$25.00
46"–55"	$30.00
56"–65"	$35.00
66"–75"	$40.00

Compute the total cost of framing each item below.

5"
7"

area: ↑ _____
perimeter: _____
regular glass: _____
backing: _____
molding: _____
total: _____

area: _____
perimeter: _____
regular glass: _____
backing: _____
molding: _____
total: _____

12"
6"

area: _____
perimeter: _____
nonglare glass: _____
backing: _____
molding: _____
total: _____

9"
10"

16"
20"

↑ area: _____
perimeter: _____
nonglare glass: _____
backing: _____
molding: _____
total: _____

©The Education Center, Inc. • *Big Book of Skill Builders* • TEC60797

Answer Key

5"

7"

area:	35 sq. in.
perimeter:	24 in.
regular glass:	$4.00
backing:	$2.50
molding:	$20.00
total:	$26.50

12"

6"

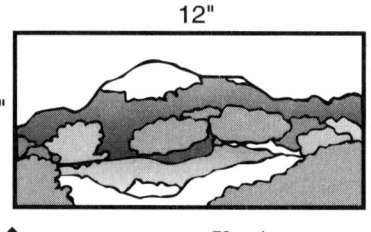

area:	72 sq. in.
perimeter:	36 in.
nonglare glass:	$12.00
backing:	$4.00
molding:	$25.00
total:	$41.00

9"

10"

area:	90 sq. in.
perimeter:	38 in.
regular glass:	$12.00
backing:	$5.50
molding:	$25.00
total:	$42.50

16"

20"

area:	320 sq. in.
perimeter:	72 in.
nonglare glass:	$40.00
backing:	$10.00
molding:	$40.00
total:	$90.00

Name _____ Slides, Turns, and Flips

Sliding, Flipping, and Turning

This page is about gymnastics—geometry gymnastics, that is! You can move a geometric figure in three ways:
- You can **slide** the figure along straight lines. (A slide is also called a **translation**.)
- You can **turn** the figure around a point. (A turn is also called a **rotation**.)
- You can **flip** the figure over a line. (A flip is also called a **reflection**.)

Look at the following examples:

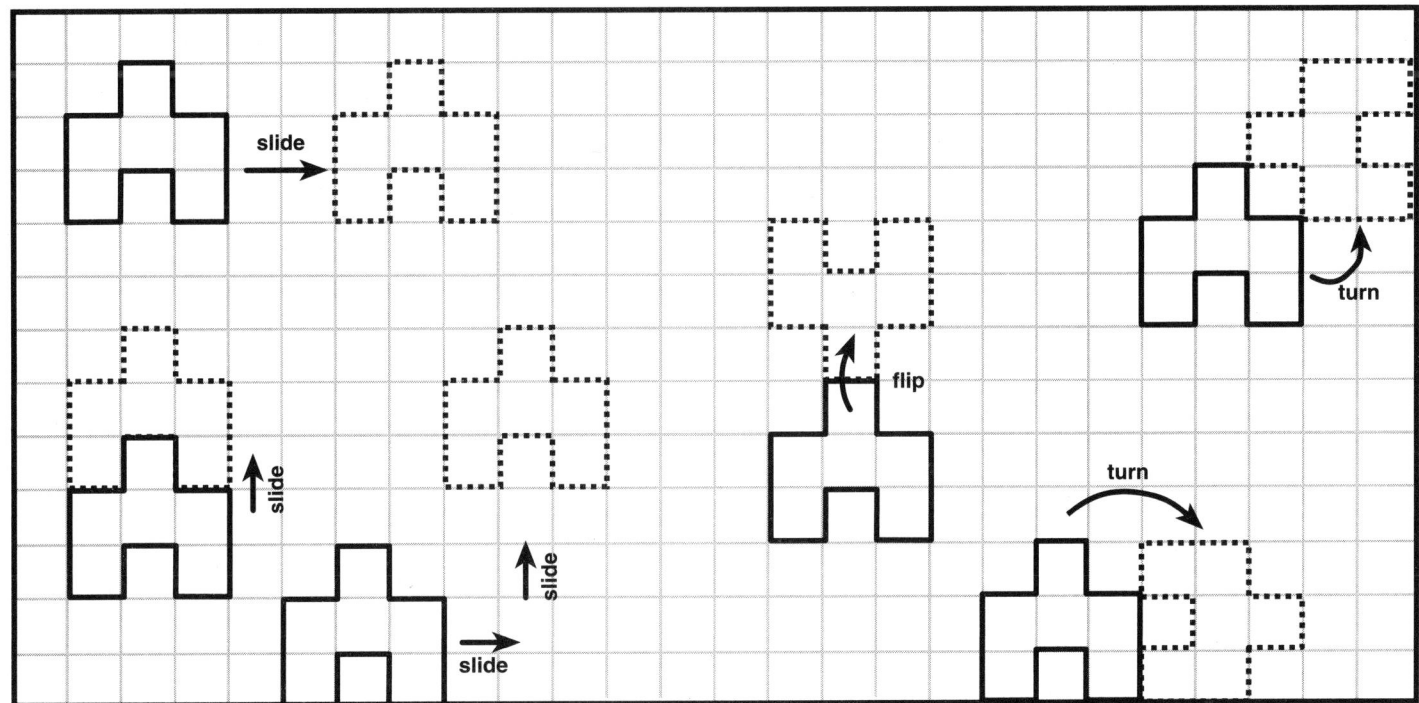

1. When you slide, turn, or flip a figure, does its size change? _____
2. When you slide, turn, or flip a figure, does its shape change? _____
3. The original figure and the final figure are _____.
4. Choose one of the shapes shown below. Cut out the shape and trace it on one-centimeter graph paper. Use slides, turns, and flips to make a design. Fill the graph paper with shapes. Color your design.

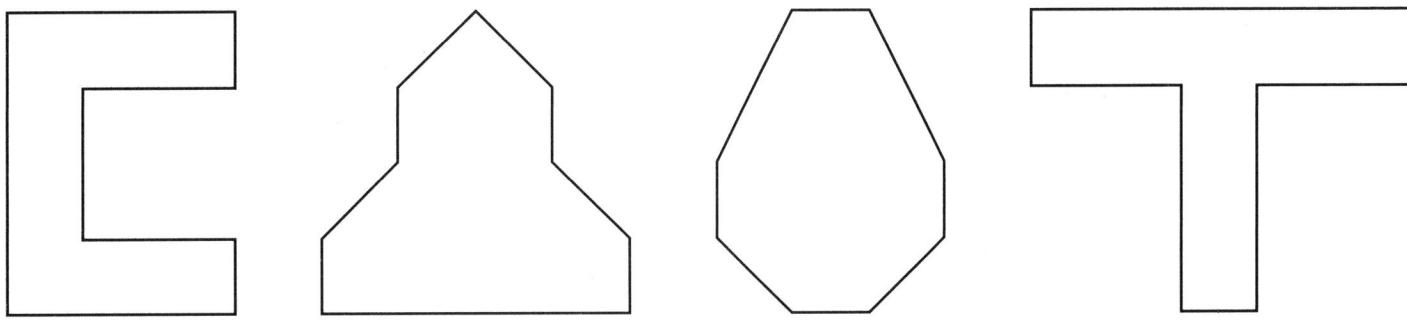

©The Education Center, Inc. • *Big Book of Skill Builders* • TEC60797

Note to the teacher: Make a supply of the one-centimeter graph paper on page 226. Cut off the answer key before making copies.

One-Centimeter Graph Paper

Name_____   Space Figures

It's What You Don't See (That Counts Too)!

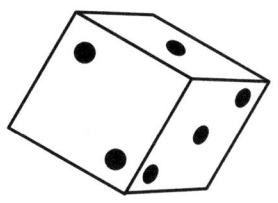

Look at the picture of the die. How many faces of the die do you see? If you held a die in your hand, could you turn it so that you could see even more of its faces? When you look at the picture, you see only three faces. But since it's a cube, you know that there are three more faces that you can't see. So a die has six faces in all, and each face is a square.

Directions: Study each shape pictured below. Each one is a solid, or three-dimensional, object. Beside each object are some two-dimensional shapes, or faces. On each shape, write the number of times it is found on the three-dimensional solid. Then write the total number of faces that the 3-D object has. The first one has been done for you. It's a cube like the die above.

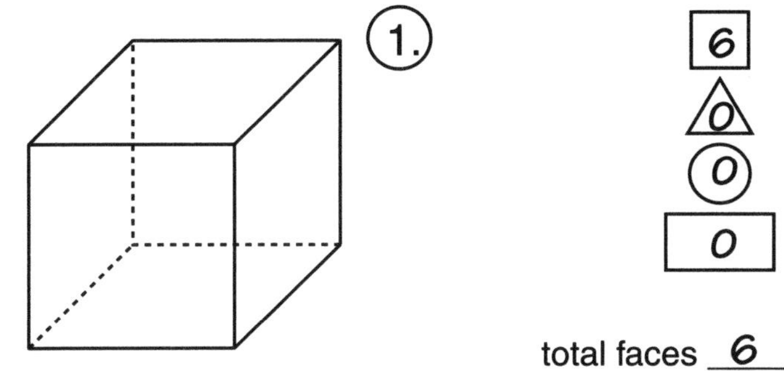

1. ☐ 6 △ 0 ◯ 0 ▭ 0   total faces **6**

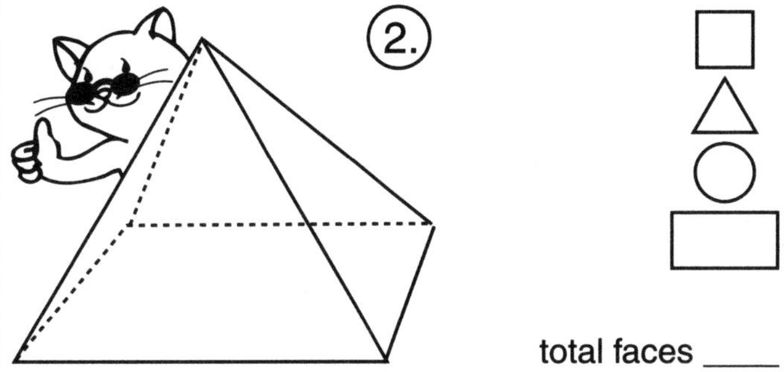

2. ☐ __ △ __ ◯ __ ▭ __   total faces ____

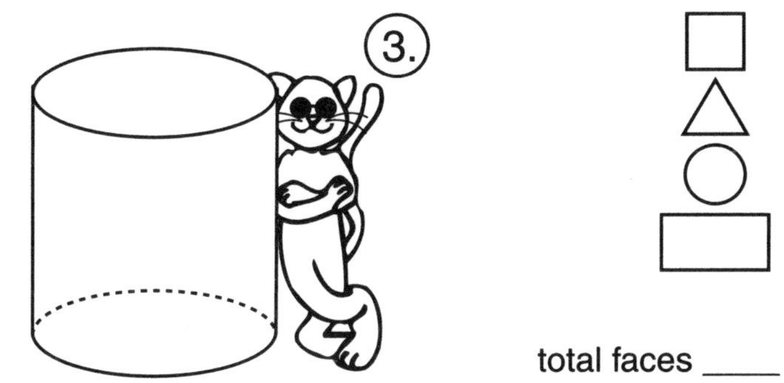

3. ☐ __ △ __ ◯ __ ▭ __   total faces ____

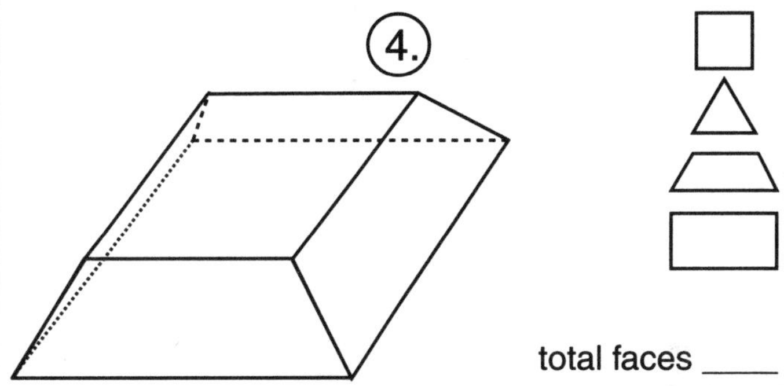

4. ☐ __ △ __ ▱ __ ▭ __   total faces ____

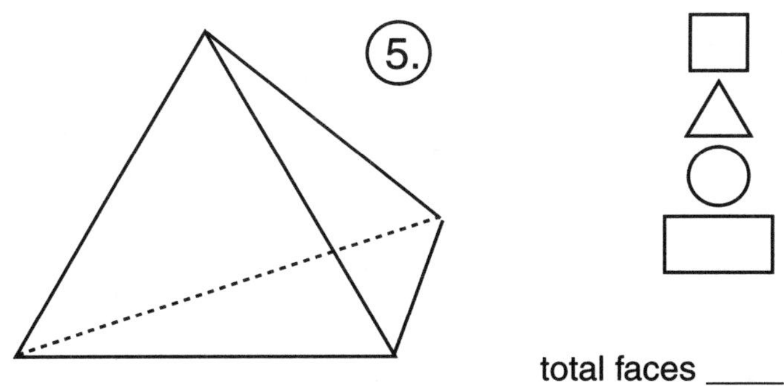

5. ☐ __ △ __ ◯ __ ▭ __   total faces ____

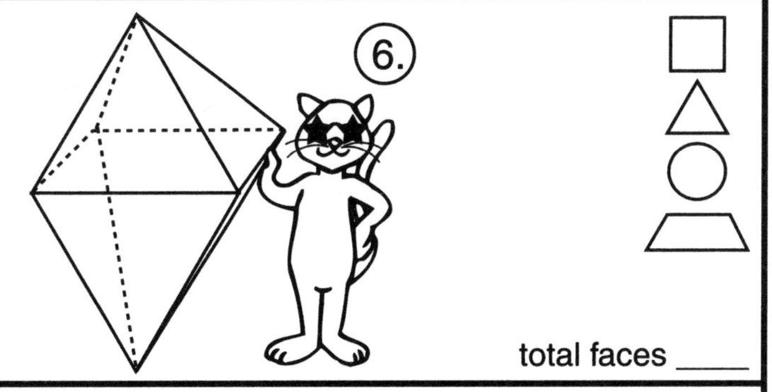

6. ☐ __ △ __ ◯ __ ▱ __   total faces ____

7. ☐ __ △ __ ▭ __ ◯ __   total faces ____

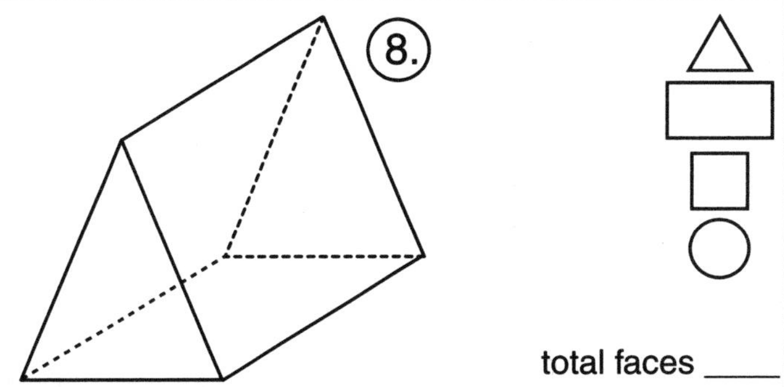

8. △ __ ▭ __ ☐ __ ◯ __   total faces ____

©The Education Center, Inc. • Big Book of Skill Builders • TEC60797   227

Answer Key

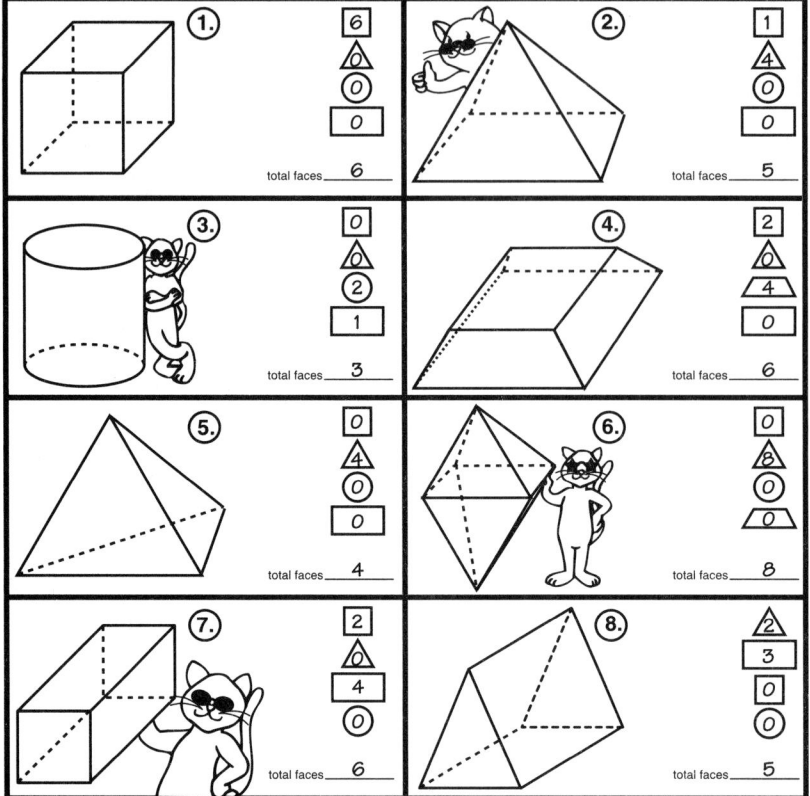

1. Like the die (a cube), this figure has six sides (or faces) that are squares.
2. This figure is a *pyramid* with a square base and four triangular sides.
3. The top and bottom of this cylinder are circles. The surface between the two circles is a curved rectangle.
4. Students might say that this figure looks like a pyramid with its top cut off. (And it is!) This particular figure is called a *frustum* of a pyramid. It has a square base and each side is a trapezoid. On a chalkboard, draw an isosceles triangle. Then draw a line segment across the triangle that is parallel to the base. Show students that the top part of the triangle is still a triangle; whereas, the bottom part is now a trapezoid.
5. This figure is also a pyramid, but it has an equilateral triangle for its base. Each of the three sides is also an equilateral triangle. This special shape—made up of four equilateral triangles—is called a *tetrahedron.*
6. Ask students what the figure in item 6 resembles. They may notice that it looks like two pyramids from item 2 that have been glued base-to-base. Thus, this figure has eight aces—all of which are congruent triangles—and is called an *octahedron*. (Did anyone include a square as a face of this shape? If so, remind students that this is a solid shape. It does have four edges that make the outline of a square. But the square is not a face of the figure.)
7. A *rectangular prism,* like a cube, has six sides. These sides are either all rectangles or a combination of rectangles and squares. So technically, if a student gives an answer of six rectangles, that should be accepted.
8. This shape—*a triangular prism*—resembles a tent or a wedge of cheese. Help students see that it has two congruent triangular bases that are joined by three rectangles. (Note: If the triangles are isosceles like the ones pictured, then two of the rectangles will be congruent. If the triangles are equilateral, then all three of the rectangles will be congruent. And if the triangles are scalene, the three rectangles will be three different sizes.)

Name _____   Types of Angles

A New Angle on Art

When you think of an artist, what tools come to mind? Paintbrushes, paint, and canvas are common answers, but how about protractors? Use what you know about the different types of angles—*acute, obtuse,* and *right*—to create some original art. Simply read the directions below. Then, using a protractor and a pencil, draw each design on a large sheet of paper. In each design that you create, outline the vertex of each acute angle in *blue,* each obtuse angle in *red,* and each right angle in *green.*

A *ray* is a part of a line that extends in one direction from a point.

An *angle* is a figure formed by two rays with a common endpoint.

A *vertex* is a common endpoint for two rays.

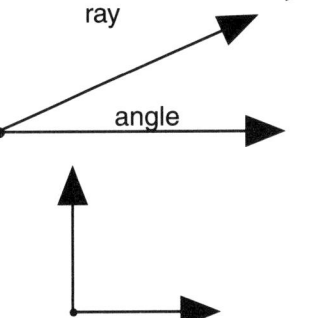

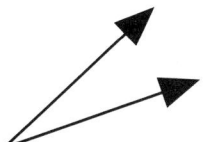   

An *acute* angle measures less than 90°.   An *obtuse* angle measures more than 90° and less than 180°.   A *right* angle measures exactly 90°.

1. Draw a flower that has eight acute angles.

2. Draw a doghouse using only right angles.

3. Design a new shoe that has at least two acute and two obtuse angles.

4. Draw a person using only acute angles.

5. Draw your favorite animal using at least two right, three acute, and three obtuse angles.

6. Design a new car using only right and acute angles.

7. Draw an alien using as many of each type of angle as possible.

8. Draw a picture of the front of your house. List how many acute, right, and obtuse angles are in your picture.

Bonus Box: Draw a picture that contains the following: two acute angles less than 45°, two acute angles more than 45°, two obtuse angles less than 150°, two obtuse angles more than 150°, and three right angles. Label each angle with its exact measurement.

How to Use Page 229

Provide each student with a copy of page 229, a protractor, colored pencils or crayons, and a sheet of 18" x 24" drawing paper. Review the terms *ray, angle, vertex, acute angle, obtuse angle,* and *right angle* with your students. Then review how to draw and measure angles using a protractor. Finally, have each student complete the page as directed. Display the completed designs on a bulletin board titled "A New Angle on Art."

Name _____ Bar Graph

Meet Me at the Zoo!

Just like no two animals are alike, the same goes for zoos! Look at the bar graph below. It shows the total acres that each zoo covers. Then answer the questions that follow.

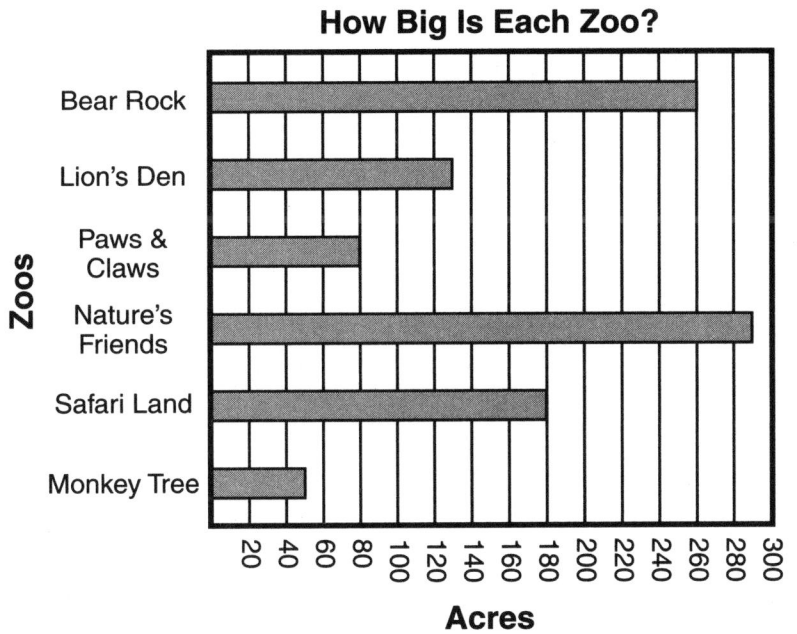

1. Which zoo is the smallest in area? _____

2. How many acres does Paws & Claws cover? _____

3. How much bigger is Bear Rock than Safari Land? _____

4. How many total acres do Monkey Tree and Lion's Den cover? _____

5. Which zoo covers 110 more acres than Safari Land? _____

So what about the animals? Make a bar graph using the information below to show how many animals are at each zoo.

Bear Rock 4,250
Lion's Den 2,000
Paws & Claws 1,250
Nature's Friends 3,500
Safari Land 2,750
Monkey Tree 750

How Many Animals Are at the Zoo?

(blank bar graph with y-axis "Number of Animals" from 0 to 5,000 in increments of 500, x-axis "Zoos": Bear Rock, Lion's Den, Paws & Claws, Nature's Friends, Safari Land, Monkey Tree)

©The Education Center, Inc. • Big Book of Skill Builders • TEC60797

Answer Key

How Big Is Each Zoo?
1. Monkey Tree
2. 80 acres
3. 80 acres
4. 180 acres
5. Nature's Friends

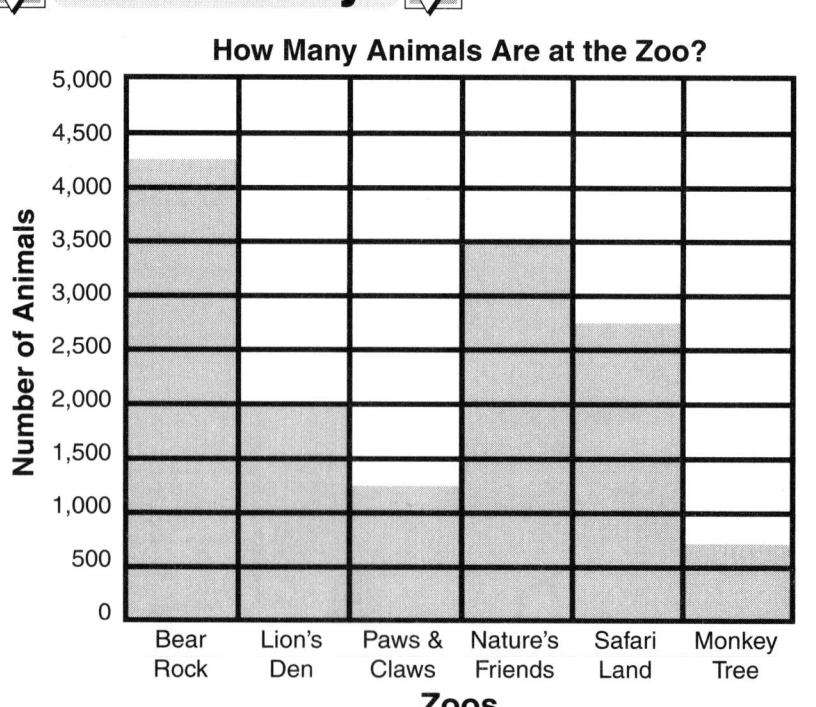

Name _____ Double Bar Graph

The Price You Pay

Can't you just see those cute, cuddly animals waiting to greet you? But you can't get in the zoo without paying for a ticket! Look at the double bar graph below. In it you will find information on ticket prices for the various zoos. Then answer the questions that follow.

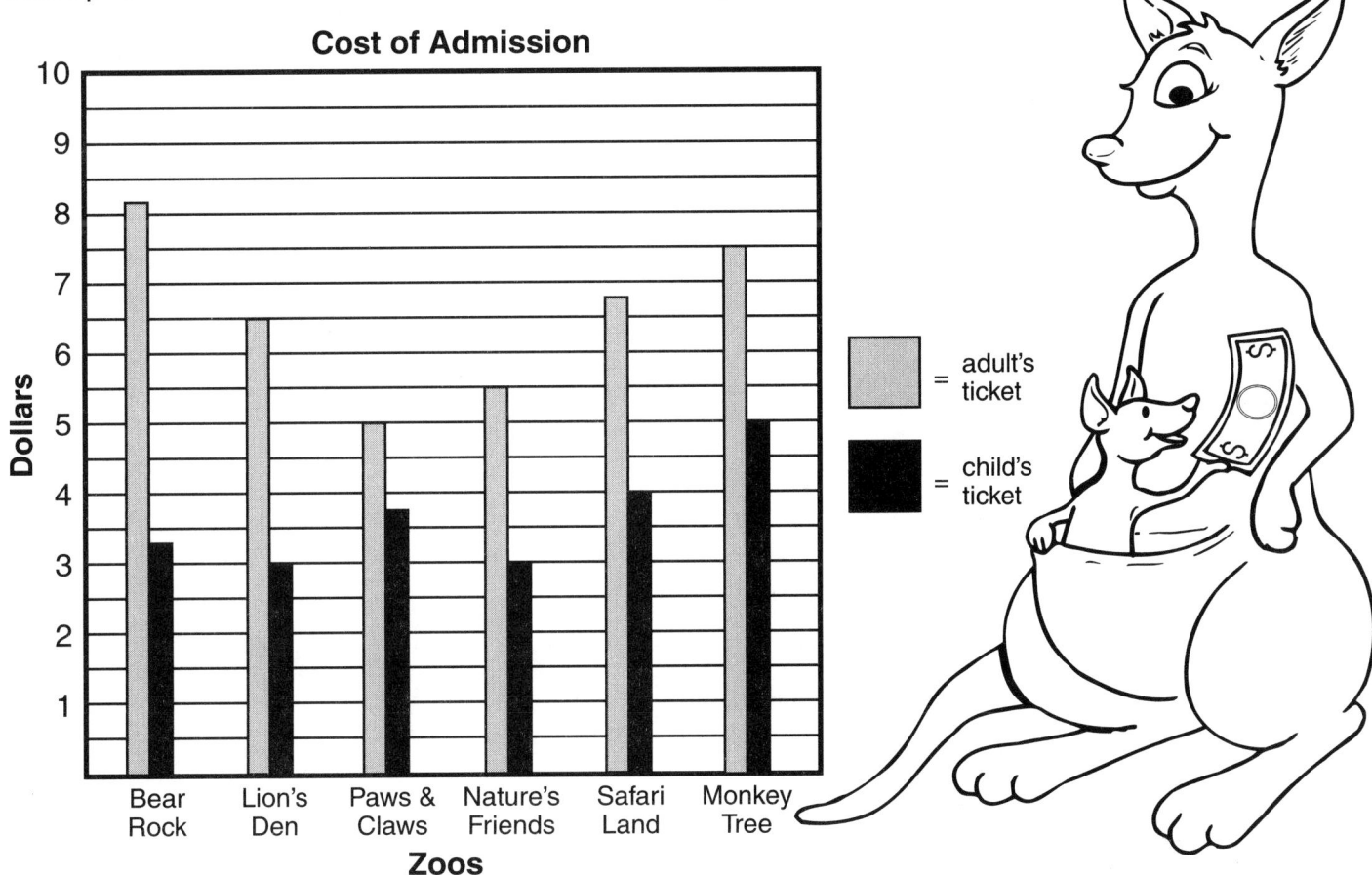

1. Which zoo charges the most for a child's ticket? _____
2. Which zoo charges the least for an adult's ticket? _____
3. At which zoo can you buy an adult's ticket for $6.50? _____
4. How much does an adult's ticket cost at Safari Land? _____
5. How much does a child's ticket cost at Bear Rock? _____
6. At which two zoos is the cost for a child's ticket the same? _____
7. How much more does it cost for an adult's ticket at Safari Land than at Paws & Claws? _____
8. At which zoo is the cost of a child's ticket $1.00 less than at Monkey Tree? _____
9. How much would it cost to buy tickets for two adults and three children at Paws & Claws? _____
10. Which zoo charges the least for one adult's ticket and two children's tickets? _____ What is the cost? _____

Bonus Box: How much would it cost for your family to buy tickets at Lion's Den?

Answer Key

1. Monkey Tree
2. Paws & Claws
3. Lion's Den
4. $6.75
5. $3.25
6. Lion's Den and Nature's Friends
7. $1.75
8. Safari Land
9. $21.25
10. Nature's Friends; $11.50

Name _____ Pictograph

Take One Home!

People who visit the Nature's Friends zoo love the animals so much that they each want to take one home! That's why the zoo store sells toy stuffed animals.

Directions: Look at the information in the chart at the right. It tells the number of stuffed animals purchased last year at this zoo. Use the information to make a pictograph to show which animals were the most popular. The first one is done for you.

Number of Stuffed Animals Sold Last Year

Elephant	43
Polar Bear	62
Giraffe	28
Lion	71
Hippopotamus	26
Gorilla	50
Kangaroo	81
Tiger	65
Deer	37

Number of Stuffed Animals Sold Last Year

Elephant	□ □ □ □ △ △ △
Polar Bear	
Giraffe	
Lion	
Hippopotamus	
Gorilla	
Kangaroo	
Tiger	
Deer	

Key   □ = 10 animals   △ = 1 animal

Bonus Box: Write five questions using the pictograph above. Give your questions to a classmate to answer.

Answer Key

Number of Stuffed Animals Sold Last Year	
Elephant	□□□□△△△
Polar Bear	□□□□□△△
Giraffe	□□△△△△△△△△
Lion	□□□□□□□△
Hippopotamus	□□△△△△△△
Gorilla	□□□□□
Kangaroo	□□□□□□□△
Tiger	□□□□□□△△△△△
Deer	□□□△△△△△△△
Key	□ =10 animals △ =1 animal

Name _____ Line Graph

The Bottom Line

Taking care of a zoo is not monkey business, but it is a business! Look at the line graph below. It shows the ticket sales over the past year for the Lion's Den and Paws & Claws zoos. Then answer the questions that follow.

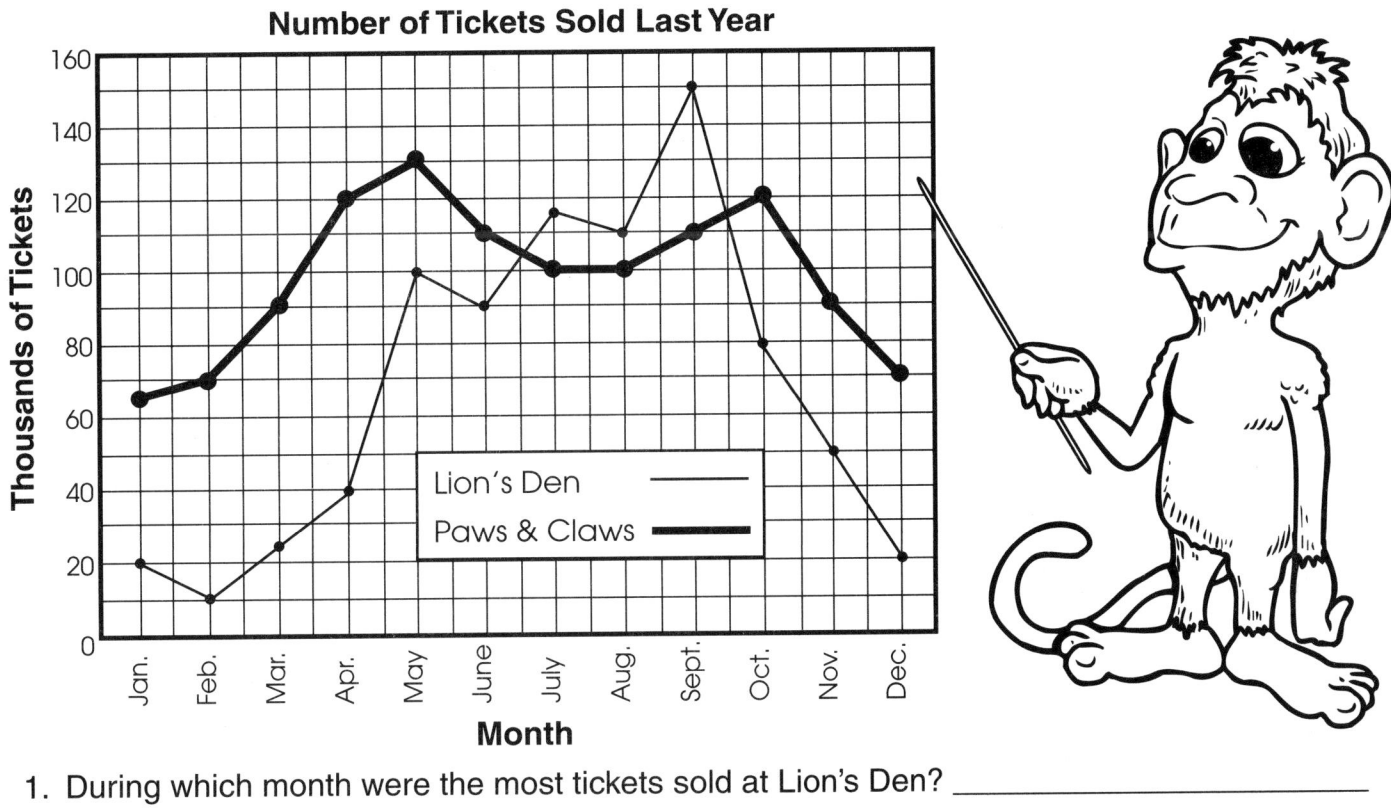

1. During which month were the most tickets sold at Lion's Den? _____
2. During which month were the least tickets sold at Paws & Claws? _____
3. Were an equal number of tickets sold at both zoos in any one month? _____
4. During which month did Lion's Den sell 115,000 tickets? _____
5. At Lion's Den, how many tickets were sold in August? _____
6. Between which two months did Lion's Den see the biggest increase in the number of tickets sold? _____ How much was the increase? _____
7. During September and October, how many total tickets were sold at Lion's Den? _____
8. How many more tickets were sold during April at Paws & Claws than at Lion's Den? _____
9. Which zoo sold more tickets in November? _____
10. During which months did Lion's Den sell more tickets than Paws & Claws? _____
    _____
11. Between which two months did Paws & Claws see the largest decrease in the number of tickets sold? _____
12. How many months did Lion's Den sell over 80,000 tickets? _____
    _____ Paws & Claws? _____

Bonus Box: What might be the reason why each zoo's sales are highest at different times of the year?

Answer Key

1. September
2. January
3. no
4. July
5. 110,000
6. April and May; 60,000
7. 230,000
8. 80,000 more
9. Paws & Claws
10. July, August, and September
11. October and November
12. five; nine

Bonus Box: Answers may vary. The following is one possible answer: The zoos may be in areas with differing climates.

Name_____   Circle Graph

Visiting the Zoo

There is so much to see and do at a zoo, how do you fit it all in? The chart below shows how one visitor spent a day at the Lion's Den zoo. Use this information and the directions below to make a circle graph showing the time spent at the zoo.

Carnivore Kingdom	4 hours
Energizing Eats & Shopping Safari	1 hour
African Plains	3 hours
Aviary	1 hour
Reptile House	1 hour
Small Mammal House	2 hours
Total	**= 12 hours**

Directions:
1. Using a ruler, divide the circle into sections that show the amount of time spent in an area of the zoo. Use the marks along the edge of the circle to help you.
2. Label each section of the circle with the name of the zoo area.
3. Use crayons to color each section a different color.

Time Spent at Zoo

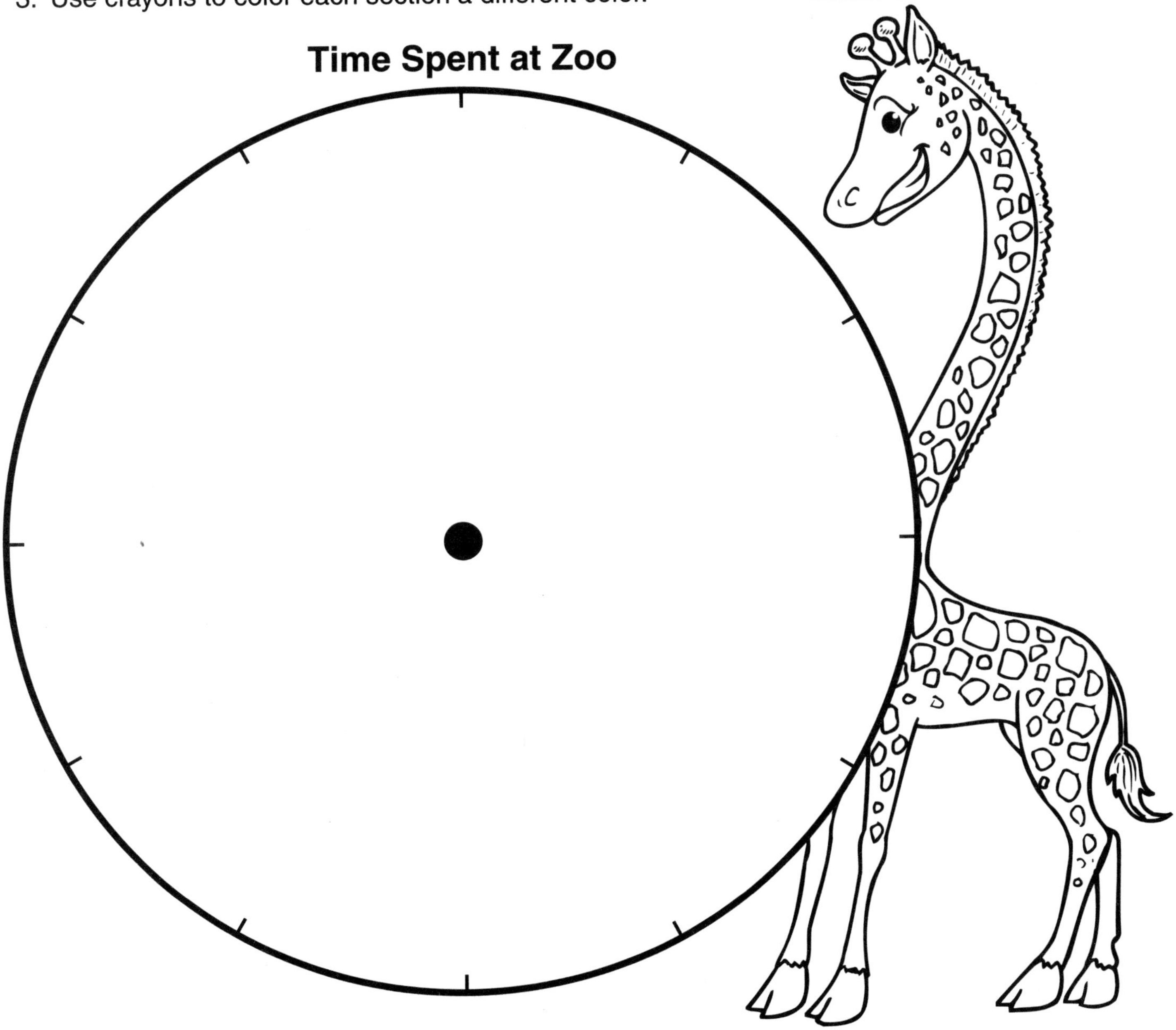

Bonus Box: On the back of this page, make a circle graph showing how much time you would spend in each of the six areas of the zoo.

©The Education Center, Inc. • *Big Book of Skill Builders* • TEC60797

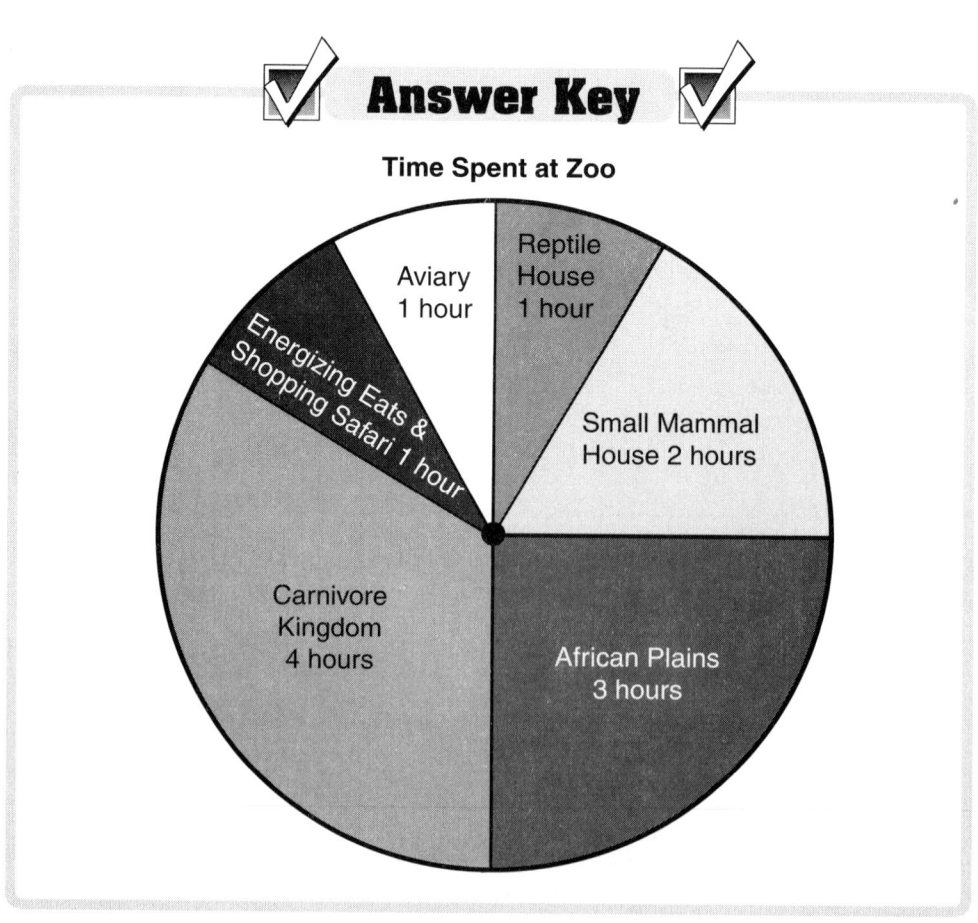

Name _____ Completing a Pattern

The Case of the Missing Manuscript

Famous mystery writer Agatha MacChristie has hired Detective Vick Tracy to track down her latest manuscript. It disappeared after Agatha had the library in her home remodeled.

Help Vick Tracy find Miss MacChristie's next best-seller by filling in the missing part of each pattern below. Next, use the secret code at the bottom of the page to learn which letter matches each answer. Arrange the vowels and consonants below to spell two words that will tell where to find the missing manuscript.

Clue 1
5, 8, 6, 9, 7, 10, 8, 11, 9, 12, ____, 13, 11,…
Letter code: ____

Clue 2
12, 9, 10, 7, 8, ____, 6, 3, 4, 1, 2
Letter code: ____

Clue 3
1, 2, 4, ____, 16, 32, 64,…
Letter code: ____

Clue 4
21, 17, 13, ____, 5, 1
Letter code: ____

Clue 5
△,△,○,□,○,△,△,___,□,○,△,△,…
Letter code: ____

Clue 6
□,___,□,□,□,△,□,□,□,△,□,…
Letter code: ____

Clue 7
1,   3,   ____,   9,   12,   15,…
Letter code: ____

Clue 8
1,   4,   ____,   16,   25,…
Letter code: ____

Clue 9
1, 1, 2, 3, 5, ____, 13, 21, 34, 55, 89, 144,…
Letter code: ____

Clue 10
1,   3,   6,   ____,   15,…
Letter code: ____

Code

C	F	I	G	A	K	D	E	R	S	W	I	N
1	2	3	4	5	6	8	9	10	○	△	□	▫

The missing manuscript is

in the __ __ __ __   __ __ __ __ __ __ __ .
       C V C C   C C V C V C

Bonus Box: Write the rule for each pattern on the back of this sheet.

Answer Key

1. 10—R
2. 5—A
3. 8—D
4. 9—E
5. circle—S
6. triangle—W
7. 6—K
8. 9—E
9. 8—D
10. 10—R

The missing manuscript is in the D E S K   D R A W E R.

Bonus Box:
The rules are:
1. add 3, then subtract 2
2. subtract 3, then add 1
3. multiply by 2
4. subtract 4
5. triangle, triangle, circle, square, circle
6. rectangle, triangle, square, square
7. The triangle-dot number pattern is made by adding one more dot to each side of a triangular dot shape so that each side has the same increasing number of dots. For example:

   1,   3,   6,   9,   12,   15, . . .

8. The square number pattern is made by putting lines of dots under and beside each other in the shape of a square. The first number has one dot. The second number has two lines of two dots in each line. The third number has three lines of three dots in each line, and so on. The pattern continues to build in the same way of adding one more line of dots and one more dot on each line for each successive number built. For example:

   1,   4,   9,   16,   25,   36, . . .

9. This is the Fibonacci Sequence. Adding each consecutive pair of numbers in succession produces the next term in the sequence: $1 + 1 = 2$, $1 + 2 = 3$, $2 + 3 = 5$, etc.

10. The stair pattern is built by putting rows of squares on top of each other. The first number has one square on a single row. The second number has two squares on the bottom row and a single square on top of the right side of the bottom row. The third number has three squares on the bottom row, two squares atop the right side of the bottom row, and one square atop the right side of the second row. For each successive number, the pattern continues to build by adding a bottom row of squares with one more square than the row above it.

    1,   3,   6,   10,   15,   21, . . .

Name _____

Identifying a Pattern

Place-Value Pumpkin Patch

Directions: Weave your way through the pumpkin patch by finding the pattern used in each vine. (Remember, a *pattern* is an arrangement of things repeated in an orderly, recognizable fashion.) Fill in each empty pumpkin with the number that fits the pattern. Then write the pattern on the blank below the vine.

Example: 9, 13, 10, 14, __11__, 15 **Pattern:** add 4, subtract 3

1. 100, 99, 97, 90
Pattern: _____

2. 250, 261, 283, 294
Pattern: _____

3. 817, 1,037, 1,257, 1,697
Pattern: _____

4. 6,006, 4,004, 3,003, 1,001
Pattern: _____

5. 10,349, 11,349, 11,349, 10,349
Pattern: _____

6. 321,121, 221,121, 211,121, 210,021
Pattern: _____

©The Education Center, Inc. • *Big Book of Skill Builders* • TEC60797

243

Answer Key

1. 100, 99, 97, <u>94</u>, 90, <u>85</u>
   Pattern: subtract 1, subtract 2, subtract 3, subtract 4, etc.

2. 250, 261, <u>272</u>, 283, 294, <u>305</u>
   Pattern: add 11

3. 817; 1,037; 1,257; <u>1,477</u>; 1,697; <u>1,917</u>
   Pattern: add 220

4. 6,006; <u>5,005</u>; 4,004; 3,003; <u>2,002</u>; 1,001
   Pattern: subtract 1,001

5. 10,349; 11,349; <u>10,349</u>; 11,349; 10,349; <u>11,349</u>
   Pattern: add 1,000; subtract 1,000

6. 321,121; 221,121; 211,121; <u>210,121</u>; 210,021; <u>210,011</u>
   Pattern: subtract 100,000; subtract 10,000; subtract 1,000; subtract 100; subtract 10

Name_____ Completing a Pattern, Attributes

Soup's On!

Some interesting patterns have formed in these bowls of alphabet soup! See if you can figure out the pattern (or the attribute) of the letters in each bowl. On the back of this sheet, write a short sentence that describes the pattern or attribute. Then answer the question in the blank below each bowl. Hmmmmmm, good!

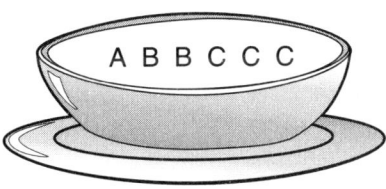

1. What letter comes next? _____

2. If A = 2, B = 4, C = 6, and so on, what is the value of H? _____

3. How many Fs are in this pattern? _____

4. In this pattern, is the letter Z lowercase or uppercase? _____

5. What letter comes next? _____

6. This well-known dozen needs three more letters to complete the pattern. What are they? _____

7. List three more letters that belong in this bowl. _____

8. Write one more letter that belongs in this bowl. _____

9. List four more letters that belong in this bowl. _____

10. Five more letters belong in this bowl of soup. What are they? _____

11. List three more letters that belong in this bowl. _____

12. These letters form a neat row of keys! What two letters are needed to complete the row? _____

13. If a = 1, b = 4, c = 9, d = 16, e = 25, and so on, what is the value of h? _____

14. Write one more letter that belongs in this bowl. _____

Bonus Bowl: What would be the 15th letter in this pattern? _____

How to Use Page 245

Duplicate page 245 for students to use during free time or as an extension of their studies of patterns and attributes. Tell students to think about how the letters in each bowl are related to each other: their order, how they are formed, how they sound, etc. Suggest that students write the alphabet on a sheet of paper, both uppercase and lowercase, to help them solve each pattern or identify an attribute.

Answer Key

Students' responses for pattern or attribute descriptions may vary.
1. *P* (Skip two letters.)
2. 16 (Count by 2s: *D* = 8, *E* = 10, *F* = 12, *G* = 14, and *H* = 16.)
3. 6 (There would be four *D*s, five *E*s, and then six *F*s.)
4. uppercase (Every even letter is uppercase. Since *Z* is the 26th letter, it is uppercase.)
5. *u* (vowel, consonant, vowel, consonant, etc.)
6. O, N, D (This set consists of the first letters of the months of the year.)
7. T, V, Z (All of the letters rhyme.)
8. *j* (Each letter has a "tail" that extends below the baseline when it's written.)
9. D, H, T, X (Each letter has at least one line of symmetry.)
10. E, K, M, V, X (All of these letters are made with straight line segments.)
11. B, J, R (All of these letters have curved line segments.)
12. o, p (These letters form the top row of letters on a computer keyboard.)
13. 64 (Each value is a square number. The value of *e* = 25, *f* = 36, *g* = 49, and *h* = 64.)
14. O (Each letter has an enclosed space.)

Bonus Bowl: *s*
The letter *b* is skipped; then two more letters (*c* and *d*) are written.
The letter *e* is skipped; then three more letters (*f, g,* and *h*) are written.
The letter *i* is skipped; then four more letters (*j, k, l,* and *m*) are written.
The letter *n* is skipped; so five more letters should be written:
   o, p, q, r, and s.
Thus the letter *s* would be in the 15th position.

Name_____ Layers of the Earth

Crust to Core

Scientists have learned that the earth is made up of different layers: *crust, mantle, outer core,* and *inner core.* Cut out the facts at the bottom of this page. Match each fact with the layer that it describes. Use reference materials for help, if needed. When you are sure of your answers, glue each fact in place.

The Crust

The Mantle

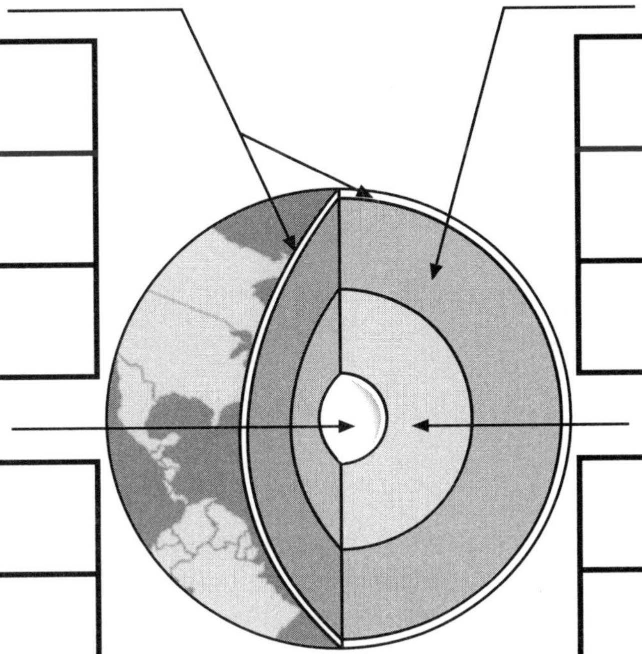

The Inner Core

The Outer Core

©The Education Center, Inc. • *Big Book of Skill Builders* • TEC60797

- -

has temperatures reaching 1,600°F—hot enough to melt rocks	is made up mostly of melted iron	has temperatures reaching up to 11,000°F	supports the crust
	contains a layer of very hot, sometimes molten, rock	is made up of solid rocks, soil, and minerals	
	ranges in thickness from 5 to 25 miles	is ball shaped and made up mostly of solid iron	
	is about 1,800 miles thick with temperatures reaching 8,000°F	is about 1,400 miles thick	
	is 4,000 miles below the surface of the earth	has temperatures as high as 13,000°F	

Bonus Box: On the back of this sheet, write a story about an imaginary journey to the center of the earth. Include at least four facts about the layers of the earth in your story.

247

Answer Key

The Crust
- ranges in thickness from 5 to 25 miles
- is made up of solid rocks, soil, and minerals
- has temperatures reaching 1,600°F—hot enough to melt rocks

The Mantle
- contains a layer of very hot, sometimes molten, rock
- is about 1,800 miles thick with temperatures reaching 8,000°F
- supports the crust

The Outer Core
- is about 1,400 miles thick
- is made up mostly of melted iron
- has temperatures reaching up to 11,000°F

The Inner Core
- is 4,000 miles below the surface of the earth
- is ball shaped and made up mostly of solid iron
- has temperatures as high as 13,000°F

Volcano Adventure

A *volcanologist* is someone who studies volcanoes and their activities. Imagine yourself to be a volcanologist for a day! Read the paragraph below. Use the boldfaced words to label the diagram of the volcano.

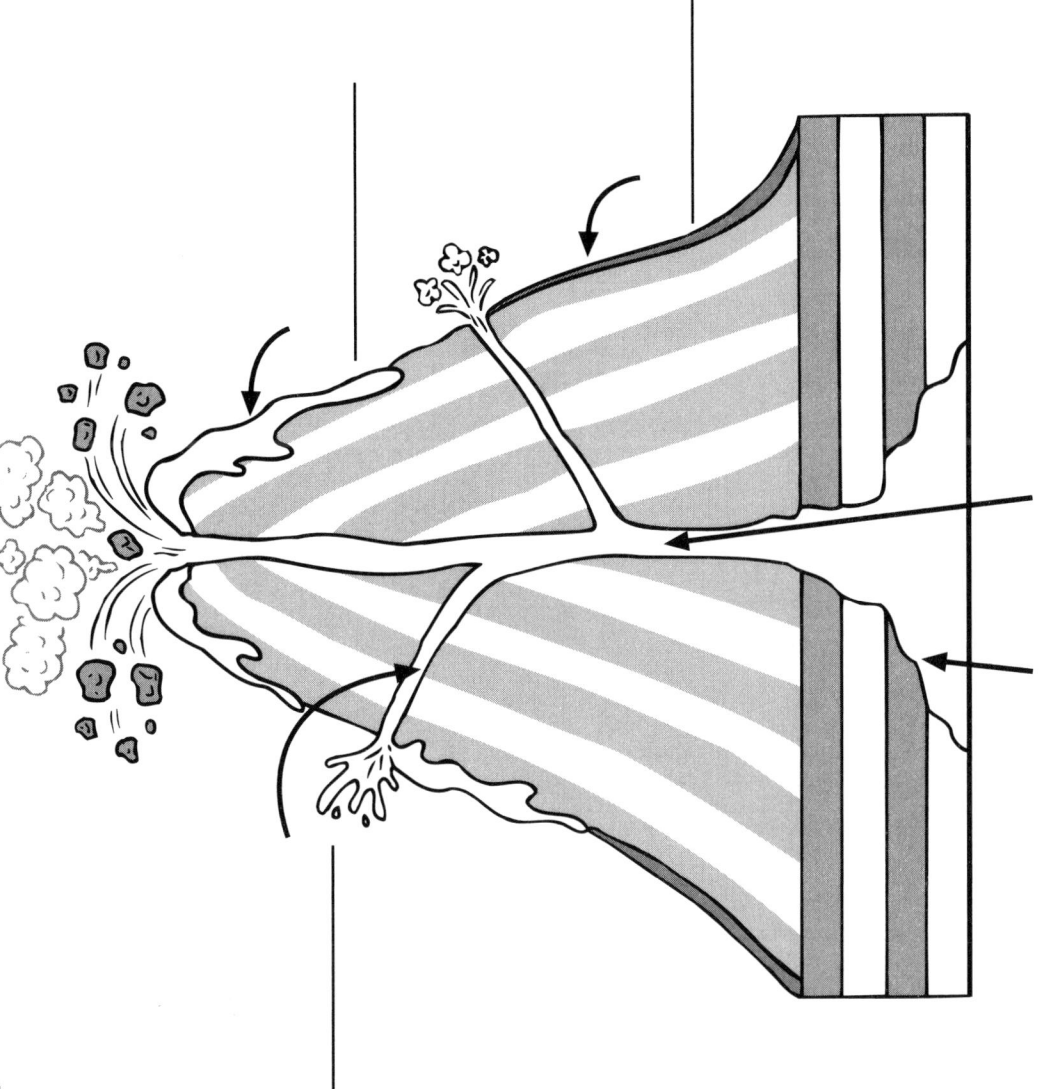

How a Volcano Is Formed

Extreme heat inside the earth melts rocks, and **magma** is formed. The melting rock produces gases, which mix with the magma. The gas-filled magma begins to rise. Pressure slowly builds as the magma pushes against surrounding rock. The magma is so hot that it melts some of the surrounding rocks along the way, forming a **conduit**, a tubelike passageway. The magma travels through the conduit until it blasts an opening, called a **vent**, through a weak area of the earth's surface. The gas is released, and the magma flows out of the vent as **lava**. The lava spills out onto the earth's surface. It eventually cools and hardens into **rock**.

Bonus Box: Find out where the word *volcano* comes from. Write your answer on the back of this sheet.

Answer Key

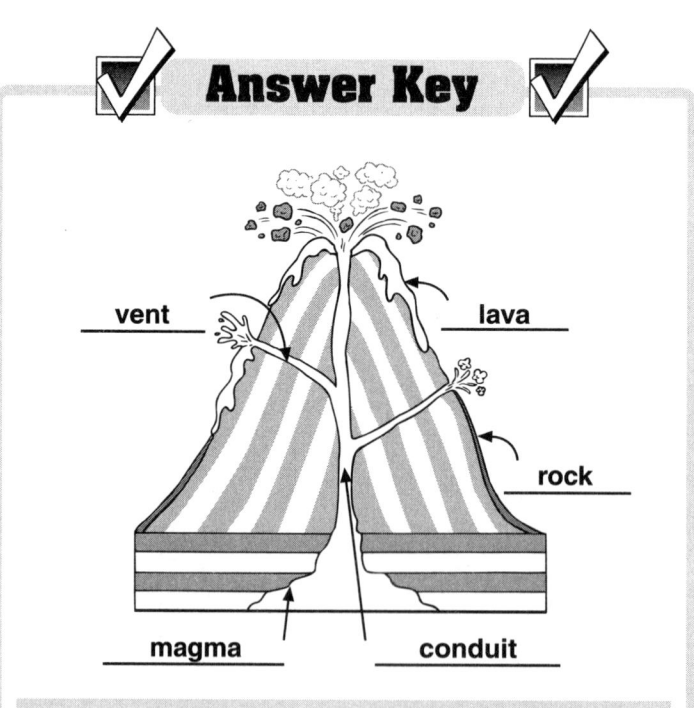

Bonus Box: The word volcano comes from the Roman god of fire, Vulcan. The ancient Romans believed that a volcano was a hot forge where Vulcan made swords and armor for the other gods.

Name _____ Earthquakes

"Earthshaking" "Facts"

Find out the facts about earthquakes. Use the word bank to help you complete each sentence.

1. An earthquake is a trembling or ☐ __ __ __ __ __ of the ground.

2. This shaking is caused by a sudden release of energy stored in the rocks __ __ __ __ ☐ __ __ the surface.

3. Earthquakes happen where the earth's crust is weak and there is a buildup of pressure under the __ __ __ __ ☐ __.

4. This pressure is caused by __ __ ☐ __ __ movements.

5. In a __ __ __ __ __ ☐ release of pressure, the rocks crack or shudder.

6. As the rocks move, they __ __ __ ☐ out vibrations that make the ground shake.

7. These vibrations, known as seismic waves, __ __ ☐ __ __ __ out from an underground point.

8. This __ __ __ ☐ __ __ __ __ __ __ point is called the focus.

9. The force of the __ ☐ __ __ __ depends on the depth of the focus, the strength of the surrounding rock, and how much the rocks move.

10. The nearer the focus is to the ☐ __ __ __ __ __, the greater the damage tends to be.

11. Two main types of waves radiate from the ☐ __ __ __ __: body waves and surface waves.

12. Body waves __ __ ☐ __ __ __ inside the earth, spreading out in all directions.

13. Surface waves travel on the earth's surface and __ __ ☐ __ __ more damage.

14. The waves sometimes make the land __ __ ☐ __ __ along a line called a fault.

15. At fault lines, rocks either slip down, get pushed up, or slide __ __ __ ☐ each other.

Word Bank

focus   split   underground
spread   shaking   cause
beneath   sudden   past
travel   waves   send
plate   surface   ground

What is the name of one of the earth's biggest faults? To find out, match the boxed letter in each sentence to a line below.
Hint: Capitalize the letters for 1, 4, and 11.

__ __ __   __ __ __ __ __ __ __
1 2 3   4 5 6 7 8 9 10

__ __ __ __ __
11 12 13 14 15

Bonus Box: Where is the fault named above located? Write your answer on the back of this sheet.

©The Education Center, Inc. • Big Book of Skill Builders • TEC60797   251

Answer Key

1. [s]hakin[g]
2. [b]ene[a][t]h
3. [g]rou[n]d
4. [p]l[a]te
5. [s]udde[n]
6. [s]en[d]
7. s[p][r]ead
8. [u]nd[e]rground
9. [w][a]ves
10. [s]urface
11. [f]ocus
12. [t]r[a]vel
13. [c]a[u]se
14. s[p][l]it
15. [p]as[t]

<u>S</u> <u>a</u> <u>n</u>   <u>A</u> <u>n</u> <u>d</u> <u>r</u> <u>e</u> <u>a</u> <u>s</u>
1   2   3   4   5   6   7   8   9   10

<u>F</u> <u>a</u> <u>u</u> <u>l</u> <u>t</u>
11   12   13   14   15

Bonus Box: off the coast of California

Name _____   Plate Tectonics

Picturing Plates

Geologists think that the earth's crust and upper mantle is not one sheet of solid rock. Instead it is divided into large pieces, called *plates.* These plates slowly "drift" around like icebergs on the ocean. Geologists have identified three types of plate boundary movements—*divergent, convergent,* and *transform.*

Directions: Study each picture below. Then read the facts about the plate movements. Color the circle(s) that matches each fact.

D = Divergent   C = Convergent   T = Transform

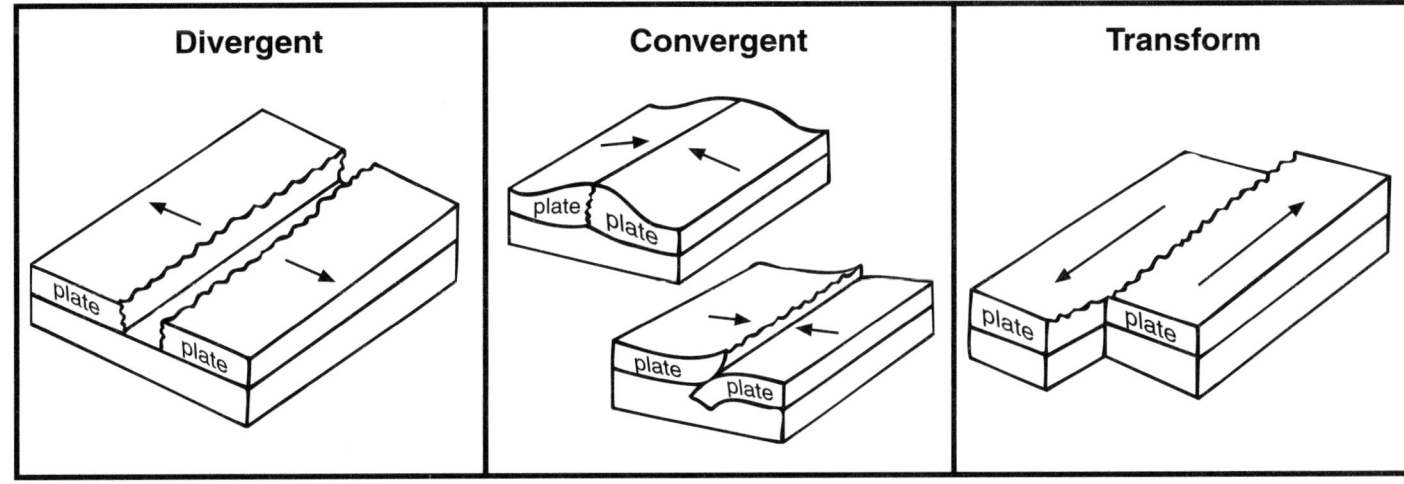

1. These plates slowly spread apart.   D C T

2. These plates *collide,* or are pushed together.   D C T

3. These plates slide past each other in opposite directions.   D C T

4. Earthquakes can accompany these types of plate movements.   D C T

5. New oceanic crust can form at places in the ocean where two plates pull apart from each other.   D C T

6. When two plates carrying continents crash into each other, the edges of both plates can crumple and form mountain ranges.   D C T

7. Sometimes these plates move sideways past each other and create a break in the earth's crust called a *fault.*   D C T

8. Volcanoes can form along the edges when these types of plate movements occur.   D C T

9. Sometimes one of the plate edges sinks below the other in this type of movement.   D C T

10. This type of plate movement may create new seas when ocean water fills the gap between the plates.   D C T

Bonus Box: An *analogy* compares a likeness between two objects that are otherwise unlike. Complete this analogy: *plate* is to _____ as *iceberg* is to ocean.

©The Education Center, Inc. • Big Book of Skill Builders • TEC60797

Answer Key

1. **D** C T
2. **D** **C** T
3. **D** C **T**
4. **D** **C** **T**
5. **D** C T
6. D **C** T
7. D C **T**
8. **D** **C** **T**
9. D **C** T
10. **D** C T

Bonus Box: *Plate* is to <u>Earth</u> as *iceberg* is to ocean.

254

Outer Space

Spotlight on Space

Name _____

Date _____

Shine your spotlight on the activities that follow to learn fascinating facts about outer space!

©The Education Center, Inc. • *Big Book of Skill Builders* • TEC60797

Spotlight on Space

Activity 1

Planetary Comparisons

Write the number for each fact in the appropriate blank. Then write <, >, or = in each circle to make the sentence true. Use an encyclopedia if you need help.

1. number of moons of Uranus _____ ◯ _____ number of moons of Neptune

2. miles Venus is from the Sun _____ ◯ _____ miles Uranus is from the Sun

3. length of Mercury's year _____ ◯ _____ length of Venus's year

4. average surface temperature of Venus _____ ◯ _____ average surface temperature of Earth

5. diameter of Neptune _____ ◯ _____ diameter of Saturn

6. number of moons of Earth _____ ◯ _____ number of moons of Pluto

7. number of days it takes Mars to orbit the Sun _____ ◯ _____ number of days it takes Mercury to orbit the Sun

8. number of outer planets _____ ◯ _____ number of inner planets

©The Education Center, Inc. • *Big Book of Skill Builders* • TEC60797

255

How to Use Pages 255-260

1. Direct each student to cut each page in half along the bold line. Have the student color the cover page, fill in the appropriate information, and compile the remaining pages in the correct order. Staple students' booklets along the left side of the pages.
2. Assign one booklet activity per day. Or assign the booklet as a week-long take-home activity. After students complete all the activities, discuss their answers.

 Answer Key

1. 15 > 8
2. 67 million < 1,780 million
3. 88 Earth days < 243 Earth days
4. 869°F > 59°F
5. 30,690 < 74,400
6. 1 = 1
7. 687 Earth days > 88 Earth days
8. 5 > 4

Outer Space

Spotlight on Space

Activity 2

Round and Round They Go

A planet is an object that revolves around a star. The nine planets in our solar system orbit the sun. Planets are dark, solid bodies while stars are huge balls of hot gases. Stars also produce their own light and heat while most planets do not. Planets are illuminated by the sun's rays and receive most of their light and heat from the sun. They can only be seen because they reflect the sun's light.

All the planets revolve around the sun in the same direction. They move in oval-shaped paths; therefore, they are a little closer to the sun at some points in their orbits than in others. Planets also rotate as they orbit the sun. The planets closest to the sun are called the *inner planets.* These are Mercury, Venus, Earth, and Mars. Jupiter, Saturn, Uranus, Neptune, and Pluto make up the *outer planets.* Except for Pluto, the outer planets are much larger than the inner planets.

Directions: Answer the following items on the back of this page.

1. Describe three features of a planet.
2. Is the sun a star? Write yes or no; then explain your answer.
3. What would happen to a planet in our solar system if there were no sun?
4. Name two differences between the inner and outer planets.
5. Find a word in the second paragraph that is a synonym for *revolve*.
6. Why is a planet closer to the sun at different times in its orbit?
7. What do you think happens when a planet is closer to the sun?
8. Look at the title of this passage. What could be another name for it?

©The Education Center, Inc. • Big Book of Skill Builders • TEC60797

Spotlight on Space

Activity 3

Out-of-This-World Analogies

An **analogy** shows a likeness between two objects that are otherwise unlike. Read each analogy below. Think about how the words in the first pair go together; then write the missing word in the second pair. Use an encyclopedia if you need help.

Example: *Cat* is to *kitten* as *dog* is to _____.
Think: A kitten is a baby cat, so what is a baby dog?
Answer: a *puppy* (They are both baby animals.)

1. *Earth* is to *planet* as *sun* is to _____.
2. *Venus* is to *hot* as *Pluto* is to _____.
3. *Moon* is to *satellite* as *Earth* is to _____.
4. *Sun* is to *planet* as _____ is to *moon*.
5. *Venus* is to *second* as _____ is to *eighth*.
6. *Earth* is to *inner* as *Jupiter* is to _____.
7. *Galaxy* is to *stars* as *forest* is to _____.
8. *Ship* is to *sea* as _____ is to *space*.

©The Education Center, Inc. • Big Book of Skill Builders • TEC60797

257

Answer Key

"Round and Round They Go"
1. A planet revolves around a star. It is dark and solid. It does not produce its own light or heat, but receives each from the sun. A planet revolves around the sun in an oval-shaped path and rotates as it revolves.
2. Yes. The sun is a star because it produces its own light and heat. The planets in our solar system revolve around it.
3. If there were no sun in our solar system, we would have no light or heat.
4. The inner planets are closer to the sun, and they are smaller than the outer planets (except Pluto).
5. *Orbit* is a synonym for *revolve.*
6. A planet is closer to the sun at different times in its orbit because the orbit follows an oval-shaped path.
7. When a planet is closer to the sun, it receives more heat and light.
8. Answers will vary. Accept reasonable responses. Another name for this passage could be "Planets and Stars."

"Out-of-This-World Analogies"
Some answers may vary. Accept reasonable responses.
1. star
2. cold
3. planet
4. planet
5. Neptune
6. outer
7. trees
8. shuttle

Spotlight on Space — Activity 4

Riddled With Space Facts

Read each clue below. Write the correct word from the word box in each blank. Then use the numbered letters to solve the riddle at the bottom of the page. Use a dictionary or encyclopedia if you need help.

Word Box
nebula crater eclipse asteroid waning fireball meteor constellation

Clues:

1. I am a bowl-shaped hole found on the moon's surface. ___ ___ ___ ___ ___ ___
                                                                        4
2. I happen when one object is in the shadow of another. ___ ___ ___ ___ ___ ___ ___
                                                                  1
3. I am a small body of burning rock or metal that travels through the solar system.
   ___ ___ ___ ___ ___ ___
         2
4. I am a cloud of dust and gas in space from which a star is born. ___ ___ ___ ___ ___ ___
                                                                              7
5. I am a group of stars that make up a pattern in the night sky.
   ___ ___ ___ ___ ___ ___ ___ ___ ___ ___ ___ ___ ___
                   8
6. I am a very large, brightly lit meteor that is often reported as a UFO.
   ___ ___ ___ ___ ___ ___ ___ ___
     6   9
7. I am one of thousands of rocky objects orbiting the sun between Mars and Jupiter. Some scientists believe I am a piece of a planet that broke apart. ___ ___ ___ ___ ___ ___ ___ ___
                                                                                              5
8. I am one of the phases of the moon. The moon appears to shrink because its face gets covered by the shadow of Earth. ___ ___ ___ ___ ___ ___
                                              3

Riddle: Why was the moon not hungry? ___ ___ ___ ___ ___ ___ ___ ___ ___ !
                                           1   2   3   4   5   6   7   8   9

Spotlight on Space — Activity 5

Mixed-Up Missions

Little Nancy Noitall was writing a research paper about five astronauts and the space missions in which they were involved. While she was stargazing one evening, Nancy's cat, Orbit, shredded her notes to pieces! Help Nancy put the pieces back together by solving the puzzle below.

Directions: Read the clues. Then match each astronaut with his or her mission by placing a ✓ in the grid. Mark an X to show each mission the astronaut did not complete.

Clues:

1. These astronauts did not participate in the following missions: John Glenn—*Gemini-Titan 2*, Neil Armstrong—Mercury *Friendship 7*, Pete Conrad—*Challenger*, Sally Ride—*Skylab*.

2. Neil Armstrong was not involved with the *Gemini-Titan 2* mission.

3. John Young was one of the four *Gemini-Titan 2* astronauts.

4. Neither John Glenn nor Neil Armstrong participated in the *Challenger* and *Skylab* missions that Nancy Noitall wrote about.

	John Glenn	John Young	Neil Armstrong	Pete Conrad	Sally Ride
Gemini-Titan 2					
Apollo 11					
Mercury *Friendship 7*					
Challenger					
Skylab					

"Riddled With Space Facts"

Clues:
1. I am a bowl-shaped hole found on the moon's surface. __c__ __r__ __a__ __t__ __e__ __r__
2. I happen when one object is in the shadow of another. __e__ __c__ __l__ __i__ __p__ __s__ __e__
                                                                        4   1
3. I am a small body of burning rock or metal that travels through the solar system.
   __m__ __e__ __t__ __e__ __o__ __r__
       2
4. I am a cloud of dust and gas in space from which a star is born. __n__ __e__ __b__ __u__ __l__ __a__
                                                                                              7
5. I am a group of stars that make up a pattern in the night sky.
   __c__ __o__ __n__ __s__ __t__ __e__ __l__ __l__ __a__ __t__ __i__ __o__ __n__
                                    8
6. I am a very large, brightly lit meteor that is often reported as a UFO.
   __f__ __i__ __r__ __e__ __b__ __a__ __l__ __l__
       6   9
7. I am one of thousands of rocky objects orbiting the sun between Mars and Jupiter. Some scientists believe I am a piece of a planet that broke apart. __a__ __s__ __t__ __e__ __r__ __o__ __i__ __d__
                                                                                                                     5
8. I am one of the phases of the moon. The moon appears to shrink because its face gets covered by the shadow of Earth. __w__ __a__ __n__ __i__ __n__ __g__
                                                                                                    3

Riddle: Why was the moon not hungry?

I	t		w	a	s		f	u	l	l	!
1	2		3	4	5		6	7	8	9	

"Mixed-Up Missions"

	John Glenn	John Young	Neil Armstrong	Pete Conrad	Sally Ride
Gemini-Titan 2	X	✔	X	X	X
Apollo 11	X	X	✔	X	X
Mercury Friendship 7	✔	X	X	X	X
Challenger	X	X	X	X	✔
Skylab	X	X	X	✔	X

Storm Smarts

So, just how high is your storm IQ? Put your storm smarts to the test! A *storm* usually refers to unpleasant or destructive weather. Listed below are 21 clues about four different storms: tornadoes, hurricanes, thunderstorms, and blizzards.

Directions: Read each clue. Decide which storm each clue describes. Write the clue under the correct storm heading. Then cross it off the list. The first one has been done for you.

- ~~can only begin in the tropics in summer~~
- are snows driven by high winds
- are also called *twisters*
- occur mostly in spring or early summer
- have winds that swirl around the *eye*, a calm area in the storm's center
- can last anywhere from a few hours to days
- contain lightning—an electrical discharge
- contain the most violent of all winds
- have wind speeds at least 35 mph and temperatures lower than 20°F
- can form in minutes with little or no warning
- have centers like vacuums
- occur when a cold air mass moves out of the Arctic
- are the most powerful electrical storms in the atmosphere
- have the strongest winds and heaviest rains surrounding their centers
- occur suddenly in polar regions
- sometimes create tornadoes
- can contain rain or hail
- form where sea temperatures are at least 82°F
- can occur in the northern U.S. Great Plains and in eastern and central Canada
- usually weaken as they move over land
- are called *waterspouts* when formed over lakes or oceans

Tornadoes:
-
-
-
-
-
-

Blizzards:
-
-
-
-
-
-

Thunderstorms:
-
-
-
-

Hurricanes:
- *can only begin in the tropics in summer*
-
-
-
-

Bonus Box: Choose a storm. Then, using the details listed, write a paragraph describing the storm. Be sure to include a main idea sentence. Write your paragraph on the back of this sheet.

Answer Key

Thunderstorms:
- contain lightning—an electrical discharge
- are the most powerful electrical storms in the atmosphere
- sometimes create tornadoes
- can contain rain or hail

Hurricanes:
- can only begin in the tropics in summer
- have winds that swirl around the *eye,* a calm area in the storm's center
- have the strongest winds and heaviest rains surrounding their centers
- form where sea temperatures are at least 82°F
- usually weaken as they move over land

Tornadoes:
- are also called *twisters*
- occur mostly in spring or early summer
- contain the most violent of all winds
- can form in minutes with little or no warning
- have centers like vacuums
- are called *waterspouts* when formed over lakes or oceans

Blizzards:
- are snows driven by high winds
- can last anywhere from a few hours to days
- have wind speeds at least 35 mph and temperatures lower than 20°F
- occur when a cold air mass moves out of the Arctic
- occur suddenly in polar regions
- can occur in the northern U.S. Great Plains and in eastern and central Canada

Name _____   Electricity

Generating Electricity

Directions: The paragraph below explains how electricity gets from power plants into homes and businesses. Each illustration at the bottom of the page shows a step in this process. Read the paragraph carefully. Then cut out each illustration. On another sheet of paper, glue the illustrations in the correct order. Then write a sentence below each illustration explaining each step.

The Development of Power Plants

In earlier days, electrical current had to be generated very close to where the electricity was going to be used. So each town or city had its own small power plant. Electricity generated at these small power plants sometimes had to be sent over long distances. But transmitting electricity over long distances caused a large amount of energy to be lost as it traveled along cables. Transmitting electricity with greater force (voltage) helped solve this problem but also created a new one. The high-voltage electricity could not be safely used in homes or businesses. In the 1880s, both the United States and Hungary developed a piece of equipment called a transformer that could increase (step up) or decrease (step down) the voltage as needed. The creation of the transformer meant that power plants near sources of energy, such as coal fields or rivers, could safely send electricity to homes and businesses hundreds of miles away.

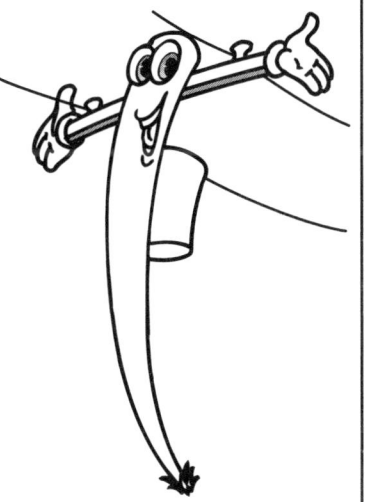

©The Education Center, Inc. • *Big Book of Skill Builders* • TEC60797

Overhead Cables
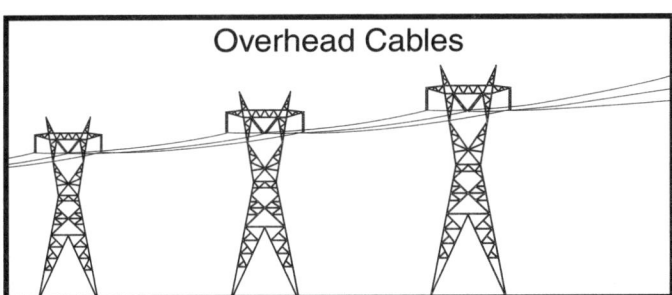

Step-Down Transformer
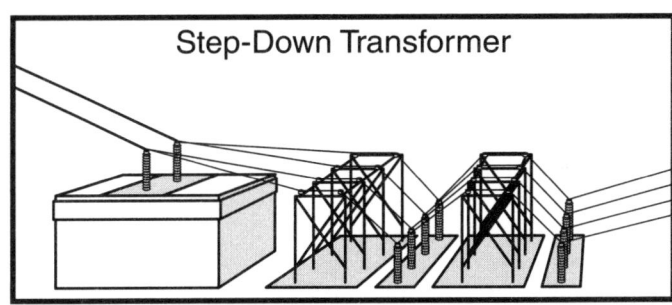

Homes or Businesses
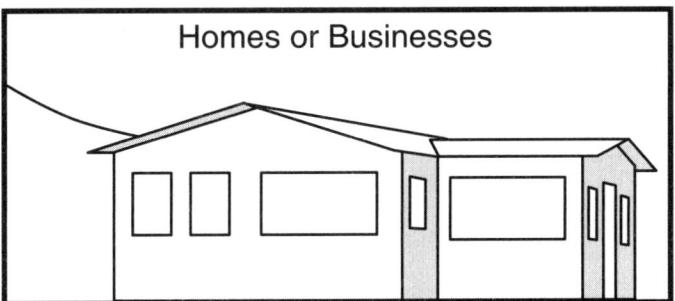

Step-Up Transformer
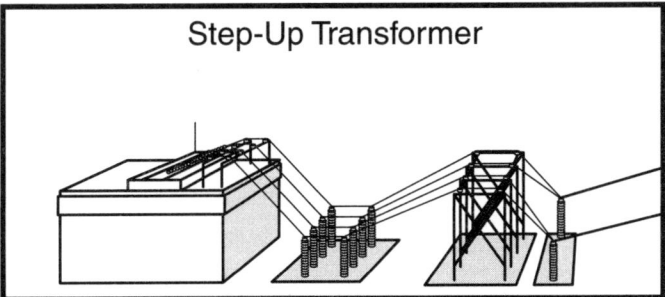

Power Plant
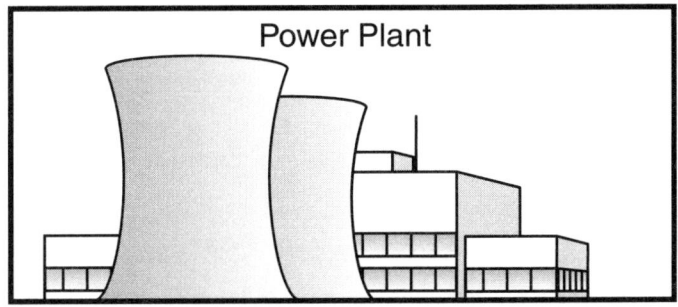

How to Use Page 263

1. Provide each student with a copy of page 263, a 9"x12" sheet of construction paper, a pair of scissors, and glue.
2. Discuss the directions on page 263. Have each student complete the page as directed; then share students' answers.

 **Answer Key**

The illustrations should be arranged in the order shown below. Students' sentences may vary.

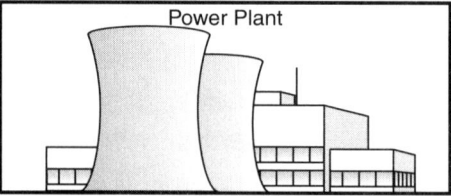

A power plant generates electricity.

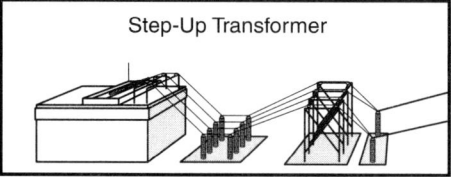

Electricity is transmitted at a high voltage from step-up transformers.

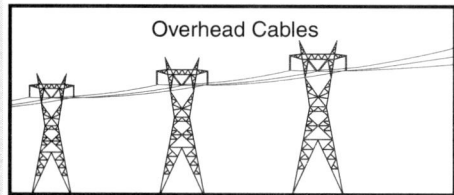

Overhead cables carry the electrical current.

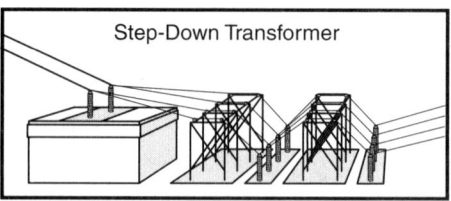

Step-down transformers lower voltage for safe use in homes and businesses.

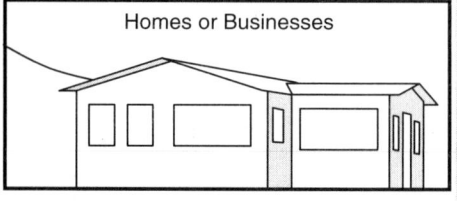

Homes and businesses receive electricity.

Name _____

Simple Circuits

How does an electrical circuit work? It's simple! In order for the circuit to work, there has to be a complete path from the source of power (the bottom of the battery) through the load, or energy receiver (the lightbulb), and back to the source.

Directions: Illustrated below are eight different ways to connect a battery and a bulb. Only four will make the bulb light up. Look at each drawing carefully. Check the "Yes" box if the connection will light the bulb. Check the "No" box if the connection will not light the bulb; then explain why it will not.

1. ☐ Yes ☐ No _____

2. ☐ Yes ☐ No _____

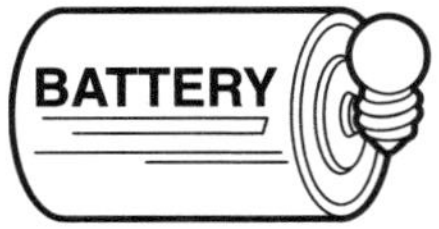

3. ☐ Yes ☐ No _____

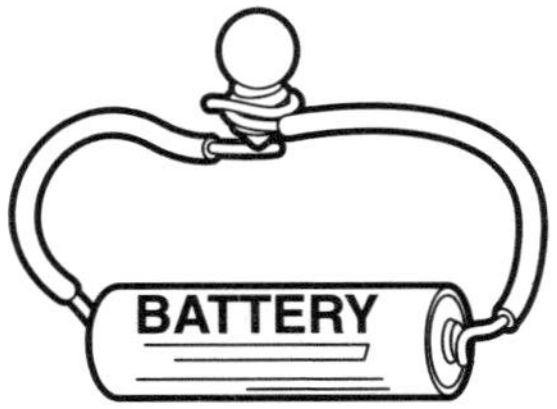

4. ☐ Yes ☐ No _____

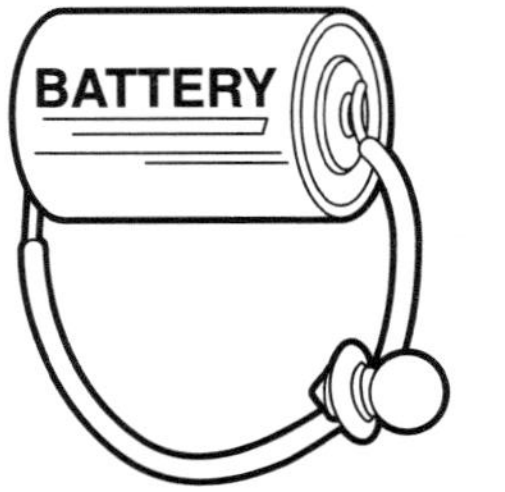

5. ☐ Yes ☐ No _____

6. ☐ Yes ☐ No _____

7. ☐ Yes ☐ No _____

8. ☐ Yes ☐ No _____

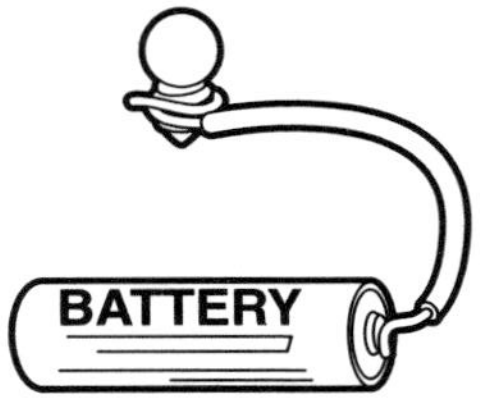

Answer Key

1. Yes
2. No—There is not a complete path from the source of power (the bottom of the battery) through the load (lightbulb) and back to the source.
3. Yes
4. No—There is not a complete path from the source of power (the bottom of the battery) through the load (lightbulb) and back to the source. Also the wire's plastic coating is still covering the wire and the wire is not touching the metal base of the bulb.
5. No—There is not a complete path from the source of power (the bottom of the battery) through the load (lightbulb) and back to the source. The wire has to be touching the metal base at the bottom of the lightbulb.
6. Yes
7. Yes
8. No—There is not a complete path from the source of power (the bottom of the battery) through the load (lightbulb) and back to the source.

Name _____ The Lightbulb

Let There Be Light!

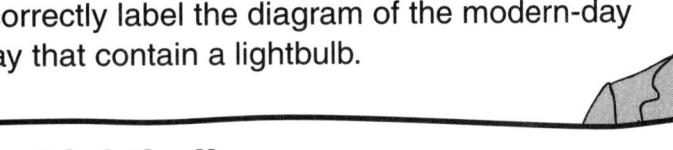

Directions: Below is a brief history of the lightbulb. Read the paragraphs carefully. Then use the boldfaced words to correctly label the diagram of the modern-day bulb. Afterward list items used today that contain a lightbulb.

The Lightbulb

At 1:30 A.M. on October 21, 1879, a group of people gathered in Thomas Alva Edison's laboratory in New Jersey. Edison was about to turn on his newest invention—a glass vacuum globe that would produce light. Edison's **bulb** contained a thin filament of carbon made by burning a thread of cotton. The **filament** was supported by a **wire frame.** The bulb and a **gas** inside the bulb kept the filament from burning out too quickly. The **base** held the bulb in its fixture and connected it to an electric circuit.

The invention worked! The bulb burned for 13 hours before the glass finally cracked. Edison knew that his invention would revolutionize the world. But, he soon realized that it wouldn't be enough to just sell everyone a bulb. There were no generating plants to supply electricity to light it. Edison turned his efforts to designing a generator and organizing a public supply of electricity.

Parts of a Lightbulb

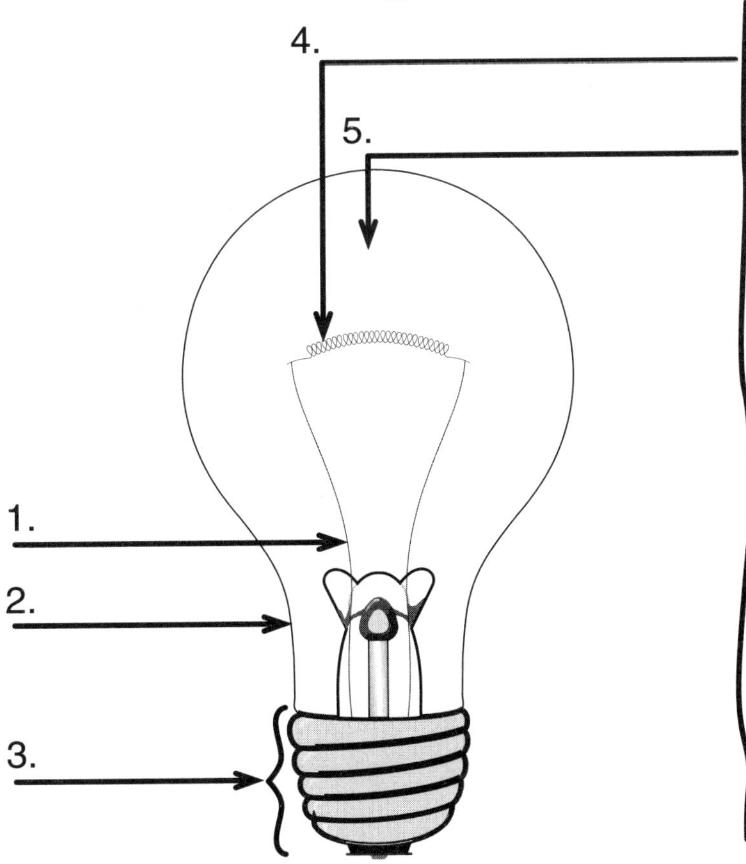

4. _____
5. _____
1. _____
2. _____
3. _____

Items That Contain a Lightbulb

1. flashlights
2. _____
3. _____
4. _____
5. _____
6. _____
7. _____
8. _____
9. _____
10. _____

Bonus Box: What would life be like if Edison's invention didn't work? On the back of this sheet, write a story describing a day in your life without the lightbulb.

Answer Key

Parts of a Lightbulb
1. wire frame
2. bulb
3. base
4. filament
5. gas

Items That Contain a Lightbulb
Answers will vary.
1. flashlights
2. night-lights
3. streetlights
4. car headlights
5. Christmas lights
6. camera flashes
7. marquees
8. lighthouses
9. pinball machines
10. refrigerators

Name _____

Animal Movement

Mammals on the Move

Pam L. Camel is having a special series showcasing how mammals move. On each clipboard below, she has written the special features a mammal may have that help it move about in its environment. Use the mammals' pictures to help Pam decide on which show each one will be featured. Write each mammal's name on the correct clipboard. The first one is done for you.

Show 1: LAND
four legs for walking or hopping
_____
_____

Show 2: TREES
hands, feet, and sometimes tails
_____
_____

Show 3: WATER
streamlined bodies, tails, and flippers
sea lion
_____

Show 4: AIR
wings made of skin and bones
_____
_____

okapi

jackrabbit

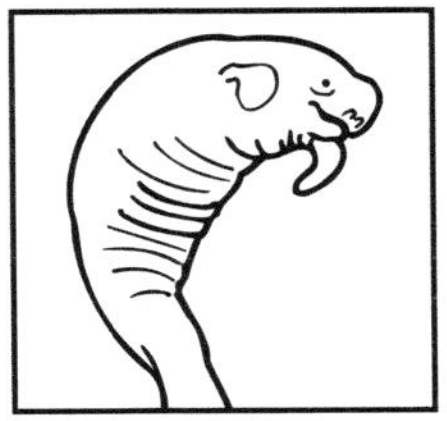

elephant seal

elephant

ring-tailed lemur

flying fox

manatee

llama

vampire bat

chimpanzee

sea lion

killer whale

Bonus Box: Which animal above do you think is a relative of the camel? On the back of this sheet, write the name of the animal and explain your answer. If desired, research your answer to see if you are correct.

©The Education Center, Inc. • *Big Book of Skill Builders* • TEC60797

Answer Key

Land: llama, elephant, jackrabbit, okapi
Trees: ring-tailed lemur, chimpanzee
Water: sea lion, manatee, elephant seal, killer whale
Air: vampire bat, flying fox

Bonus Box: the llama

Name_____ Animal Movement

SPEEDY SOLUTIONS!

Sometimes a speedy getaway is the best way for an animal to defend itself against an enemy! Study the graph and read the problems below. Fill in each blank with a word or phrase from the Word Bank that completes the problem. Use each word or phrase once.

Animal Speeds in Miles per Hour

Animal	Speed
killer whale	35
cheetah	70
sailfish	68
dragonfly	36
zebra	40
rabbit	35
grizzly bear	30
squirrel	12
impala	50
cat	30

Word Bank

greater   twice   increase   decreased
half   more than   in all   equal

1. A cheetah's speed is _____ as fast as a killer whale's.

2. If an impala runs 25 miles per hour, it's running _____ as fast as its top speed.

3. If a sailfish swimming at its fastest speed slows to 40 mph, it has _____ its speed by 28 mph.

4. To catch up to a zebra running at top speed, a dragonfly must _____ its speed by four mph.

5. A rabbit fleeing a grizzly bear must run _____ 30 mph.

6. If a killer whale increases its maximum speed by 33 mph, it will travel at a speed _____ to a sailfish's top speed.

7. An impala that runs for 150 miles at a speed of 50 mph has run three hours _____.

8. If a human being can run about 28 mph, nine of the animals can travel at _____ speeds.

©The Education Center, Inc. • Big Book of Skill Builders • TEC60797

Answer Key

1. twice
2. half
3. decreased
4. increase
5. more than
6. equal
7. in all
8. greater

Name _____ Animal Adaptations

FITTING FEATURES

Do you remember what the Big Bad Wolf told Little Red Riding Hood after she said he had very big eyes? ("Better to see you with, my dear!") Well, what the wolf said was very fitting! Animals have special body parts or features that help them **S**ense their environment, **M**ove, **E**at, **C**ommunicate, and **D**efend themselves. Together these features help animals survive.

Directions: Read each animal feature described below. Then fill in the footprint that shows how the feature helps the animal in its environment. (**S** = Sense their environment, **M** = Move, etc.) The first one is done for you.

	S	M	E	C	D
1. The tree-inhabiting gibbon has arms twice as long as its body and long, curved fingers.		●			
2. An African elephant has huge earflaps that it moves in different positions.					
3. Alligators have eyes that stick up above their skulls.					
4. Some goats living in the mountains have hooves with very sharp edges and hollows in the soles.					
5. An armadillo is covered with small plates made of toughened skin.					
6. Beavers have webbed back feet and tails like paddles.					
7. The African fish eagle has sharp talons.					
8. The male mandrill has a bright scarlet and blue face.					
9. The long-eared bat's ears are almost as long as its body.					
10. A snowshoe rabbit's broad feet have long hairs along the sides and between the toes.					
11. The honey possum's tongue is covered with tiny, brush-like bristles.					
12. The star-nosed mole has 22 small tentacles surrounding its nose.					

Bonus Box: If you were an animal, what features would you have to sense the environment, move, eat, communicate, and defend yourself? Write a description of each feature on the back of this sheet.

©The Education Center, Inc. • *Big Book of Skill Builders* • TEC60797

Answer Key

Accept reasonable responses.

1. **M;** The long arms help the gibbon move quickly through trees by swinging. Its long, curved fingers allow it to firmly grip branches.
2. **C and D;** Elephants beat their earflaps on their backs to communicate with their young. They also spread out their earflaps to scare off their enemies.
3. **S;** This feature allows alligators to see above the water while their bodies are below it.
4. **M;** The sharp edges of their hooves help goats dig into the cracks of rocks. The hollows in their soles act as suction cups. Both features give the goats secure footholds.
5. **D;** The armadillo rolls up into a ball and uses the plates to protect itself if threatened.
6. **M;** These features help the beaver to move about in the water.
7. **E;** The African fish eagle uses its talons to snatch up fish.
8. **C and D;** The male mandrill has a bright scarlet and blue face to scare off its rivals.
9. **S and E;** The long-eared bat uses its ears to locate prey in the dark.
10. **M;** The rabbit's broad feet keep it from sinking in the snow. The hairs help it grip the ground.
11. **E;** Pollen sticks to the possum's bristly tongue as it feeds.
12. **S;** The tentacles help the mole find its way underground by touch.

Name _____   Animal Defenses

WHAT'S THEIR DEFENSE?

Agent Armadillo is a member of the CSA (Central Security Agency). He needs help determining the different ways animals protect themselves. Read each animal action described below. Decide which defense listed on the briefcase the animal is using. Write your answers in the spaces provided. Use each answer once.

Animal Defenses

- avoidance
- camouflage
- chemical defense
- escape
- fright
- group defense
- playing dead
- protective body parts
- special weapons

1. A skunk squirts a horrible-smelling liquid on its attacker.

2. A hedgehog rolls up into a ball. Its sharp spines cover the softer parts of its body.

3. A frilled lizard raises its special folds of skin. It makes an attacker think it is larger.

4. A leaf insect looks almost exactly like a leaf.

5. Musk oxen defend their calves by standing in a circle with their horns facing outward.

6. A North American opossum closes its eyes and becomes totally limp in the presence of an enemy.

7. Caribou have antlers that are large enough to fend off grizzly bears.

8. An impala can run at a speed of 50 miles per hour.

9. A gibbon stays off the ground. It spends its entire life in the trees.

Bonus Box: Look at the picture of Agent Armadillo. What feature does he have to protect himself from an attacker? Write your answer on the back of this sheet. Then name two other animals that use the same defense.

©The Education Center, Inc. • Big Book of Skill Builders • TEC60797   275

Answer Key

1. chemical defense
2. protective body parts
3. fright
4. camouflage
5. group defense
6. playing dead
7. special weapons
8. escape
9. avoidance

Bonus Box: The armadillo is covered by small plates of toughened skin to protect more delicate parts of its body. A turtle and a crab also have tough outer coverings.

Name _____ Skeletal System

This Joint Is Jumpin'!

You've got the moves, and it's your joints that give 'em to you! A *joint* is a place in your body where two or more bones meet. There are two main types of joints: fixed joints and movable joints. Follow the directions below to help you learn more about these movable mechanisms in your body.

Directions: Use the Joint Jukebox to help you correctly label each joint location in the diagram. Next read the descriptions of the three main kinds of movable joints. Then, using the color code, lightly color each box to correctly identify the joint type.

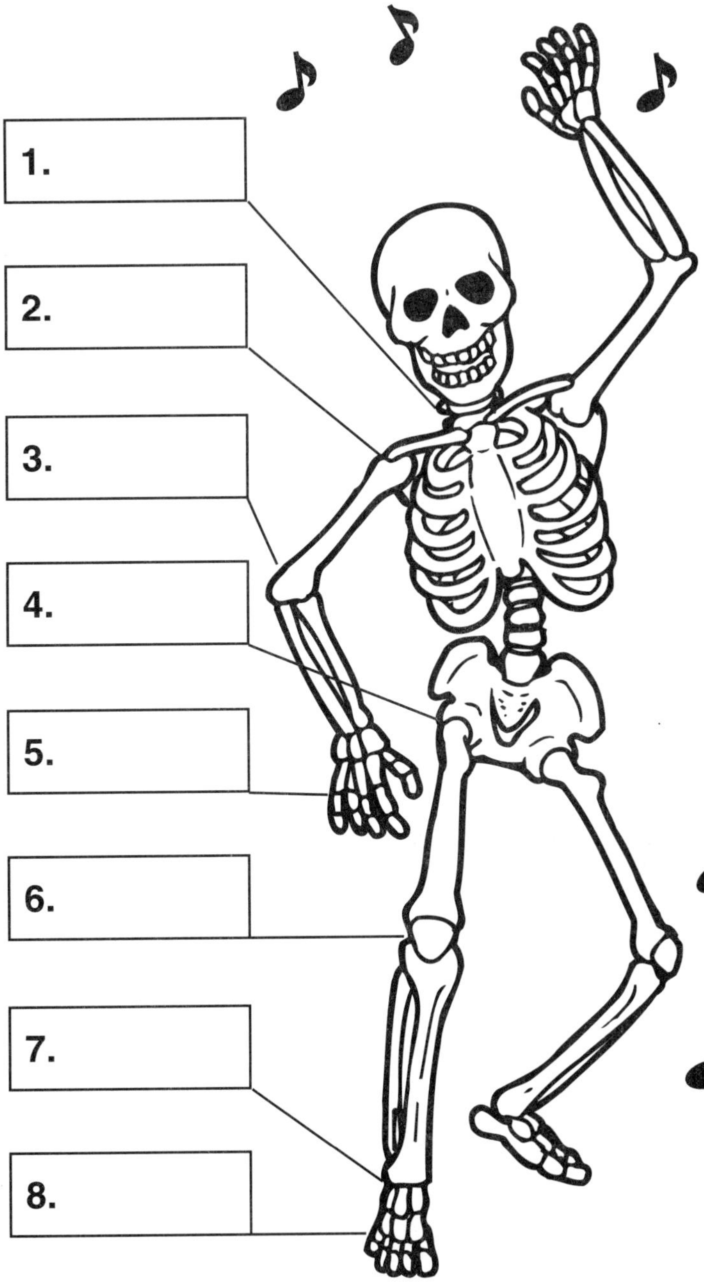

Joint	Description	Color
Ball-and-socket	Ball-shaped bone rotates in a cup-shaped bone, allowing movement in any direction	Blue
Hinge	Allows bending and straightening only, like the hinges that allow a door to open and close	Red
Pivot	Rod of one bone fits into a ring of another, allowing a swiveling or rotating motion	Green

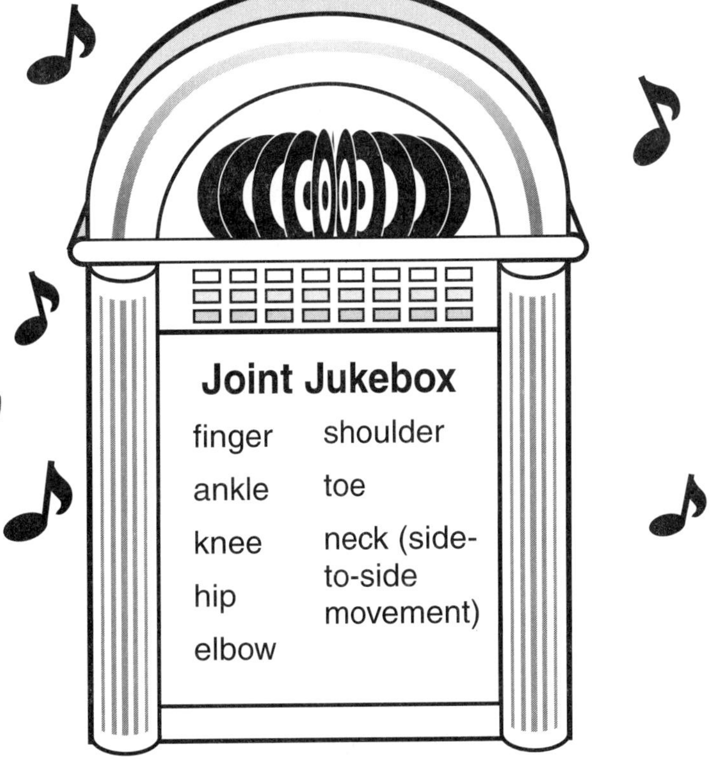

1. _____
2. _____
3. _____
4. _____
5. _____
6. _____
7. _____
8. _____

Joint Jukebox

finger   shoulder
ankle   toe
knee   neck (side-to-side movement)
hip
elbow

Bonus Box: Choose one of the joints in your skeletal system. Imagine that it suddenly changes into another type of joint. Describe the effects of the change on what you could and could not do.

©The Education Center, Inc. • Big Book of Skill Builders • TEC60797

Answer Key

1. neck: pivot (green)
2. shoulder: ball-and-socket (blue)
3. elbow: hinge (red)
4. hip: ball-and-socket (blue)
5. finger: hinge (red)
6. knee: hinge (red)
7. ankle: hinge (red)
8. toe: hinge (red)

Name _____   Respiratory System

The Respiratory Shuffle

Step to the rhythm of the respiratory shuffle and find out just how this system works! Cut out the steps of respiration at the bottom of the page. Place each step in the correct order. Use reference materials for help, if needed. When you are sure of your answers, glue each step in place.

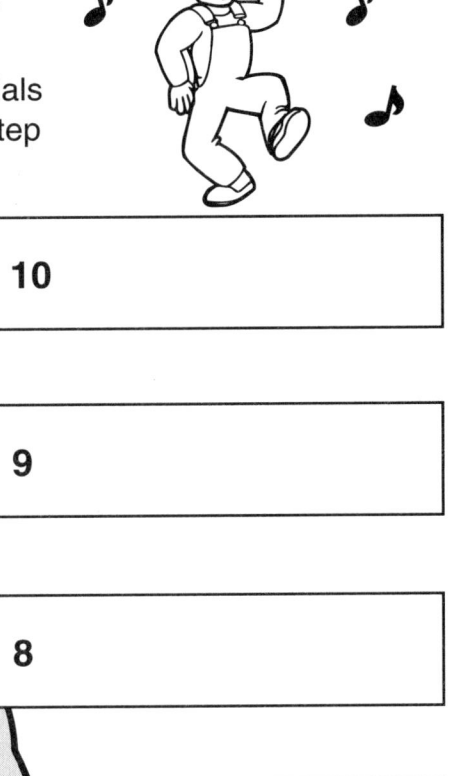

1.
2.
3.
4.
5.
6.
7.
8.
9.
10.

Bonus Box: Explain how smoking and air pollution cause problems with the respiratory system.

©The Education Center, Inc. • *Big Book of Skill Builders* • TEC60797

- Carbon dioxide leaves the body when you exhale.

Oxygen leaves the air sacs and passes into the bloodstream through capillaries.	Carbon dioxide enters the lungs by way of the capillaries and air sacs.
Air travels through many smaller branches from the bronchial tubes.	Air travels down two bronchial tubes, each leading to a lung.
Carbon dioxide is passed from the air sacs into the bronchial tubes.	Carbon dioxide, a waste product, is picked up from body tissues and carried through the bloodstream to the lungs.
Air enters the nose as you inhale.	Air enters the windpipe, or *trachea*.

- Air flows into the air sacs at the end of the tiny branches.

Answer Key

1. Air enters the nose as you inhale.
2. Air enters the windpipe, or *trachea*.
3. Air travels down two bronchial tubes, each leading to a lung.
4. Air travels through many smaller branches from the bronchial tubes.
5. Air flows into the air sacs at the end of the tiny branches.
6. Oxygen leaves the air sacs and passes into the bloodstream through capillaries.
7. Carbon dioxide, a waste product, is picked up from body tissues and carried through the bloodstream to the lungs.
8. Carbon dioxide enters the lungs by way of the capillaries and air sacs.
9. Carbon dioxide is passed from the air sacs into the bronchial tubes.
10. Carbon dioxide leaves the body when you exhale.

Bonus Box: Students' answers may vary. Smoking and other pollutants can cause damage to the lungs by making it harder to breathe, making the lungs work harder and less efficiently.

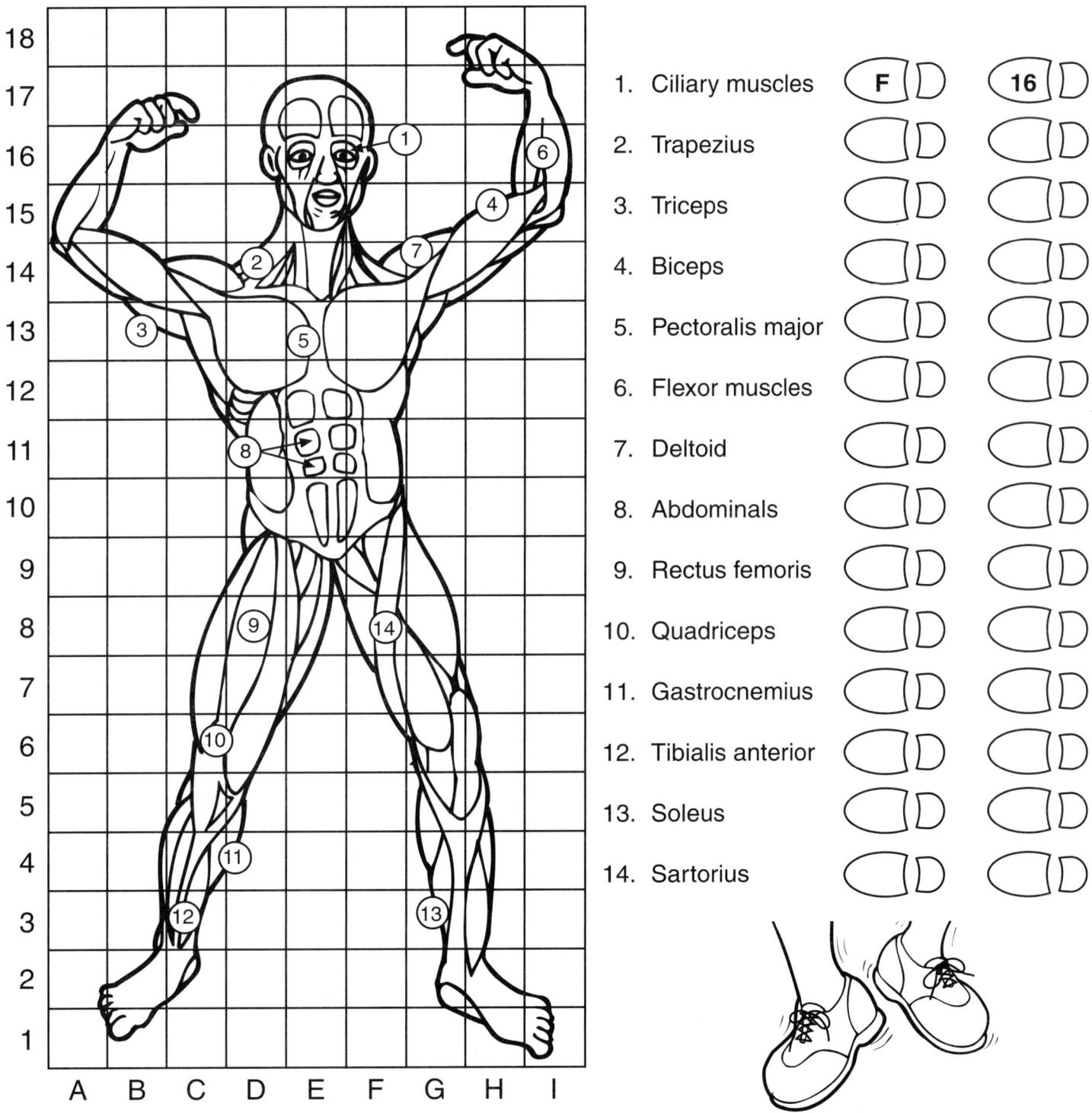

Movin' to the Muscle Music

Name _____ Muscular System

Put a little wiggle in your work and move your muscles to the beat! Then identify the location of major muscles in your body by following the directions below.

Directions: Locate each muscle on the coordinate grid. Then write the coordinate pair in the shoe print patterns next to the muscle. The first one has been done for you.

1. Ciliary muscles — F, 16
2. Trapezius
3. Triceps
4. Biceps
5. Pectoralis major
6. Flexor muscles
7. Deltoid
8. Abdominals
9. Rectus femoris
10. Quadriceps
11. Gastrocnemius
12. Tibialis anterior
13. Soleus
14. Sartorius

Bonus Box: Muscles help your body move. Think about the location of each muscle above. On the back of this page, write how each muscle helps you move.

Answer Key

1. F, 16
2. D, 14
3. B, 13
4. H, 15
5. E, 13
6. I, 16
7. G, 14
8. E, 11
9. D, 8
10. C, 6
11. D, 4
12. C, 3
13. G, 3
14. F, 8

Bonus Box: Answers may vary. Accept reasonable responses.
1. Ciliary muscles—change the shape of your lens so rays of light can be focused
2. Trapezius—raises, pulls back, and rotates the shoulder blades
3. Triceps—straightens arm
4. Biceps—bends arm
5. Pectoralis major—moves shoulder
6. Flexor muscles—move hand
7. Deltoid—moves shoulders
8. Abdominals—bend the body forward
9. Rectus femoris—pulls the leg forward, flexes the hip, extends the knee
10. Quadriceps—straightens leg
11. Gastrocnemius—pulls on the ankle to point the foot
12. Tibialis anterior—flexes the ankle joint to pull the feet up
13. Soleus—helps to steady the leg for standing
14. Sartorius—bends leg

Name _____   Digestive System

Doin' the Digestive Dance

If you're going to get down and boogie, you've gotta have energy! The digestive system changes the food you eat into the energy you need. Unscramble the letters to discover the part of the digestive system where each process takes place. Then, in the diagram at the right, label each part of the digestive system with its matching number. The first one has been done for you.

1. takes food into the body H M O T U M O U T H

2. releases solid wastes from the body
   S A U N __ __ __ (O) __

3. absorbs nutrients into the bloodstream
   M L A L S S T T N E I N I E
   __ __ __ __ (O) __ __ __ __ __ __ __ __ __

4. stores food, breaks down food, and kills bacteria from food
   M S T H O A C __ __ (O) __ __ __ __

5. makes bile, a liquid that breaks down fats
   V L E I R __ __ __ __ (O)

6. produces digestive juices and insulin
   A A C N P R S E __ __ __ __ __ __ __ __

7. carries food from the mouth to the stomach
   P S E G U O H A S __ __ __ __ __ __ __ (O) __

8. removes water and salts from waste materials
   G L R A E E I N I E N T T S
   __ __ __ __ __ __ __ __ __ __ __ __ __

9. stores bile
   L G A L E D L B D A R
   __ __ __ (O) __ __ __ __ __ __ __

10. stores solid waste material until removal from the body
    M U C E T R __ __ __ __ __ __

Bonus Box: Unscramble the circled letters from above to find out another name for the esophagus.

Answer Key

1. MOUTH
2. ANUS
3. SMALL INTESTINE
4. STOMACH
5. LIVER
6. PANCREAS
7. ESOPHAGUS
8. LARGE INTESTINE
9. GALLBLADDER
10. RECTUM

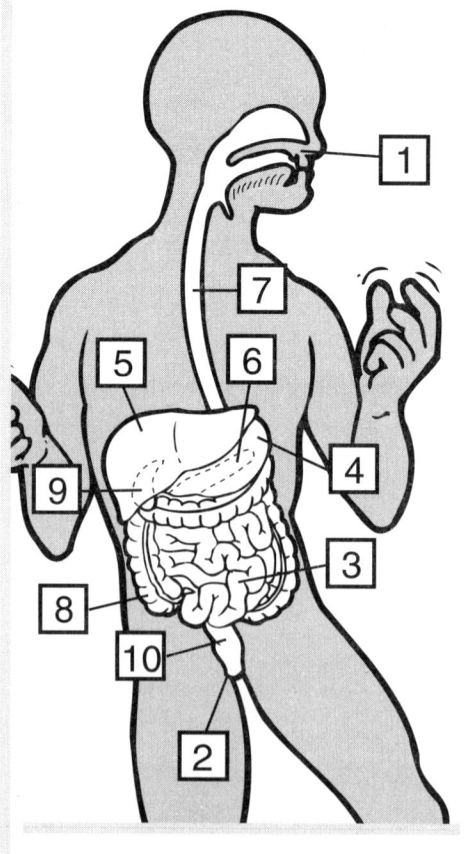

Bonus Box: GULLET

Name _____

Circulatory System

I've Got the Rhythm in Me!

Get your pulse pounding! Discover the effects of different actions on your circulatory system by following the directions below.

Directions:
1. Practice taking your pulse by following the steps in the box at the right.
2. Next, complete the first activity for one minute.
3. Take your pulse for 15 seconds. Multiply by four to get the number of beats per minute.
4. Rest for three minutes. Follow the same procedure for each remaining activity.
5. Then display your results on the bar graph below.

Taking Your Heart Rate
1. Lay your arm on a table with the palm of your hand up.
2. Place the fingertips of your other hand below the thumb on your upturned wrist.
3. Gently press until you can feel your heartbeat. *(Note: You may have to move your fingertips around the area until you feel your heartbeat.)*

Heart Rate Graph

(Bar graph: Beats per Minute, 0–180, vs. Activity 1–8)

Activity #1: Sit very still in your chair.
____ beats per minute

Activity #2: Carefully swing your arms back and forth.
____ beats per minute

Activity #3: March in place.
____ beats per minute

Activity #4: Jog in place at a slow pace.
____ beats per minute

Activity #5: Jog in place at a moderate pace.
____ beats per minute

Activity #6: Jog in place at a fast pace.
____ beats per minute

Activity #7: Walk slowly around the room.
____ beats per minute

Activity #8: Sit very still in your chair.
____ beats per minute

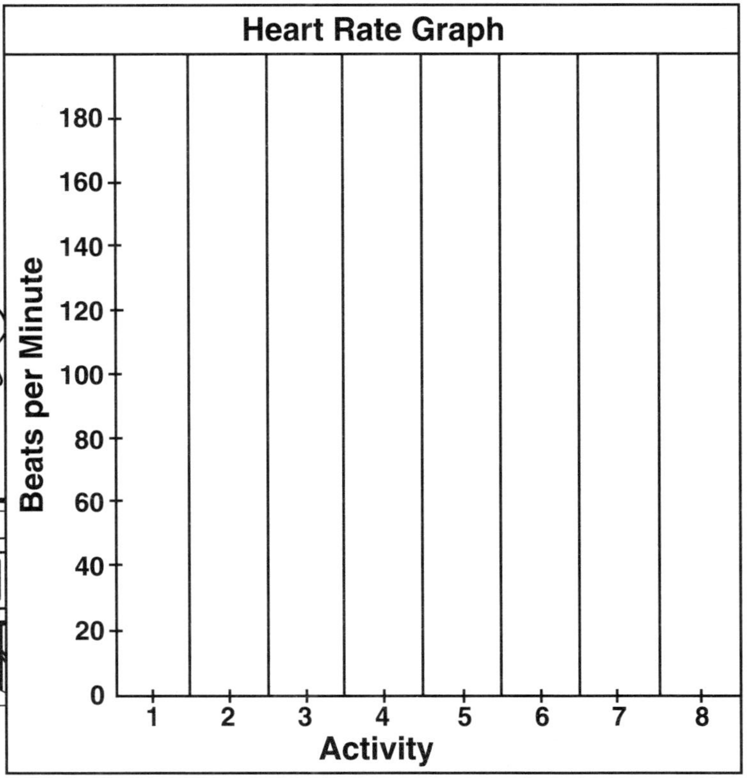

©The Education Center, Inc. • *Big Book of Skill Builders* • TEC60797

Name _____ Cardinal and Intermediate Directions

Boning Up on Directions

A **compass rose** shows the four **cardinal directions**—*north, south, east,* and *west.* It can also show **intermediate directions** that lie between the cardinal directions. The intermediate directions are *northeast, northwest, southeast,* and *southwest.*

Help Boomer find a special treat. Use the compass rose to help you.

- Begin at the dot labeled *start.*
- Move 2 spaces north and draw a dot. Connect the two dots.
- Next, move 1 space northwest and draw another dot. Then connect the dots.
- Continue with the steps below in the same manner to reveal Boomer's special treat.
- Check off each step as you complete it.

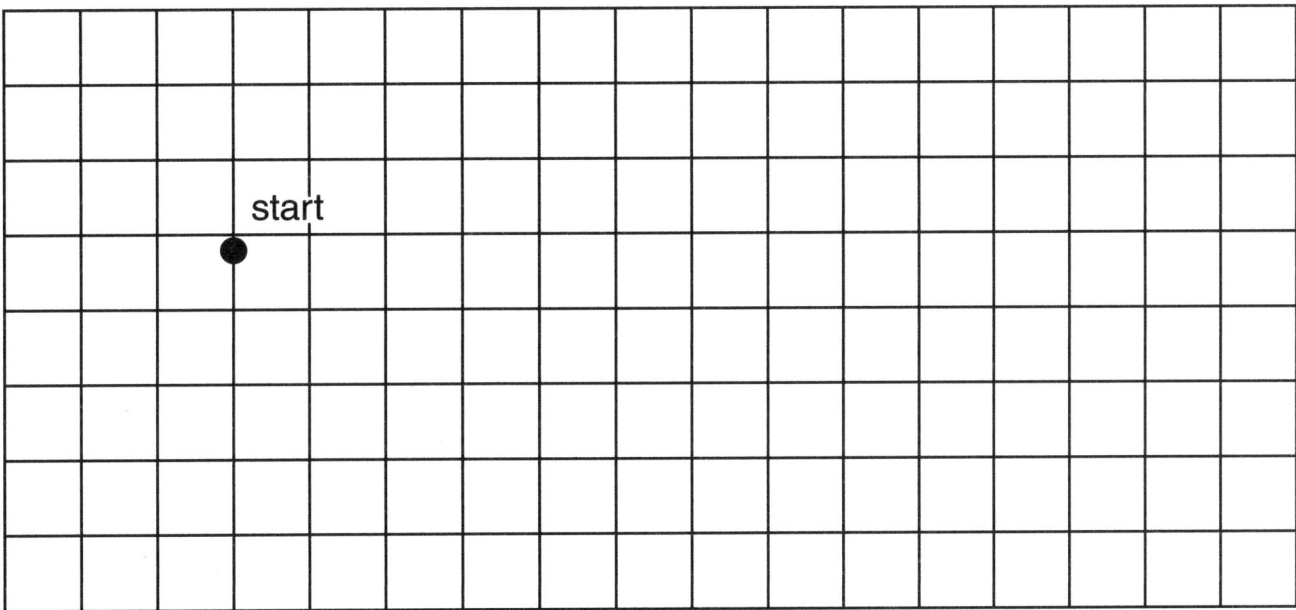

___ 1. Move 1 space southwest.
___ 2. Move 2 spaces south.
___ 3. Move 1 space southeast.
___ 4. Move 1 space southwest.
___ 5. Move 2 spaces south.
___ 6. Move 1 space southeast.
___ 7. Move 1 space northeast.
___ 8. Move 2 spaces north.
___ 9. Move 11 spaces east.
___ 10. Move 2 spaces south.

___ 11. Move 1 space southeast.
___ 12. Move 1 space northeast.
___ 13. Move 2 spaces north.
___ 14. Move 1 space northwest.
___ 15. Move 1 space northeast.
___ 16. Move 2 spaces north.
___ 17. Move 1 space northwest.
___ 18. Move 1 space southwest.
___ 19. Move 2 spaces south.
___ 20. Move 11 spaces west.

Boomer's special treat is a _____.

©The Education Center, Inc. • *Big Book of Skill Builders* • TEC60797

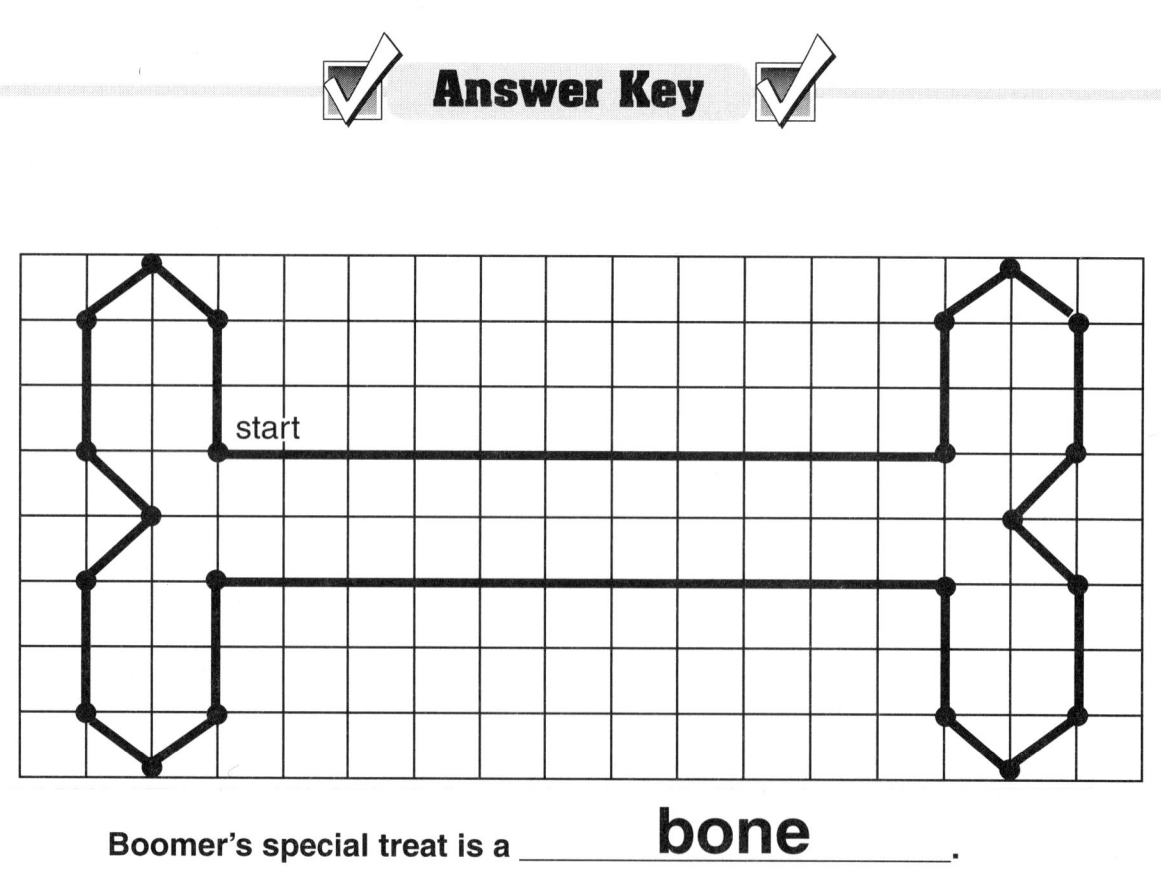

Boomer's special treat is a **bone**.

Name _____ Map Scale

Hot on the Trail

Frankie the Fox has been stealing chickens from farmers all over Canine County. Help Boomer track down Frankie by following the clues below.

Directions:
- Cut out the ruler at the bottom of the page.
- Use the ruler and the map scale to help you.
- Draw a line from place to place to show Boomer's route.
- Write each distance (in km) Boomer traveled on the map.

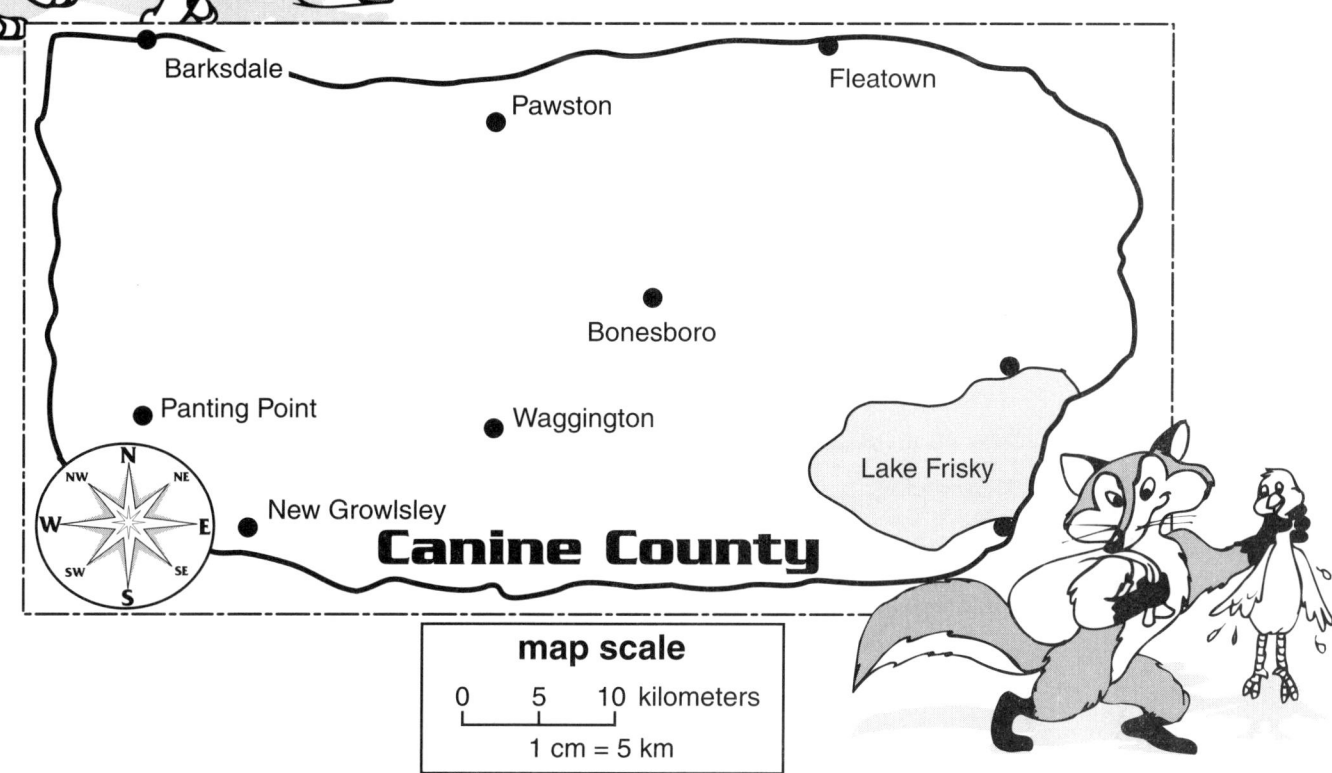

1. Boomer began his quest in Bonesboro. He traveled _____ km northeast to Fleatown.
2. From Fleatown Boomer trekked _____ km southeast to the north shore of Lake Frisky.
3. Boomer swam _____ km across Lake Frisky.
4. Boomer then hiked 50 km west to _____.
5. The next leg of Boomer's adventure led him _____ km northwest to Panting Point.
6. Boomer journeyed 25 km north to _____.
7. Boomer sniffed his way _____ km southeast to Waggington.
8. Boomer's keen sense of smell finally led him 20 km north to _____, where he found Frankie and his secret chicken coop.
9. Boomer freed the chickens. Then he handcuffed Frankie and marched him _____ km southeast back to Bonesboro, where he put him in jail.
10. Find the total distance Boomer traveled on his journey. _____

✅ Answer Key ✅

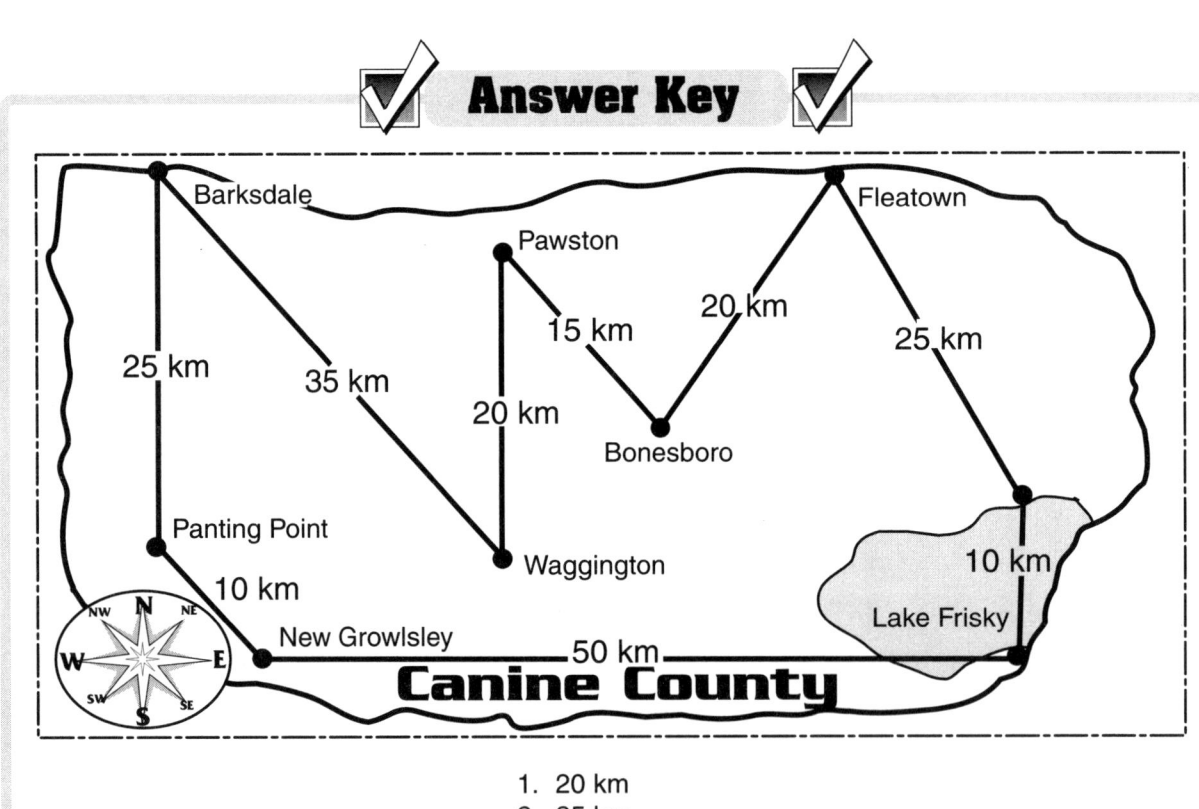

1. 20 km
2. 25 km
3. 10 km
4. New Growlsley
5. 10 km
6. Barksdale
7. 35 km
8. Pawston
9. 15 km
10. 210 km

Name _____

Latitude and Longitude

Vacation Wonders

Looking for a great place to vacation? How about visiting some of the natural wonders of the world? Follow the directions below to learn more about these wonderful vacation spots. The first one is done for you.

A. Victoria Falls
B. Himalayas
C. Olympus
D. The Matterhorn
E. Lake Titicaca
F. Grand Canyon
G. Niagara Falls
H. Mont Blanc
I. Mount Everest
J. The Great Barrier Reef

Directions:
1. Use the latitude and longitude coordinates below to locate each place on a world map.
2. Match the coordinates with the natural wonder's name from the cloud. Write its matching letter on the line.
3. Find the natural wonder's description in one of the airplanes below. Write its letter on the airplane's nose.

1. _H_ 45.5° N 6.5° E
2. ___ 17.5° S 25.5° E
3. ___ 16° S   69° W
4. ___ 40° N   22.5° E
5. ___ 27.5° N 86.5° E
6. ___ 29° N   84° E
7. ___ 36° N   112.5° W
8. ___ 16° S   146° E
9. ___ 45.5° N 7.5° E
10. ___ 43° N   79° W

Airplane descriptions:
- the highest mountain range in the world
- the highest navigable lake in the world
- a 355-foot waterfall a 277-mile-long, on the Zambezi River in Africa
- the highest point on Earth
- a beautiful mountain known for its pyramidlike shape
- the highest peak in Greece
- the highest mountain in western Europe
- a 277-mile-long, 1-mile-deep 18-mile-wide canyon carved by the Colorado River
- the most famous waterfall in North America
- the world's longest group of coral reefs

Bonus Box: Select one of the above natural wonders to visit. In which direction would you have to travel if you left from your house?

Answer Key

1. **H;** the highest mountain in western Europe
2. **A;** a 355-foot waterfall on the Zambezi River in Africa
3. **E;** the highest navigable lake in the world
4. **C;** the highest peak in Greece
5. **I;** the highest point on Earth
6. **B;** the highest mountain range in the world
7. **F;** a 277-mile-long, 18-mile-wide, 1-mile-deep canyon carved by the Colorado River
8. **J;** the world's longest group of coral reefs
9. **D;** a beautiful mountain known for its pyramidlike shape
10. **G;** the most famous waterfall in North America

Name_____ Cardinal and Intermediate Directions

Cruising Through the Caribbean

Ella just returned from a Caribbean cruise that was so long she can't remember all the places the ship stopped! Read the clues below to help Ella map out the ship's course. Then draw a line on the map to show the ship's course and place an X on each place where the ship stopped.

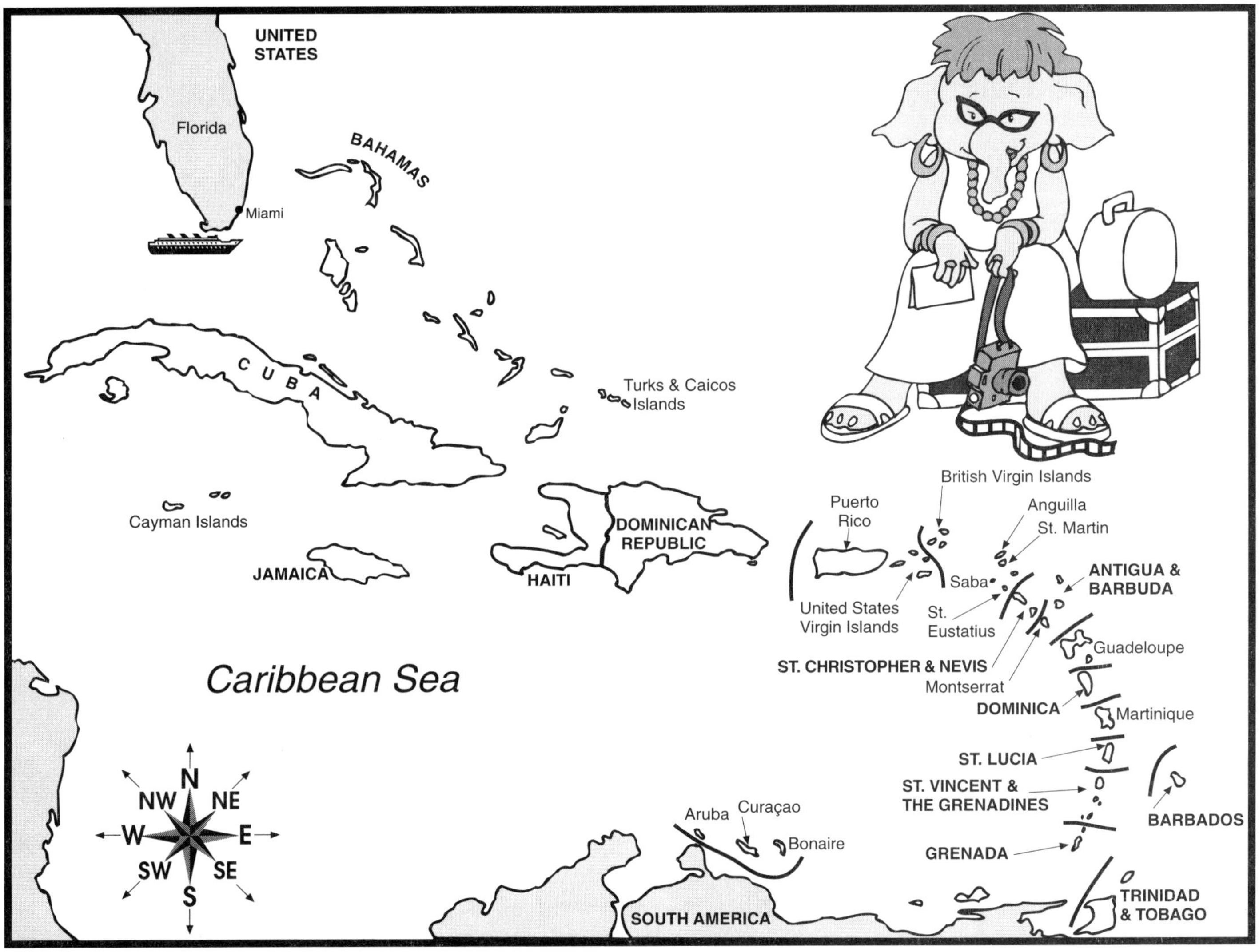

⚓ Leaving Miami, Florida, the ship sailed **SW** around Cuba, then **SE** to a group of islands **S** of Cuba.

⚓ From there, the ship headed **SE** and docked at a group of three islands **N** of South America.

⚓ Next the captain steered the ship **N** to a large island located **SE** of Cuba.

⚓ From there the ship sailed to an island located **W** of Haiti.

⚓ The next port of call was an island located **NW** of Barbados and **S** of Martinique.

⚓ Then it was off in the **NW** direction to an island located **W** of the U.S. Virgin Islands and **E** of the Dominican Republic.

⚓ From there the ship sailed to a group of islands located **E** of Cuba and **N** of Haiti.

⚓ Before returning to Miami, the ship stopped at a large group of islands located **N** of Cuba and **SE** of the United States.

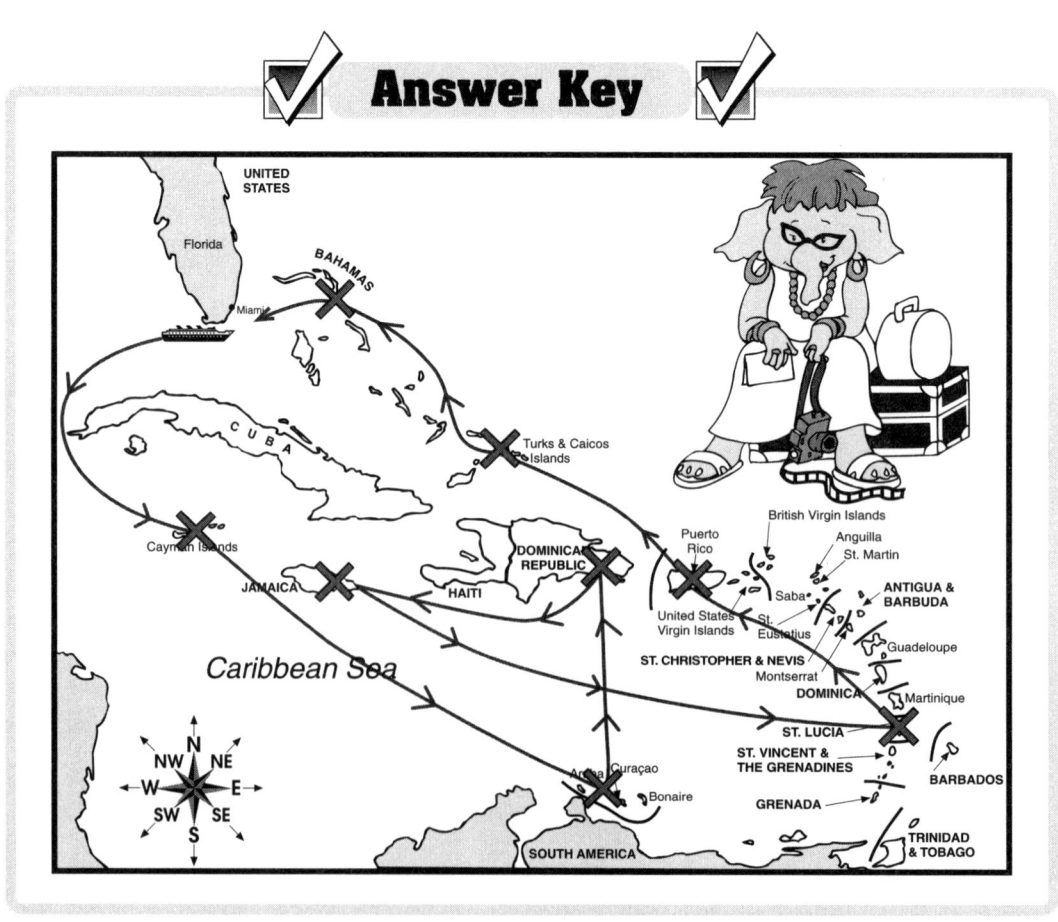

Answer Key

Name _____ Map Symbols

Exciting Excursions

Ella is a vacation dreamer! She wants to visit so many places in the United States that she labeled them on a map for herself. Use Ella's map to answer the questions below. Write your answers on the lines provided. Use an atlas for help if needed.

Key
- ★ city
- ☐ national park or monument
- △ theme park
- ● historical site
- ▲ natural landmark
- ○ museum

1. In which three states does Ella want to visit a theme park? _____

2. Suppose Ella wants to leave Pennsylvania and visit Scotts Bluff National Monument, the Pro Football Hall of Fame, and Devils Tower all in a one-way trip out West. In which order should she plan to see these sites? _____

3. Name the three cities that Ella wants to visit. _____

4. Texas and Alabama have which similar type of place marked? _____

5. If Ella is in North Carolina, what is the closest museum on her map? _____

6. Name the natural landmarks that Ella wants to see. _____

7. How many national parks or monuments did Ella include on her map? _____

8. If Ella is at the Gettysburg National Military Park, in which direction would she need to travel to get to the closest natural landmark? _____

9. How many states have two different types of places? _____

10. Which theme park is closest to the Gateway Arch? _____

©The Education Center, Inc. • *Big Book of Skill Builders* • TEC60797

Answer Key

1. Texas, Tennessee, and Florida
2. Pro Football Hall of Fame, Scotts Bluff National Monument, Devils Tower
3. San Diego, New Orleans, Savannah
4. Historical site
5. Kentucky Derby Museum
6. Great Salt Lake, Grand Canyon, Niagara Falls
7. 9
8. north
9. 3
10. Dollywood

Name _____

State Trivia Trek

Directions: Read each topic below. At your teacher's direction, find a different classmate who can correctly answer each item. Write each classmate's answer in the square. Score one point for each correct answer.

State-Study Game

Total Points: _____

A city or town with five letters in its name	Colors in the state flag	State postal abbreviation	Famous person from the state
State's nickname "Just call me 'Lone Star'!"	Natural resource found in the state	Largest city in the state	Famous state landmark
State waterway or landform	State tree	Sports team from the state	State's average temperature
Something for which the state is well known	State motto	Popular state vacation site	State capital
State governor	Number of regions in the state	State flower	Interesting fact about the state

©The Education Center, Inc. • Big Book of Skill Builders • TEC60797

How to Use Page 297

1. Duplicate page 297 for each student.
2. Discuss with students the directions on that page. Point out that if a student agrees with a classmate's answer, he should move on to the next item. If the student does not agree, he should find another classmate who can answer it correctly.
3. Determine a starting and stopping time; then begin the game.
4. At the end of the game, if desired, have each student use reference materials to check any answer about which he is unsure.
5. Discuss the answers as a class. Give each student who scores at least 15 points a special treat.

Name _____

"Geog-ing" Around Your State

Get out your running gear for a whirlwind tour of your state's geography and culture!

Directions: At your teacher's direction, answer the questions on the track below. Answer as many as possible before the time limit expires. The player or team with the most correct answers when the time limit expires is the winner.

State-Study Game

A is for average.
The average annual temperature in our state is _____.

B is for business.
_____ is one of the largest industries in our state.

C is for capital.
The capital of our state is _____.

D is for dining.
_____ is a type of food for which our state is known.

E is for energy.
Our state gets most of its energy from _____.

F is for festival.
_____ is a festival held in our state.

G is for geographic.
_____ is a geographic feature for which our state is known.

H is for historical.
_____ is a famous historical site in our state.

I is for interstate.
An interstate that runs through our state is _____.

J is for justice.
Our state court is located in _____.

K is for kindness.
_____ is a program that helps the less fortunate in our state.

L is for lake.
_____ is a lake in our state.

M is for music.
_____ is a musical group from our state.

N is for natural resources.
_____ is an important natural resource in our state.

O is for official.
Our official state bird is _____.

P is for park.
_____ is a park located in our state.

Q is for quality.
Our state is known for having the best _____.

R is for river.
_____ is a river that runs through our state.

S is for school.
_____ is a college found in our state.

T is for travel.
It is about _____ miles from east to west in our state.

U is for urban.
_____ is the largest urban area in our state.

V is for vegetation.
_____ is a plant that grows naturally in our state.

W is for west.
_____ is located to the west of our state.

X is for X ray.
_____ is a large hospital found in our state.

Y is for yearly.
The average yearly rainfall in our state is _____ inches.

Z is for zoo.
There is a zoo in _____ in our state.

How to Use Page 299

1. Duplicate page 299 for each student or team. If desired, supply resource materials for students to use to complete the activity.
2. Determine a time limit for completing the activity; then begin the race.
3. After the time limit expires, or when the first student or team completes the race, stop the game and discuss students' answers.

Name _____

Natural Resources

Resource Roundup

Use the map and key to identify which natural resources can be found in each region of the United States. Then choose a region. Write a different resource from this region on each of the blanks provided. Then write two products that could be made from it.

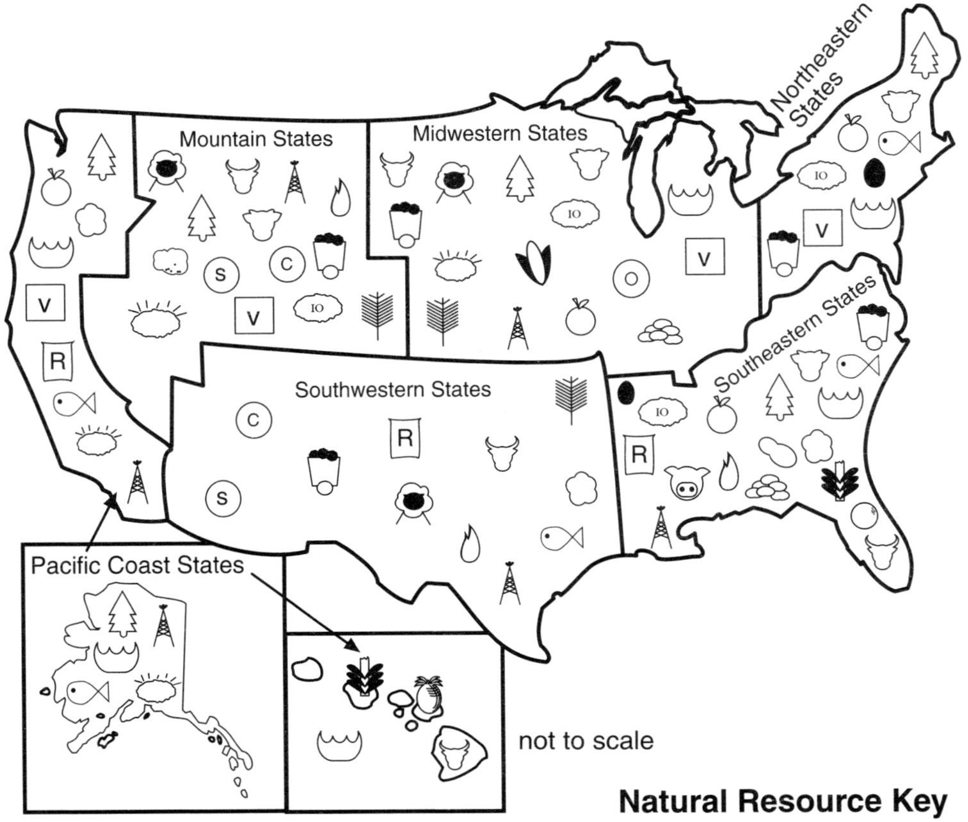

Region: _____

Resource: _____ **Products:**

_____ ⟩ _____

_____ ⟩ _____

_____ ⟩ _____

_____ ⟩ _____

_____ ⟩ _____

_____ ⟩ _____

_____ ⟩ _____

_____ ⟩ _____

Natural Resource Key

- beef cattle
- coal
- copper
- corn
- cotton
- dairy cattle
- forests
- fruits
- gold
- hogs
- iron ore
- natural gas
- oats
- oil
- oranges
- peanuts
- pineapple
- potatoes
- poultry
- rice
- seafood
- sheep
- silver
- soybeans
- sugarcane
- vegetables
- water
- wheat

not to scale

©The Education Center, Inc. • *Big Book of Skill Builders* • TEC60797

How to Use Page 301

1. Give each student a copy of page 301.
2. Define the terms *natural resources* (all things in the natural environment that are useful to people) and *products* (things that can be made using the resources). Assess students' understanding of the page by asking them various questions, such as the following: In which regions would you find cotton and oil? (southeast, southwest, and Pacific coast) Name three resources found in the mountain region. (Examples include dairy cattle, copper, and sheep.)
3. Ask students to name several products that can be made from the resources in one of the regions discussed in Step 2. For example, cheese can be produced using dairy cattle, and clothing can be produced using sheep.
4. Discuss the directions on page 301 with students. Then have each student complete the page as directed. Provide assistance and allow students to use encyclopedias as needed.
5. If desired, follow up this activity by having students complete the activity on page 303.

 Answer Key

Possible answers include the following:

beef cattle—hamburgers, leather goods
coal—steel, electricity
copper—jewelry, coins
corn—popcorn, corn chips
cotton—clothing, upholstery
dairy cattle—cheese, leather goods
seafood—soup, frozen foods
forests—furniture, paper
fruits—ice cream, snack foods
gold—jewelry, electrical items
hogs—ham, soap
iron ore—steel, tools
natural gas—fuel for cooking and heating
oats—cereal, crackers
oil—paint, gasoline
oranges—juice, marmalade
peanuts—peanut butter, peanut oil
pineapple—canned fruit, juice
potatoes—French fries, potato chips
poultry—eggs, fried chicken
rice—cereal, flour
sheep—clothing, blankets
silver—jewelry, tableware
soybeans—candles, milk
sugarcane—sugar, candy
vegetables—canned foods, frozen foods
water—drinking, power
wheat—cereal, bread

Name_____ Natural Resources

Resourceful Responses

Use the map below to help you write a question for each answer.
Use other reference books if you need help.

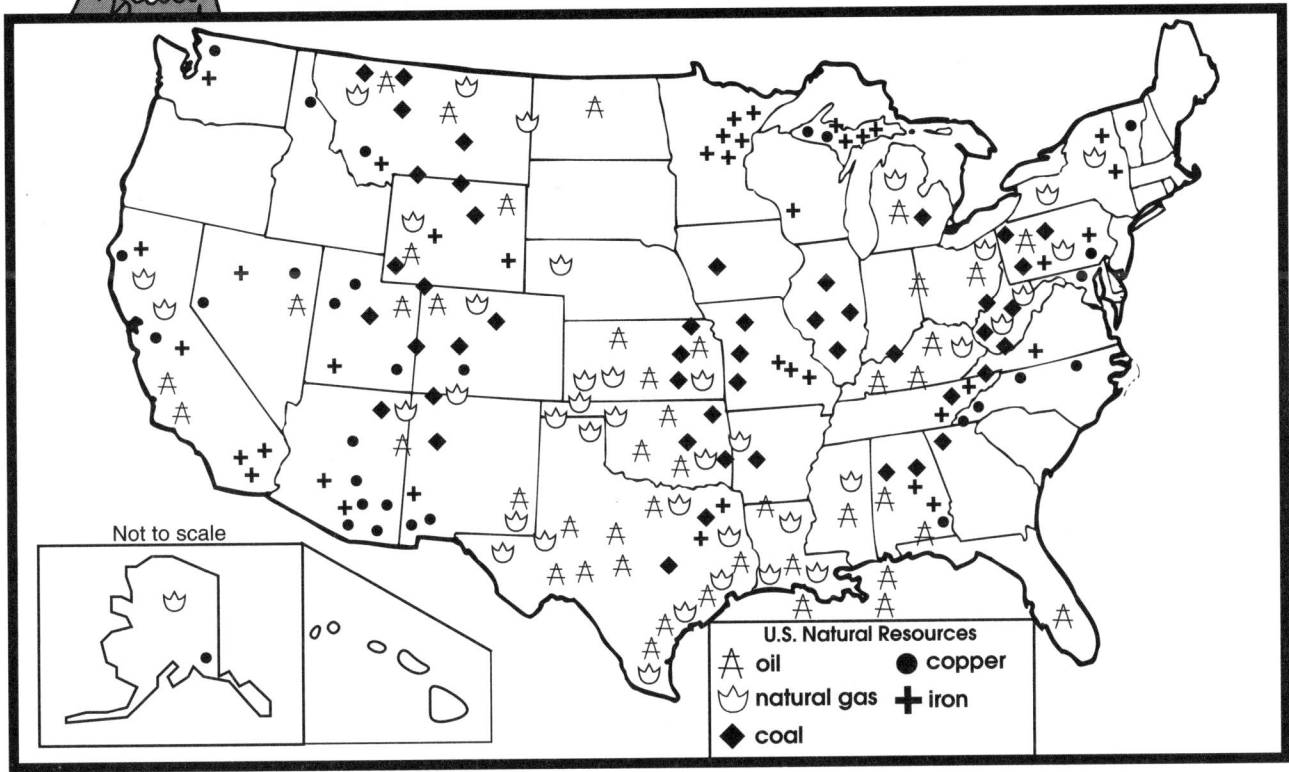

1. These resources are found in abundance along the Gulf of Mexico.
   _____

2. These natural resources are some of the fossil fuels found in the United States.
   _____

3. Much of this resource is found in the Rocky Mountains and Appalachian Mountains.
   _____

4. This resource is not mined in states that border the Pacific Ocean.
   _____

5. Large amounts of these resources are mined in the southwest region of the United States.
   _____

6. These natural resources are two important metals mined in the United States.
   _____

7. Minnesota produces more of this resource than any other state.
   _____

8. Texas, Oklahoma, and Kansas are leading producers of these resources.
   _____

9. Large deposits of this resource are found in West Virginia and Pennsylvania.
   _____

10. This resource is not found in the Plains region.
    _____

Bonus Box: Use the map to help you write five questions about natural resources in the United States. Write the answers to your questions. Give your answers to a classmate and ask him to come up with questions to match them.

©The Education Center, Inc. • Big Book of Skill Builders • TEC60797

Answer Key

Responses may vary. Sample questions are given below:
1. What are oil and natural gas?
2. What are oil, natural gas, and coal?
3. What is coal?
4. What is coal?
5. What are copper and iron?
6. What are copper and iron?
7. What is iron?
8. What are oil and natural gas?
9. What is coal?
10. What is copper?

States and Capitals Game

Capital Play

MD	NV 	OR 	NH	MO 	NJ	KY
NM	MI	TX	WA	AL	FL	PA

Left column (top to bottom): UT, MS, NC , IL, ND, CA, CT, AZ, TN, CO, DE, LA, MA, IN

Right column (top to bottom): OK, VA, WI , VT, WY , WV, ID , NY, MN , GA, ME , NE

New England
Augusta
Montpelier
Concord
Boston
Hartford
Providence

Middle Atlantic
Albany
Harrisburg
Trenton
Annapolis
Dover

Upper Southeast
Charleston
Richmond
Frankfort
Raleigh
Nashville
Columbia

Lower Southeast
Atlanta
Tallahassee
Montgomery
Jackson
Baton Rouge
Little Rock

Great Lakes
Columbus
Indianapolis
Springfield
Lansing
Madison
St. Paul

Southwest
Austin
Oklahoma City
Santa Fe
Phoenix

Plains
Bismarck
Pierre
Lincoln
Topeka
Des Moines
Jefferson City

Rocky Mountain
Helena
Boise
Cheyenne
Carson City
Salt Lake City
Denver

Pacific
Olympia
Salem
Sacramento
Juneau
Honolulu

Bottom row: MA , KS , SC , IA , HI , OH , Go! (to any box!)
IN, RI, SD, AK, AR, MT

©The Education Center, Inc. • *Big Book of Skill Builders* • TEC60797

How to Use Page 305

Duplicate page 305 for every two to four students. In addition, duplicate the directions below for each group of players.

Game Directions

Capital Play

Materials needed:
- different color of marker or pencil for each player
- die
- key for checking (if necessary)
- game marker for each player

How to play:
1. Place all game markers on "Go!"
2. Roll the die to see who goes first. The player with the lowest roll is Player 1.
3. Player 1 rolls the die.
4. Player 1 moves his marker the same number of spaces as his roll.
5. When Player 1 lands on a space, he must:
   - choose one of the two state postal abbreviations in that space,
   - name the state that matches that abbreviation, and
   - name the capital of that state.
6. If both of Player 1's answers are correct, he marks through that state capital on the gameboard with his colored marker or pencil.
7. If either of Player 1's answers is incorrect, he stays on that space until it's his turn again.
8. Play continues with Player 2 rolling the die.
9. The game continues until:
   - a player marks through all of the capitals listed in a region, or
   - a player marks through at least one capital in each of the nine regions.
10. Whenever a player lands on "Go!", he may move his game marker to any space on the gameboard. He then follows the directions in step 5.

©The Education Center, Inc. • *Big Book of Skill Builders* • TEC60797

Name _____

Amendments

Those Amazing Amendments!

The *amendments*, or additions, to the U.S. Constitution list the rights of the American people that cannot be taken away. Read the summary of each amendment below. Decide if it applies to an individual freedom or to the general welfare of our country. Put a star by each amendment that applies to an individual freedom.

1. People have the freedom of religion and the freedom of speech.
2. People have the right to own guns and protect themselves.
3. The government cannot force people to keep soldiers in their homes.
4. People have the right to privacy in their homes.
5. People accused of crimes have certain rights.
6. People accused of crimes are to have fair trials.
7. A person is guaranteed a trial by jury.
8. People accused of a crime cannot be treated cruelly.
9. People have many other rights not listed in the Constitution.
10. States have powers not belonging to the national government.
11. A citizen from one state cannot sue another state.
12. The candidate with the greatest number of votes becomes president.
13. Slavery is unlawful.
14. All citizens have rights regardless of race.
15. All male citizens have the right to vote regardless of race.
16. The government has the right to collect taxes.
17. People have the right to elect state senators.
18. Alcoholic beverages are illegal.
19. Women have the right to vote.
20. A president's term in office begins at noon on January 20.
21. Alcoholic beverages are legal.
22. A president cannot serve more than two terms.
23. Residents of Washington, DC, have the right to vote in a presidential election.
24. A person cannot be denied the right to vote for failing to pay a tax.
25. If the president becomes sick or dies, the vice president takes over.
26. The voting age is changed from 21 to 18.
27. Pay raises for members of Congress are delayed.

Answer Key

Students' answers may vary. Accept reasonable responses.

★ 1 ★ 13
★ 2 ★ 14
★ 3 ★ 15
★ 4 ★ 17
★ 5 ★ 18
★ 6 ★ 19
★ 7 ★ 21
★ 8 ★ 23
★ 9 ★ 24
★ 11 ★ 26

Name _____

Amendments

★★★ Power to the People ★★★

What guarantees that the American people have some power over government? The U.S. Constitution!

Directions: Read each problem below. Decide which amendment was written to solve this problem. Write the amendment number in the correct space. Then write how this amendment helps people today.

Before the Amendment	Amendment	After the Amendment
1. At the time of the American Revolution, the British forced colonists to keep soldiers in their homes.		
2. People were forced to work against their will as slaves.		
3. Women were not allowed to vote in elections.		
4. People wanted to make sure they were free to criticize the government without fear of punishment.		
5. Some people were denied the right to vote because of their race.		
6. Americans were against Great Britain's past practice of holding unfair trials.		
7. President Eisenhower became very ill, causing citizens to worry who would take over his job if he wasn't able to do it.		
8. Because the Church Of England was Virginia's official church during the colonial period, Baptists and Methodists were often thrown into jail.		
9. People living in Washington, DC, thought it was unfair that they were not allowed to vote.		
10. Eighteen-year-olds were made to fight in a war, but could not vote in an election.		

Bonus Box: Make a list of ten rights that you have, such as the right to an education. Write your rights on the back of this sheet.

©The Education Center, Inc. • *Big Book of Skill Builders* • TEC60797

309

Answer Key

Accept reasonable responses for students' explanations of how the amendments help people today.

1. 3; Today people's homes are private. The government cannot force them to keep soldiers in their homes.
2. 13; No one has the power to own another person.
3. 19; Women have the right to vote.
4. 1; People have a right to speak out about things they believe.
5. 15; A person cannot be denied the right to vote because of his race.
6. 6; If a person is charged with a crime, he can get a lawyer and have a fair trial.
7. 25; If something should happen to the president and he can't do his job, then the vice president takes over.
8. 1; People have the right to go to church wherever they choose.
9. 23; If a person lives in Washington, DC, he can vote in the presidential elections.
10. 26; When a person turns 18 years old, he has the right to vote.

Name _____

Checks and Balances

The Constitution created a strong government that united all the states. It also created a system of *checks and balances* to keep the three federal branches of government from becoming too powerful.

1. Each box contains one of the three branches of the federal government. Research to find the answers for each box.

2. The system of checks is represented by the white and shaded arrows going to and coming from each box. Research how each branch checks up on the other branches. Write your findings inside the arrows.

Executive Branch

President

List three duties of the president:

1. _____
2. _____
3. _____

Legislative Branch

Congress

List three duties of Congress:

1. _____
2. _____
3. _____

Judicial Branch

Supreme Court and Federal Courts

What is the job of the Supreme Court?

_____
_____
_____

Bonus Box: On the back of this page, explain why you think the founding fathers were wise to include a system of checks and balances in the Constitution.

©The Education Center, Inc. • *Big Book of Skill Builders* • TEC60797

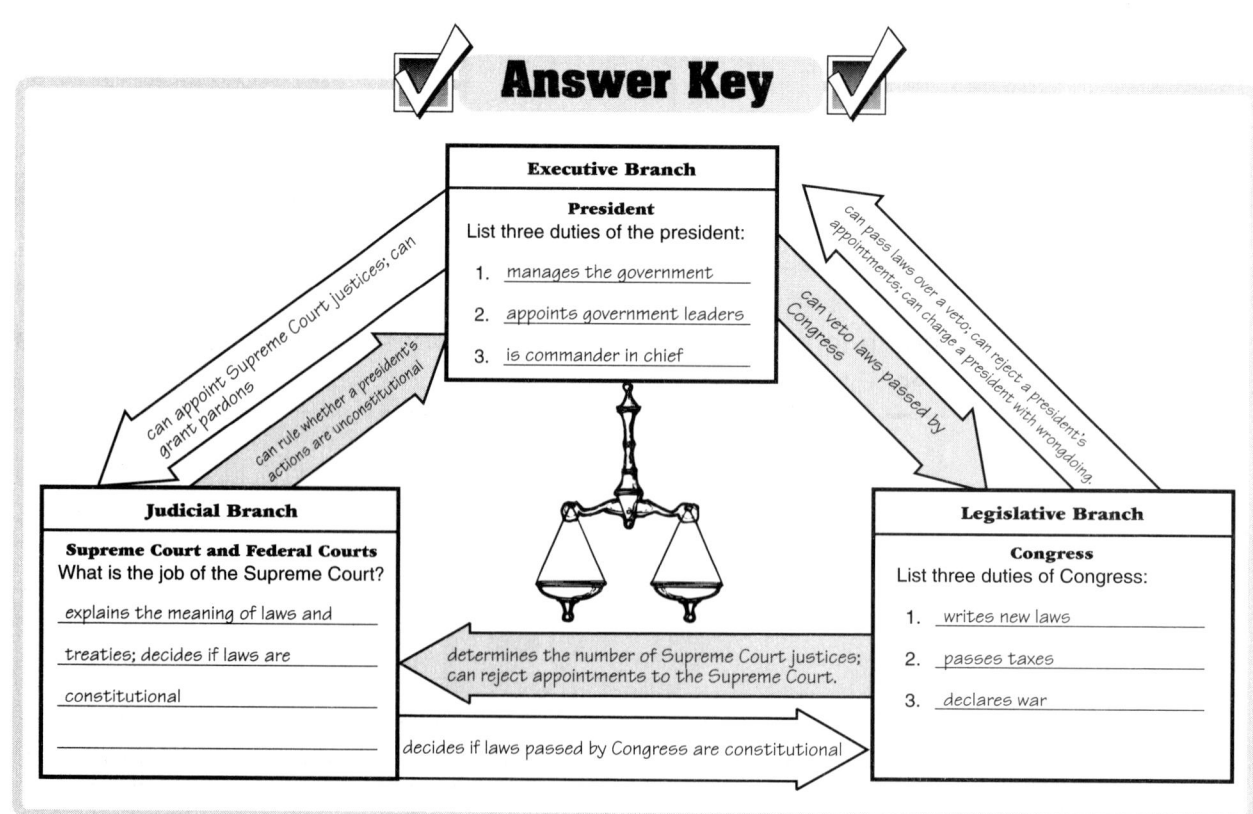

Name _____ The Preamble

The Preamble

The Preamble is a 52-word sentence that introduces the Constitution. This very long sentence explains the purpose for writing the Constitution. Read the Preamble; then follow the directions below.

"We the people of the United States, in order to form a more perfect **Union**, establish **justice**, insure **domestic tranquility**, provide for the **common defense**, promote the **general welfare**, and **secure** the blessings of liberty to ourselves and our **posterity** do **ordain** and **establish** this Constitution for the United States of America."

Find the meaning of each word below in a dictionary. Use the context of the Preamble above to pick the best definition for each word. Write the definitions in the appropriate boxes.

1. Union: _____

2. justice: _____

3. domestic: _____

4. tranquility: _____

5. common: _____

6. defense: _____

7. general: _____

8. welfare: _____

9. secure: _____

10. posterity: _____

11. ordain: _____

12. establish: _____

Now it's your turn to update the Preamble. Use the definitions above to help you write a more modern version of the Preamble in the space below.

_____

Bonus Box: Write a preamble for your classroom rules on the back of this page. Be sure your preamble represents the goals and needs of your class.

 **Answer Key**

1. Union—a political unit such as the 13 former colonies
2. justice—rights according to the law
3. domestic—originating from our own country
4. tranquility—a state of calmness
5. common—relating to the community at large
6. defense—protecting oneself
7. general—involving the whole
8. welfare—referring to good fortune, happiness, well-being, and prosperity
9. secure—guarantee
10. posterity—all future generations (offspring)
11. ordain—to establish by law
12. establish—to institute permanently by enactment or agreement

Updating the Preamble
Answers will vary.

Americans want to work together. Everyone should be treated fairly. We want to get along with each other and defend ourselves. We want freedom for ourselves and our children. These are the reasons for writing the Constitution of the United States of America.

Name_____   Economics Vocabulary

What'$ the Word?

Become a word wizard in no time by completing the vocabulary activities below!

A. Read each definition. Then read each group of words that follow. Based on the definitions, decide which word does not belong in the group and draw a line through it.

- **budget**—a plan of how much money is available and how it will be spent
- **consumer**—a person who buys and uses goods and services
- **demand**—consumers' desire for goods and services
- **goods**—real items, such as tennis rackets and televisions
- **needs**—things necessary for people to live
- **producer**—the person or business that provides goods and services
- **profit**—the money remaining after expenses have been paid
- **services**—work that is done for others, such as teaching and nursing
- **supply**—the amount of goods or services available to consumers
- **wages**—money paid to an employee for work completed
- **wants**—things people would like to have but can live without

1. consumer
   shopper
   customer
   store owner

2. money
   consumer
   cash
   wages

3. goods
   supply
   merchandise
   items

4. spend
   save
   needs
   loan

5. budget
   outline
   wants
   plan

B. Read each analogy below. (Remember, an *analogy* shows a likeness between two objects that are otherwise unlike.) Think about how the words in the first pair go together; then choose a word from the list above that completes the second pair. Write the word in the blank.

6. *Work* is to *services* as *items* are to _____.

7. *Consumer* is to *shopping* as _____ is to *selling*.

8. *Merchandise* is to a *producer* as *money* is to a _____.

9. *Air* is to *needs* as *candy* is to _____.

10. *Consumer* is to *demand* as *producer* is to _____.

11. *Punishment* is to *crime* as _____ are to *work*.

©The Education Center, Inc. • *Big Book of Skill Builders* • TEC60797

Answer Key

1. store owner
2. consumer
3. supply
4. needs
5. wants
6. goods
7. producer
8. consumer
9. wants
10. supply
11. wages

Name _____ Supply and Demand

Confused about the concept of *supply* and *demand*? Make the connection by completing the activity below!

Directions: Cut out each sentence fragment along the bold lines. Then read each fragment carefully. On another sheet of paper, arrange three fragments to make a complete sentence. Continue until nine sentences have been formed. Then glue the sentences into place. **Hint:** The first fragment of each sentence begins with a capital letter. The last fragment ends with a period.

A store owner	is greater than the demand,	there would be a surplus of it.
People pay higher prices	his prices too high,	because they are rare.
If the demand for goods or services	for bread	the price goes up.
If the supply of goods or services	sets the prices	he can raise prices.
If a store owner wants	stopped buying bread,	of his merchandise.
If a store owner raises	to increase his profit,	the price would go up.
If people	for diamonds	because there is a large supply of it.
People pay lower prices	became scarce,	the price goes down.
If bread	is greater than the supply,	people might not shop in his store.

©The Education Center, Inc. • *Big Book of Skill Builders* • TEC60797

 **Answer Key**

A store owner sets the prices of his merchandise.

If the demand for goods or services is greater than the supply, the price goes up.

If the supply of goods or services is greater than the demand, the price goes down.

People pay higher prices for diamonds because they are rare.

If a store owner raises his prices too high, people might not shop in his store.

If a store owner wants to increase his profit, he can raise prices.

If people stopped buying bread, there would be a surplus of it.

People pay lower prices for bread because there is a large supply of it.

If bread became scarce, the price would go up.

Name _____ Wants and Needs

Wishing for Wants and Needs

Oh no! You're stranded on a desert island, all alone and with nothing but the clothes on your back. The good news is that a genie has appeared and will grant you ten wishes. The only thing you must do is decide if each wish is a *want* or a *need*. Follow the directions below to make your wishes come true.

Directions: Read the wish list below. In the blank next to each item, write an *N* if the item is something you need or a *W* if the item is something you want. Next, choose ten items from the list for which to wish. List the ten items in the order you would wish for them on the lines below. Then write the reason for your choice in the space that follows.

Wish List

- ___ clean water
- ___ books
- ___ radio
- ___ batteries
- ___ binoculars
- ___ food
- ___ knife
- ___ comic books
- ___ rope
- ___ paper and pencil
- ___ blanket
- ___ suntan lotion
- ___ sunglasses
- ___ deck of cards
- ___ hat
- ___ first aid kit

1. Item: _____ Reason: _____
2. Item: _____ Reason: _____
3. Item: _____ Reason: _____
4. Item: _____ Reason: _____
5. Item: _____ Reason: _____
6. Item: _____ Reason: _____
7. Item: _____ Reason: _____
8. Item: _____ Reason: _____
9. Item: _____ Reason: _____
10. Item: _____ Reason: _____

©The Education Center, Inc. • *Big Book of Skill Builders* • TEC60797

Answer Key

Answers may vary. Accept reasonable responses.